THE PEOPLE'S HOTEL

Working for Justice in Argentina

KATHERINE SOBERING

THE PEOPLE'S HOTEL

Duke University Press Durham and London 2022

Printed in the United States of America on acid-free paper ∞
Designed by Aimee C. Harrison
Typeset in Minion Pro and Helvetica Neue by Westchester
Publishing Services

Library of Congress Cataloging-in-Publication Data
Names: Sobering, Katherine, [date] author.
Title: The people's hotel : working for justice in Argentina /
Katherine Sobering.
Description: Durham : Duke University Press, 2022. |
Includes bibliographical references and index.
Identifiers: LCCN 2021049289 (print) LCCN 2021049290 (ebook)
ISBN 9781478015635 (hardcover) ISBN 9781478018261 (paperback)
ISBN 9781478022862 (ebook)
Subjects: LCSH: B.A.U.E.N. Hotel (Buenos Aires, Argentina) | Employee
ownership—Argentina—History—21st century. | Hotels—Argentina—
Buenos Aires. | BISAC: SOCIAL SCIENCE / Anthropology / Cultural &
Social | HISTORY / Latin America / South America
Classification: LCC HD8039.H82 A7 2022 (print) | LCC HD8039.H82
(ebook) | DDC 331.7/6164794098212—dc23/eng/20220120
LC record available at https://lccn.loc.gov/2021049289
LC ebook record available at https://lccn.loc.gov/2021049290

Cover art: Photo by BAUEN Cooperative.

In memory of Don, Fred, Arminda, Horacio, and Luisita

Contents

Acknowledgments

This research was made possible by the many people in Argentina who included me in their work and invited me into their homes. First and foremost, to my compañeros in the BAUEN Cooperative, thank you for sharing your experiences with me, trusting me to enter your organization, and embracing me as part of your community.

Without the steadfast support, intellectual guidance, and friendship of Javier Auyero, this project would not have been possible. He has been involved from the very beginning, inspiring me to return to graduate school in sociology; reading countless versions of applications, articles, and books; and giving careful attention to this manuscript. Thank you, Javier, for investing your time in me, training me to be an ethnographer, and sharing your enthusiasm (and anxiety) for sociological research. I cannot thank you enough for helping me evolve and mature my ideas about work and social change, pushing me to improve as a writer, and teaching me to never make excuses for my ideas and passions.

I have benefited from insightful feedback from teachers, mentors, friends, and colleagues who supported this project over the years. My greatest thanks go to George Cheney, Jennifer Glass, Christine Williams, and Michael Young, who provided support and guidance during most of my data collection and initial analysis. Thank you also to Rob Crosnoe, Henry Dietz, Kathy Edwards, Joyce Rothschild, and Sharmila Rudrappa for their generous mentorship and to Joseph Blasi for welcoming me into the Beyster community and supporting important interdisciplinary dialogues about employee ownership. I am especially grateful to Christine Williams for constantly pushing me to think broadly about my case and to start publishing before I thought I was ready.

I became an ethnographer as a graduate fellow of the Urban Ethnography Lab at the University of Texas at Austin, and I am indebted to the collaborative training I received from my professors and peers. My writing groups over the years have been critical in helping me articulate my thoughts and think broadly about social theory. To Kate Henley Averett, Nino Bariola, Caitlyn Collins, Kristine Kilanski, Megan Tobias Neely, and Marcos Pérez: I can't thank you enough for your time, support, and encouragement. In particular, the consistency and accountability provided by weekly writing sessions with Carolyn Fornoff, Laura Smithers, and Sarah Stanlick made writing fun as I pushed this project across the finish line. I would also like to acknowledge other colleagues and friends who commented on earlier iterations of this work, including Jacinto Cuvi, Jorge Derpic, Matías Dewey, Daniel Fridman, Katherine Jensen, Amanda Stevenson, and Esther Sullivan. Dustin Avent-Holt, Pablo Lapegna, Joan S. M. Meyers, and Trevor Young-Hyman provided thoughtful feedback on chapters that now appear in this book. Many thanks are also due to Gisela Fosado and Ale Mejía at Duke and the anonymous readers who provided invaluable feedback on this book. Finally, Letta Page and my mom, Cindi Sobering, helped me catch the errors and typos I could no longer see after so many years of writing and revision, and Melissa McWilliams helped me create the original illustrations for this book. Thank you all!

I presented parts of this project at meetings of the American Sociological Association, the Eastern Sociological Society, the International Sociological Association, the Society for the Advancement of Socio-Economics, and the

Latin American Studies Association. Many thanks to the organizers—Dana Britton, Katherine Chen, José Itzigsohn, Megan Tobias Neely, Aliya Rao, and Joyce Rothschild—for including me. This project benefited greatly from the insightful feedback of the participants, discussants, and panelists, especially Adam Reich and Rachel Sherman. Thank you also to Dani and Javier for including me in the workshop Argentina en Perspectiva Sociológica at the University of Texas at Austin and to the participants, especially Claudio Benzecry, Mariana Heredia, Amalia Leguizamón, and Luisina Perelmiter, for their constructive feedback.

I received financial support for this project from the National Science Foundation (#1519204), the Fulbright Commission to Argentina, and the Department of Sociology, College of Liberal Arts, and International Office at the University of Texas at Austin. I am particularly grateful for early funding from Sheldon Ekland-Olson and the Teresa Lozano Long Institute for Latin American Studies at the University of Texas at Austin that allowed me to explore my initial idea for this project. Thank you also to Héctor Palomino, Brenda Pereyra, Natalia Polti, and especially Andrés Ruggeri at the University of Buenos Aires for their guidance at different stages of my fieldwork in Buenos Aires. I brought this project to completion at the Sociology Department at the University of North Texas. Thank you to my colleagues for providing an intellectual home, and especially to Donna Barnes, who created a genuinely supportive environment for me as a junior professor.

This book is the product of many years living between Texas and Argentina. To the people who helped bridge the distance, thank you. In particular, to Diego and Vero for welcoming me into their families; to Caitlin, Emma, and Natalie for their love from near and far; to Marla, Marcos, and Lindsey for getting me out of the house; and especially to Carina, for opening her beautiful home to me and being a steadfast friend. I also owe a great deal to my family: to my mom for editing countless drafts; to my dad for keeping me busy with projects; to my sister for giving me the most wonderful gift in my niece, Julia; to my grandparents for believing in me; and to my in-laws for their patience as I moved my family across the globe.

Finally, I would like to acknowledge Melissa, who has been the most important source of support throughout this project. Thank you for brainstorming with me, reading almost everything I have ever written, sharing your humor and lightheartedness, and keeping my heart and mind focused on what is most important. For all of this and so much more, thank you.

xi

Parisians would not have stormed the Bastille, Gandhi would not have challenged the empire on which the sun used not to set, Martin Luther King would not have fought white supremacy in the "land of the free . . . ," without their sense of manifest injustices that could be overcome.
—AMARTYA SEN, *The Idea of Justice*

Introduction

In 1919 Conrad Hilton used his life savings to buy a hotel in the small town of Cisco, Texas. At the height of an oil boom, he turned a quick profit and kept buying hotels, establishing what would become the international brand of Hilton Hotels. Hilton's story is a classic entrepreneurial tale: Through hard work, smart decisions, and a bit of luck, a plucky veteran of the Great War turned a humble Texas hotel into a global hospitality corporation. This narrative is seeded with assumptions about how businesses in capitalist economies begin and grow: A boss starts and owns the company, makes decisions unilaterally, and expands to turn an even bigger profit. But there is more than one way to run a business. Some are owned collectively, run democratically, and driven not only to make money but also to advance social values. Yet as you walk along, peeking into shops or hurrying past storefronts, you're unlikely to notice all these different organizational possibilities. That's just not how we think about business.

Now let's imagine you're walking around the densely populated capital city of Buenos Aires, Argentina. An eclectic mix of homes, businesses, schools, and offices line the sidewalks, punctuated by busy bus stops and subway entrances. At the intersection of Corrientes and Callao (pronounced *ca-jao*) Avenues, you stand within blocks of major national landmarks: Argentina's Congress, the tall white obelisk marking the city's four hundredth year, and the nation's Supreme Court, to name a few. Turning off Corrientes, known as "the street that never sleeps," you pass a restaurant window temptingly arrayed with rows of fresh empanadas, a newspaper stand, and an English language school before approaching a street-side café. The windows of the modest Utopia Café are usually covered in seasonally themed decals— pastel flowers in spring, turning leaves in fall—that welcome guests as they step in from the busy street for a cup of coffee and buttery croissants called *medialunas*. What is not immediately evident is that the Utopia Café, with the adjoining Hotel Bauen, is run exclusively by its workers, who make decisions democratically, share tasks and rotate jobs, and pay members equally (see figure Intro.1). Here in Argentina hundreds of companies have adopted a different way of organizing work that centers on democracy, equality, and social needs over expansion and profit. Conrad Hilton presumably would be appalled.

While many people accept Hilton's approach to business as legitimate and even desirable, sociologists who study inequality are concerned with the consequences of such practices. In research on everything from workplaces and neighborhoods to families and schools, sociologists ask: How do inequalities manifest in everyday life? And what are the causes and consequences of unequal conditions? Understanding how inequality operates, who it affects, and why it persists is critically important. It does not, however, shed much light on how we might promote a more just society.[1] In writing this book, I set out to ask a different set of questions: How can we produce and sustain equality? How might organizations broadly distribute opportunities and resources? Why are some businesses motivated to do this? And what challenges do they confront in the process?

Equality is widely agreed upon as worthy—at least in theory. From revolutions of the past to social movements of the present, calls for democracy, justice, and equality can be heard ringing from the halls of government to

2

Intro.1 Entrance to the Utopia Café. Photo by BAUEN Cooperative.

protests in the streets. But there is little consensus on what equality means in practice. In sociology, scholars often use the term *equality* to refer to an ideal or as a synonym for the reduction of inequality. This is an oversimplification. In a field that embraces *inequality* research as core to its disciplinary endeavors, sociologists need to be every bit as attentive to our understanding of *equality* and its effects. Equality, I argue, is not only an important ideal but is a central sociological concept in its own right. In this chapter I introduce the concept of an equality project to bridge abstract debates about equality in principle with the need for empirical studies of equality in practice.

When Work Disappears

In 2002 the entrance to the Hotel Bauen was boarded up, covered in graffiti, and plastered with political propaganda (see figure Intro.2). The year prior, Argentina had experienced one of the worst economic crises in its history. After a decade of rising unemployment and worsening poverty—much of it caused by policy changes that sharply devalued the Argentine peso—investors were skittish and ready to pull their money out of the country. So, in a dramatic turn of events, the government froze all bank accounts.

3

Intro.2 Entrance to the Hotel Bauen after it closed in 2001. Source unknown.

Foreign investors were stymied, but so were regular Argentines, now locked out of their savings. Thousands of outraged people took to the streets, banging pots and pans and chanting, "¡Que se vayan todos!" (Out with them all!). Amid these social mobilizations, the private owners of the Hotel Bauen quietly closed their doors and fired the remaining seventy employees.

Gisela was in her early sixties when she was fired from the Hotel Bauen in 2001. "It was an aberration," she said. "I still get emotional when I remember it. It was the saddest thing. . . . I had been there for twenty years, and [they knew] I didn't have [another] job, that they weren't going to pay a single peso. Imagine how you would feel?"[2]

On her last day at work, Gisela collected uniforms from her fellow employees. A seamstress by trade, she explained, "I was [working] with the linens, we distributed uniforms. . . . They had to turn in all their uniforms before they left, and each person came and said goodbye to me . . . crying bitterly." At the end of the day, Gisela remembered, "they gave me cardboard boxes and told me to put all the uniforms in them. . . . I left everything organized in my sector and locked up."

Towering twenty stories over the streets of Buenos Aires, the Hotel Bauen was once a symbol of luxury (see figure Intro.3). Gisela vividly remembered its glitzy 1978 opening: "Impressive, impressive. I started a month before [it opened]. It was a five-star hotel, but really five stars because it . . . opened when the World Cup was here in Argentina." From the elegant lobby, affluent guests could descend a spiral staircase to an underground nightclub where the walls were tiled with small mirrors that made the whole room look like a disco ball. Or they could take a glass elevator from the ground floor to the second-story bar and restaurant, finding some privacy in its intimate

4

Intro.3 An aerial view of the Hotel Bauen. Photo by Martin Barzilai/Sub Cooperative.

booths shrouded in heavy curtains. Overnight guests enjoyed downtown views from the twenty-story tower and access to a deck and pool that felt like an oasis amid the bustle of urban life.

A single mother of three, Gisela had worked in a perfume shop before learning about the job openings at the Hotel Bauen. She explained, "I had the opportunity to come to this hotel where I could dedicate myself exclusively to making things, and I really liked it . . . the production of curtains, pillowcases, tablecloths, everything related to hotels. It was 1978, the year that [the hotel] opened." Gisela, like many others, knew the history of the Hotel Bauen well. It had been financed with public loans granted by a US-backed military dictatorship, which took power on the pretext of controlling communism.[3] Gisela recalled, "It was the era of the military and the repression, a time when they killed a lot of people . . . but [the hotel] was really nice, a luxury organization. . . . We didn't realize what was happening outside."

It must have been quite a contrast, this constructed facade of luxury juxtaposed against the brutal reality taking place in the streets. Human rights organizations estimate that thirty thousand people were disappeared— kidnapped, tortured, and murdered—by the state during the five-year military dictatorship. After the country returned to democracy in 1983, Gisela said,

5

she gradually became more aware of what had happened: "The girls and boys who were involved in politics, they were the people they [the military] disappeared during that time." But even then, Gisela admitted, "I was never political. I never organized with any [political] party, I was more of a worker." Gisela's understanding of her work as a seamstress as outside of politics would change dramatically in the years to follow.

When Gisela lost her job in 2001, she decided to retire early. But she soon made a startling discovery about her longtime employer: "When I started to do the paperwork to retire, [I realized] they had not contributed to my retirement. . . . They kept the money [even though] they deducted my contribution." As Gisela sought to resolve her retirement situation, she was in contact with other former coworkers negotiating with the bankruptcy judge in charge of the hotel's case to receive the unpaid wages they were owed. When talks stalled, former Bauen employees looked for other options. It became clear to many that losing their jobs was not an individual failure but a byproduct of a greedy employer and a neoliberal political and economic crisis.

Unemployment can be an isolating experience. When work disappears, as William Julius Wilson (1996) puts it, people often feel alone and defeated as life becomes disorganized in the absence of steady jobs. But a very different series of events took place in Argentina. As unemployment rates rose, social movements blossomed all around the country.[4] Residents formed neighborhood assemblies to organize basic services. Unemployed workers known as *piqueteros* blocked streets to demand jobs and social services.[5] And, responding to the wave of bankruptcies, former employees illegally entered and occupied businesses, forming what are called *worker-recuperated businesses* to fight for their rights and revive their source of work.

That's just what organizers from the National Movement of Recuperated Businesses (MNER) suggested to former Bauen employees who reached out to them in 2002: *illegally enter and occupy the shuttered hotel to demand the money they were owed.*[6] Gisela remembered the initial conversations among her former coworkers that took place during visits to occupied factories across the city of Buenos Aires: "I went to the first meeting [when] they started to say that we were going to take the hotel. . . . At that time there were a bunch of recuperated businesses, but the most important thing was that this was not a small hotel or a hotel in the background or in the province. It was in the middle of downtown. It was a really important thing to take it."

In these meetings Gisela saw her former coworkers for the first time in months. She was struck by the hardships they faced: "They didn't have milk to bring home, they couldn't find any work . . . so they couldn't eat. They didn't have any other alternative. . . . This was the only way that they [the owners] would pay their debt to us: to go and plant ourselves inside the hotel until they paid us." After consulting with her family, she decided to join the group. Using a term more typically applied to social movement coparticipants than coworkers, Gisela described her choice: "I decided with a lot of determination, even though I was sixty or so years old. I still feel strong. I still say I'm going to fight for my compañeros."[7]

On March 21, 2003, over a year after the hotel closed, Gisela arrived at the corner of Callao and Corrientes. She trembled as she waited for the others—former coworkers, MNER organizers, workers from other recuperated businesses, students, and neighbors. Gisela knew the Hotel Bauen like the back of her hand, so when the group decided to enter through an underground parking garage, she and a small cadre of women led the way. If they were stopped by the police, they reasoned, older women would certainly garner more respect than younger men. They might even avoid police repression for their trespassing. Approaching the entrance, the group broke the lock and entered a dark underground corridor. They proceeded through the lower levels of the hotel and up the staff stairs, following the light shining in through the floor-to-ceiling windows in the lobby. "When we got there," Gisela said, the women "began to cry and hug because we never thought that we would return to the hotel." They were overwhelmed by what they'd done.

In the months that followed, the group occupied the hotel around the clock, panhandling for spare change on the street corner and sharing what little income they made from working odd jobs. After their appeals to their former employer stalled, the group started the process of forming a worker cooperative to negotiate with the judge as a collective. They decided to keep the hotel's original name but make it into an acronym. *Bauen*—a German word meaning "to construct"—became BAUEN, standing for Buenos Aires, a National Company (Buenos Aires, una Empresa Nacional).[8] It didn't take long for the group to realize there was little hope that they'd ever receive their unpaid wages. So members of the newly formed BAUEN Cooperative set their sights on a more ambitious goal: to reopen the hotel *sin patrón* (without a boss). Rather than returning to an employment relation of dependence, becoming members of a worker cooperative allowed them to share ownership of the company. In the new BAUEN, they would be "worker-owners."

In 2005 the cooperative reopened the hotel to the public and operated it continuously until the state-mandated closure in 2020 during the coronavirus pandemic. During its operation the BAUEN Cooperative succeeded in providing work for many. From 30 founding members in 2003, the BAUEN

Cooperative soon grew to over one hundred members. Their success none-theless came with a big caveat: the cooperative never received the legal right to use the property. In a perplexing series of events, different state actors offered and then withdrew support, passed favorable laws and then vetoed them, and ultimately left the cooperative in a legal limbo for the entire time it operated the downtown hotel.

Equality Projects

Through the process of reorganizing work, members of the BAUEN Coop-erative initiated what I call an *equality project*, a term that is central to un-derstanding the story of this hotel. As mentioned, in sociology the word equality is commonly used to refer to inequality reduction.[9] If we decrease inequalities—so the logic goes—we can promote equality in society. Reduc-ing inequalities is certainly a worthy goal (and the implicit moral project behind much social science research).[10] But equality is not simply the ab-sence of inequality. So what exactly is equality?[11]

Equality often describes situations where people are treated interchange-ably regardless of their differences.[12] Take the idea of political equality, which refers to a system in which each person by virtue of their group membership has an equal influence, may it be through a democratic vote (one person, one vote), equality before the law, or free speech. Political equality is a cor-nerstone of democratic republics, but it is possible in practice only if groups address social and economic differences.[13] Research on everything from vot-ing and enfranchisement to the legal system and law enforcement attests that political equality is rarely upheld in our daily lives.

Efforts to define equality as an ideal are also closely tied to theories of dis-tributive justice, which propose various schemes for distributing resources and opportunities in society.[14] To create a just society, do we equalize basic resources like food and shelter? Should we compensate people for situations outside their control? Or try to make up for the harms of "brute luck"?[15] Eliza-beth Anderson (1999) argues that debates over how to fairly divvy up resources have lost sight of the political aim of distributive efforts: to create *relations of equality* to end oppression. Equality, Anderson argues, requires considering demands for recognition and respect as well as principles of distribution.[16]

Across these egalitarian debates, consensus about how to promote equal-ity in practice has remained elusive.[17] As journalist Joshua Rothman (2020) observed in the *New Yorker*, "The complexities of egalitarianism are espe-

8

cially frustrating because inequalities are so easy to grasp. C.E.O.s, on average, make almost three hundred times what their employees make; billionaire donors shape our politics; automation favors owners over workers; urban economies grow while rural areas stagnate; the best health care goes to the richest." Rothman points out what social scientists have documented well: people and groups vary in their access to human capital, resources, and opportunities, and that variance has major consequences.[18] Just documenting that inequality is real and consequential, however, doesn't tell us how to promote equality in our families, workplaces, and economies.

Plenty of inequalities, after all, are widely considered legitimate.[19] Take the issue of CEO pay that Rothman brings up. In the United States, CEOs of public firms make 278 times the salary of a typical worker (a whopping US$17.2 million per CEO per year, on average).[20] The Occupy movement, which emerged in response to widening socioeconomic gaps following the 2008 recession, identified the disproportionate power of such superhigh incomes—the "1 percent"—and encouraged the 99 percent to recognize income inequality as a social problem.[21] Indeed, extreme wage gaps like those between CEOs and the typical workers at their firms now stir a sense of injustice. As Amartya Sen so cogently states in the epigraph of this chapter, identifying disparities as social problems is key to motivating efforts for social change. Still, very few people question the underlying principle that workers are paid differently in the first place. Managers earn more than their employees, architects more than construction workers, tenured professors more than adjuncts, and so on. We might think this is perfectly normal. But this also reveals that what constitutes equality is closely tied to our collective determinations about which inequalities are unjust.[22]

In this book, I show how equality can be fostered through social interactions and inscribed in organizations.[23] Rather than an idealized end point or distributional achievement, I argue that equality should be understood as a *project*: an effort to promote more egalitarian relations between people by revaluing the categories that orient social practice.[24] A relational understanding of the social world focuses on relationships between people, positions, and organizations and the categories that are produced therein. In their rigorous account of relational inequality theory, Donald Tomaskovic-Devey and Dustin Avent-Holt (2019) argue that inequalities become durable when categorical distinctions map onto organizational divisions of labor.[25] The resources, relations, practices, and cultural models that constitute an organization's distinctive "inequality regime" are key to explaining how inequalities

9

emerge and persist.[26] Equality projects turn our attention to how organizations might *question, redefine, or even dismantle* categorical distinctions in order to promote more equal interpersonal relations.

Back in Argentina, workers occupied businesses to create better jobs and more equal workplaces—in other words, to initiate equality projects. Capturing the sentiment, one worker said, "We formed the cooperative with the criteria of equal wages and making basic decisions by assembly; we are against the separation of manual and intellectual work; we want a rotation of positions and; above all, the ability to recall our elected leaders" (quoted in Lavaca Collective 2007b: 8). In the following chapters, I examine one equality project in depth, considering how workers in the BAUEN Cooperative reorganized work to promote relational equality and the dilemmas they confronted along the way. I focus on four workplace practices that change not only how work is done but also how people interact: democratic decision-making, workplace participation, job rotation, and pay equality. Through these practices workers have directly confronted categorical distinctions that are common in workplaces: power differences justified by ownership and authority; differential access to opportunities justified by skill, training, and experience; and unequal compensation justified by what types of work are valued over others.

To understand the inner workings of this equality project, I visited and worked at the Hotel Bauen on and off for nearly a decade. I washed linens alongside workers in the laundry room, answered phones at the reception desk, cleaned guest rooms with housekeepers, and observed how co-op members made decisions, organized their money, and interacted with clients, suppliers, politicians, and supporters. Through an analysis of organizational efforts to democratize decision-making, facilitate participation, rotate jobs, and equalize pay in the BAUEN Cooperative, I identify a series of organizational and cultural mechanisms that help us understand how equality is produced and sustained. *Inclusion* refers to the shifting of power dynamics that results from disrupting relations of domination based on ownership and integrating people into the value added by their efforts.[27] *Opportunity distribution* refers to the sharing of resources between members of bounded groups and those outside their network. Finally, *symbolic leveling* refers to the discursive emphasis on peoples' equivalent ability to participate in decision-making, learn new skills, and contribute value to a group (Sobering 2019a).

This book cannot provide a one-size-fits-all prescription for how to produce equality.[28] Across time and space, an organization's context and people's assessments of their circumstances vary tremendously. Any examination into how people go about creating more equal relationships requires attention to *why* they are doing so, whether they are motivated by a collective commitment to democratic participation or a sense of manifest injustice fomented by some feature of the status quo. In this sense, I use the word *project* intentionally in two ways. First, projects are the building blocks that connect what equality means in a particular context with the ways that everyday experiences are organized based on that meaning.[29] Second, the term signals the ways that we *project* into the future.[30] This notion of an equality project builds on efforts to advance democratic egalitarian goals that Erik Olin Wright (2010) calls "real utopias."[31] By combining the words *real* (something that exists) and *utopia* (a place that cannot exist), Wright purposely plays with the oxymoron to describe the dynamic interaction of hope for the future and daily social practice in actual attempts to create social institutions free from oppression. Wright's broad definition of real utopias runs the gamut from participatory governance to gender equality, though, while my notion of equality projects focuses specifically on how to facilitate more equal relations in organizations, including practices aimed at material and symbolic distribution and cultures that develop an "egalitarian ethos."[32]

How We Do Business

Let's now consider work in political terms. The institution of employment is not only undemocratic (most people have limited—if any—voice in their workplaces) but also authoritarian (most employers exercise arbitrary and unaccountable power over their workers' lives).[33] Conventional capitalist workplaces are oddly close to popular portrayals of communist dictatorships: the dictator is the boss, the organization owns all the assets, planning is centralized and hierarchical, and the ultimate punishment of exile is being fired.[34] What if work organizations were democratic instead?

Worker cooperatives partially answer this compelling question.[35] As businesses that are owned and operated by their workers, cooperatives have a long history rooted in practices of collective production, forms of mutual aid, and indigenous social organization.[36] By the Industrial Revolution, cooperatives offered an alternative to capitalist work arrangements based on a critique of the exploitation and alienation inherent to working in a relation of dependence in which workers labor under the authority of a boss. Legally and operationally, members of worker cooperatives share ownership as worker-owners, breaking the classic distinction between those roles. While specific legal classifications vary by locality, contemporary cooperatives are guided

11

by the shared principles of self-responsibility, democracy, equality, and solidarity.[37] Cooperatives span industries and borders, from small, relatively unstructured self-help organizations like your local food co-op to large, transnational businesses that adopt hierarchies to produce goods and services, like the famous Mondragón Corporation in Spain (comprising over 250 cooperative companies in the finance, industrial production, retail, and knowledge industries).

A dynamic and growing body of scholarship has examined cooperatives as organizational levelers.[38] Among research that has detailed the inner workings of workplace democracy, many studies have focused on the ways that organizations—even cooperatives—end up *reproducing* inequalities.[39] Indeed, as ongoing efforts, equality projects do not and cannot eradicate all inequality. Organizations are not neutral arenas in which we can identify and stamp out social problems but racialized and gendered structures that create and maintain inequalities.[40] Researchers tend to look at cooperatives in terms of whether or not they uphold purist, cooperative ideals in every aspect of doing business (Is this *really* a co-op?) rather than focusing on what they might teach us about efforts, however imperfect, to reorient social practice.[41] Worker cooperatives cannot eliminate all inequality, but cooperative organizational practices can be powerful leveling tools. Cooperative groups can question, resist, and reconfigure formal and informal practices and cultural models that shape how people interact, offering possible progressive paths toward more just and democratic workplaces.

The relative silence about workplace equality also comes from interdisciplinary research on organizations. Much of this focuses on generalizable findings, reporting how organizations mimic each other, adopt similar practices, and reproduce inequalities in generic ways.[42] A focus on social interaction within stable organizations can certainly illuminate local dynamics and patterns of meaning making. Yet organizations aren't passive recipients of their environment; people within organizations actively modify, emulate, and sometimes break institutional expectations.[43] Here Joan Acker (1989, 5) offers helpful advice: scholars should *also* focus on moments of organizational transformation—both large and small—that can expose deep-set interests and assumptions that guide people's actions.[44]

Worker-recuperated businesses are unique in this respect. They are organizations in which inequalities became starkly visible, motivating workers to question business-as-usual practices and reorganize their work.[45] In the twenty-first century, thousands of workers in Argentina have occupied closed businesses—nearly four hundred in total as of 2018—and converted

12

them into worker-run cooperatives.[46] The project of workplace recuperation is also underway in countries around the world.[47]

Arriving at the Hotel Bauen

On a cold January night in 2006, I sat in a dark room at the University of Michigan to watch a screening of *The Take*, a vivid documentary about Argentine businesses being occupied and converted into worker cooperatives.[48] As a member of a student housing cooperative, I had made the trek from Austin, Texas, to Ann Arbor for our annual conference.[49] After a busy day learning all sorts of facts and figures about cooperatives, I left the film screening bubbling over with questions that none of the panels and breakout sessions could answer: *Why was this happening in Argentina? What was the experience like for workers? Would the cooperatives survive?* When I had the opportunity to study abroad, Argentina was my first pick.

During my first stay in Buenos Aires in 2008, my academic adviser put me in contact with Alberto, a member of the BAUEN Cooperative. We'd come to know each other well over the next decade, but in those days Alberto was working in the press sector at the Hotel Bauen. He was the first line of contact for journalists and students like me interested in learning about the recuperated business. During our first conversations, Alberto told me about the origins of the cooperative and showed me around the hotel. I spent the next month visiting the press sector a couple of times a week, helping in any way I could (mostly translating documents into English), and attending public events and meetings at the hotel. Those weeks marked the beginning of what would become my decade-long project on the BAUEN Cooperative and the movement of worker-recuperated businesses in the city of Buenos Aires.

My research eventually involved observing work processes and interactions, interviewing members of cooperatives, attending rallies and events in the Hotel Bauen and across the city, and doing actual shift work for ten months in the BAUEN Cooperative. I spoke with local experts on worker-recuperated businesses and spent hours combing through organizational and university archives to better understand their history. I closely followed local news and public policy to track the status of ongoing challenges confronting worker-recuperated businesses in Argentina. In the appendix I detail my fieldwork, the selection of the Hotel Bauen as my case study, and my process of data analysis.

By the time I arrived at the Hotel Bauen, it had undergone a complete transformation from its origins as a privately owned and operated hotel.

13

When the BAUEN Cooperative reopened the facility, workers adopted democratic practices to organize their operations. Over the years, it had also become a leader in the movement of worker-recuperated businesses owing to its organizing efforts, central location, and ability to host events, press conferences, and visits from other groups. No other organization in Argentina has been this prominent, which helps explain why it received such extensive local, national, and international news coverage. The cooperative's struggles have been meticulously documented by its own members, local scholars, and national policy makers. Its guest rooms and ballrooms have been photographed for the *New York Times* and a host of similarly high-profile media outlets.[50] Its stories have been told in movie theaters and on the radio, including a full-length documentary film (Grupo Alavío 2015). These snapshots generally depict the cooperative during moments of crisis, focusing on inspiring, if carefully practiced, portrayals of efforts to advocate for workers' rights and overcome adversity.

This book takes a more holistic view of the Hotel Bauen, offering a look at not just moments of crisis but also the quotidian interactions and everyday operations of the cooperative hotel over many years. Unlike most outsiders, I committed early on to showing up, over and over again, to understand how and why workers were recuperating the business. This book is not the product of a single uninterrupted period of fieldwork but the result of extensive longitudinal research conducted over series of visits and revisits, each lasting anywhere from two weeks to a full year.[51] For nearly a decade, I returned to Buenos Aires year after year to observe and participate in working life in the hotel. When my periods of in situ fieldwork would come to a close, I didn't stop collecting data but shifted methods. I stayed in touch with my participants through WhatsApp and social media, and I followed the local news to track political and legal issues impacting the BAUEN Cooperative. Studying organizations as dynamic entities benefits from marshaling multiple types of data: observations, interviews, internal documents, and external coverage, from court files to financial reports to news media.

This approach to social scientific research is time-consuming and logistically complicated. Yet this type of long-term ethnography is crucial to both developing social theory and practicing ethical research. Throughout this book you will see how (and why) sociological theories that frequently focus on the exploitative nature of work and the stability of organizations can be elaborated through the fine-grained study of how workers redesign work and attempt to change, rather than play by, the rules of the game. All this is to say, studying one workplace over an extended period provided more

14

than just a rich description of a single case—it allowed me to consider the dynamic processes and changing web of relationships that constituted the organization.

Investing time and attention to understand lived experiences is also valuable because it opens doors to building meaningful relationships with the people we study. Given the BAUEN Cooperative's leadership role in the movement of recuperated businesses, longtime members were accustomed to recounting their history to outsiders. These practiced narratives were important, because they showed me how the cooperative presented itself to the public. But through my repeated visits, I was able to develop the trust needed to move beyond these scripts and into the complexities of members' experiences. Perhaps most tellingly, I embraced the cooperative ethos of mutual accountability and made sure to stay connected to the community I studied. After drafting this manuscript, I returned to the Hotel Bauen in 2019 to share my arguments and publishing plans with members of the cooperative. It was the first time I ever stayed as a guest in the hotel, and I provide a reflection on this experience in the epilogue.

Overview

The next chapter introduces the movement of worker-recuperated businesses through the fascinating history of the Hotel Bauen. I pick up where Gisela left off, when she and her coworkers occupied the hotel and began to transform it into a worker cooperative. Equality projects require that people question the status quo, collectively define what equality means for them, and take actionable steps to change how they interact. Chapter 1 explains how workplaces can undergo significant changes and how these moments of change can imprint transformative practices on existing organizations.

The subsequent chapters detail the equality project in the BAUEN Cooperative, charting how workers broadly distributed power, opportunities, and resources. Chapter 2 explains how collective decision-making took place in the BAUEN Cooperative. Structural changes to the workplace provided the legitimacy and rationale for workers to reconfigure power dynamics, sharing the authority previously held by owners and managers among the newly minted worker-owners. Drawing on many hours of observations in meetings, as well as meeting notes since the cooperative's earliest days, I show how formal efforts to broadly distribute power can sometimes be supported and at other times undermined by informal dynamics through which workers identify obstacles to participation and negotiate the meanings of fairness at work.

15

Chapter 3 moves from the spaces of formal decision-making—what scholars refer to as an organization's *governance*—to the ways that workers learned to participate in the everyday *management* of the hotel. For members of the BAUEN Cooperative, participation was about more than voting in meetings; they had to adopt a different approach to work itself. Workers in the hotel were encouraged to self-manage: to organize their own daily routines, problem-solve as issues arose, express their opinions, and invest their time and energy in the workplace. Formal policies enshrined this equality project in the organization's structure, but the BAUEN Cooperative also experienced cultural changes as it sought to cultivate an egalitarian ethos among its membership. As people became worker-owners—or compañeros, as they called each other—they developed an awareness of their work as a political act.

Equality projects require a lot of reflection and planning. Members must question the ways organizational practices reinforce, redefine, or even dismantle categorical distinctions in order to justify more equal interpersonal relations. In the BAUEN Cooperative, this involved confronting how everyday inequalities—many of which were widely legitimated in society—played out at work. A primary way that organizations perpetuate social inequality is by segregating people into different jobs by categories like race, class, and gender. In chapter 4 I show how the BAUEN Cooperative developed a system of job rotation to allow people to change jobs across the hotel. For housekeepers to move to accounting positions, and receptionists to move to maintenance, the cooperative had to grapple with the meaning and importance of *skill*, breaking down commonsense ways of understanding who should fill which job and affording workers a broader understanding of the organization across social differences. I also rotated jobs from sector to sector during my longest period of fieldwork in the hotel, and in doing so, I found that the practice was implemented informally. Elected officers thus exercised great discretion over job rotation. As in so many organizations, such a discretionary policy was a double-edged sword: it facilitated a more flexible and holistic approach to collective decision-making, even as it allowed bias and discrimination in its implementation.

Job rotation in the Hotel Bauen was made possible by the fact that all members were paid the same base salary. Chapter 5 delves into the politics of equal pay. I explore how the organization navigated its commitment to pay equity in a context of scarcity by developing a system of what I call *survival finance*. Survival finance addresses three primary ways that workers benefit from full-time employment: wages, credit, and time. As a key part of its equality project, the cooperative's effort to broadly distribute resources

16

was a straightforward reflection of the organization's values. Despite spirited debates and lofty ideals, however, workers in the BAUEN Cooperative continually put in long hours doing physically demanding labor. Chapter 6 explores the effects of this overwork and discusses how workers reconciled their emotional and physical pain with their broader purpose as members of a worker-recuperated business.

The BAUEN Cooperative's remarkable success was never easy. From day one, the cooperative navigated twists, turns, roadblocks, and dead ends. Throughout its operation until its closure in 2020, the cooperative's use of the Hotel Bauen remained legally unresolved. In chapter 6 I explain why the hotel survived and continued to pursue its equality project for so long. The BAUEN Cooperative was able to remain open for business not because politicians neglected its appeals, nor because the government lacked the resources to enforce the law. Rather, I argue that it survived due to the state's *unwillingness* to resolve its situation.

The cooperative's trials and tribulations in securing its legality cannot be separated from its equality project. At the Hotel Bauen, joining the cooperative provided both a source of work and inside access to a social movement that questioned the legitimacy of private property and challenged state authority. By chronicling efforts to legalize their occupation, I show how this long-term campaign led workers to incorporate social movement practices into their everyday work routines. Equality projects, I argue, can transform organizations into activist workplaces in which production and resistance combine to transform the meanings and practices of paid work.

In the conclusion I reflect on the broader lessons of the BAUEN Cooperative and revisit the theoretical and political issues they raise. Returning to the idea of equality projects as a way to understand social change in and beyond the workplace, I advocate for scholarship that not only explains inequality and exclusion but also analyzes the creative solutions people adopt to address social problems. The epilogue provides an update on the status of the Hotel Bauen at the time of publication and explores the potentials of workplace recuperation in and beyond Argentina.

Somos presente y futuro
A resistir y ocupar
El Bauen hoy no se cierra
Lo vamos a levantar

We are the present and the future
To resist and occupy
The "Bauen" doesn't close today
We are going to lift it up

—CHANT IN THE HOTEL BAUEN

1   Recuperating the Hotel Bauen

"The hotel was born bad and ended worse," Lacunza told me one afternoon in the Hotel Bauen. He knew its history well: he had started working here soon after it opened and eventually became a founder of the cooperative. Now in his fifties, he had worked as a receptionist for over thirty years, nearly twenty of them at the Hotel Bauen. When I ran into Lacunza on the third floor, he was hard at work plastering the walls of an unused office in preparation for new tenants. I joined him as he sat down to evaluate his progress. Showing me his work, he reiterated that the hotel "was born bad from the moment it was constructed." Sure, the office looked good with a fresh coat of plaster, but Lacunza insisted the hotel needed far more than cosmetic repairs. I noted that his assessment hearkened back to Argentina's recent and turbulent history. It also suggested the very real possibility for an organization, even this one, to change over time.

The birth of an organization—what scholars refer to as its *founding moment*—is key to understanding how it operates and evolves over time. Founders draw on technical, economic, political, and cultural resources available to them, and they imprint this founding context onto their fledgling organization.[1] What resources they incorporate or avoid are not predetermined but patterned by the founders' interactions with external stakeholders.[2] Research usually emphasizes the persistence of these originating structures and practices, yet it's fascinating to consider how these imprints might impact an organization's ability to transform and change over time.[3]

Worker-recuperated businesses like the Hotel Bauen, for instance, were originally founded as privately owned firms that converted into worker-run cooperatives with new ownership arrangements, decision-making structures, divisions of labor, and workplace cultures. In such moments of change, we get a glimpse into a second founding moment that *reimprints* new characteristics onto existing workplaces.[4] These cannot obviate the past; instead, for workers at the Hotel Bauen, the business's origins became the inspiration for radical change in the second founding.[5] Not only can organizations change, but reimprinting can also turn critiques of the past into justifications for novel organizational forms.

The primary purpose of this chapter is to lay the historical foundation for how and why workers initiated an equality project in the BAUEN Cooperative. Indeed, the shared history and collective commitments bound up in organizational reimprinting are key to understanding why certain workplace problems are identified as unjust and which tools workers draw on when they set out to reconfigure workplace relations. Telling the history of the Hotel Bauen also reveals a story of organizational evolution. As the cooperative reorganized work, its collective choices were shaped by other important actors, from politicians and social movement activists to fellow recuperated businesses and cooperatives. Throughout this chapter, I trace the lasting impacts of the Hotel Bauen's two founding moments: the hotel's creation in the 1970s and its reorganization as a worker cooperative twenty years later. The dynamics between these two moments show how the cooperative founders used the hotel's origin not as a guide for persistence but as a motivation for change.

The Hotel Bauen's story begins during Argentina's last military dictatorship (1976–1983). For thirty years, the business would trace broad political and economic shifts. As the country returned to democracy in the 1980s, the hotel

20

was bought and sold by multinational firms, stable jobs were replaced with contract work, and cost cutting eventually whittled away the once luxurious accommodations. The hotel's 2001 closure could have been its concluding chapter, but its workers were ready to rewrite the script. In a time of dramatic social unrest marked by an explosion of social movement participation, the prospect of occupying the closed business and forming a cooperative seemed increasingly feasible. With the support of external stakeholders, the founders of the BAUEN Cooperative occupied the hotel, demanded their rights, and ultimately resuscitated their source of work for another two decades.

Bauen (German): To Build, to Construct

The World Cup soccer tournament is a much-anticipated megaevent—and, for some, that might even be an understatement. In Argentina, a country known for its love of the sport, the prospect of hosting the 1978 World Cup was intoxicating, if controversial. Just two years earlier, a group of military officers had led a coup, ending the government of President Isabel Perón.[6] Once in power, a military junta made a series of economic, legal, and political reforms that immediately impacted daily life in Argentina. Political opposition was prohibited, wages were frozen, collective bargaining agreements were voided, and the right to strike was suspended. In preparation for the spotlight that would accompany the World Cup, the military leaders initiated a flurry of preparations, including the construction of hotels to accommodate the influx of soccer fans. A businessman named Marcelo Iurcovich seized the opportunity, forming the Bauen Corporation to construct a four-star hotel in Buenos Aires.

The military coup and resulting junta had by this time violently targeted union organizers, students, academics, and members of left-leaning political parties. Police abducted people from their homes and public spaces, systematically torturing and then executing them in a network of 340 clandestine detention centers secreted around the country. As historian Luis Alberto Romero (2002, 219) explains, the objective of these state operations was not only to "eliminate all political activism, including social protest" but also to target the living, to atomize and isolate people such that "the whole of society . . . [would] be controlled and dominated by terror." Between 1976 and 1983, it is estimated that this state-sponsored campaign disappeared over thirty thousand people.[7] Memorials to this time can be found throughout Argentina today. Just a block from the Hotel Bauen, a commemorative tile (*baldosa por la memoria*) is set into the sidewalk in remembrance of two Argentines kidnapped off the street, never to be seen again.

During the military dictatorship, the minister of the economy took steps toward a massive economic transformation. The background: In the years following World War I, Argentina had become one of the world's wealthiest countries by implementing a program of Keynesian reforms that included import substitution, industrialization, and strong state intervention in the economy. These policies cultivated national growth and were subsequently expanded during the presidency of Juan Domingo Perón (1946–1955), Argentina's most important twentieth-century political figure. Perón added strong cultural and political elements to policies aimed at redistributing income to the working class and generating full employment to support the growth of the middle class. By the end of the 1970s, however, state retrenchment began. Governing forces had now identified the welfare state as the source of political and social instability and instead promoted an economic program based on free-market economics. Where business, labor, and the government once vied for state resources, the new economic team of the military junta concentrated power among business groups and national and transnational corporations. "Dismantling the instruments of state planning, regulation, and control of the economy that had been assembled since 1930" included deregulating interest and credit rates, removing currency exchange controls, and dismantling tariff protections, which ultimately allowed the private sector to grow at the expense of public firms and state-sponsored services (Romero 2002, 231; see also Jozami, Paz, and Villareal 1985).

Profiting Off Democracy

For businessmen like Marcelo Iurcovich, the opening of the economy and the concentration of power in the military intertwined to offer both financial and political support. Public funding was made available to prepare the country, particularly its capital city, for the World Cup, and Iurcovich ultimately received a generous loan from the state to build his hotel. Flush with cash, the Hotel Bauen inaugurated an era of luxury consumption and high-end service. On its opening day, the opulent hotel featured seven ballrooms, an auditorium, a restaurant, a bar, a nightclub, a pool, and over two hundred guest rooms with downtown views. Even twenty years later, longtime employees recalled the glass elevator in the lobby, the intimate upper-story bar known for its bottle service, and the staircase that spiraled down into an underground, mirror-bedecked nightclub.

Lacunza reflected on the glitz and glamor, telling me that the owners went all-out hoping to attract affluent international visitors rather than domestic clientele. He even believed the builders purposefully chose materials "that were too sumptuous and expensive for the Argentine market. . . . Because they needed to spend money. They needed Carrara marble . . . so that they could use [the hotel] for every international event."

Many of Iurcovich's shady business dealings would eventually be exposed by his former employees.[8] By 2015 Lacunza and others who worked in the Hotel Bauen had discovered that all this luxury had a dark source. As we shared yerba maté in the half-plastered office, Lacunza continued telling me the hotel's origin story:

> The construction of this monster cost millions and millions of pesos from the famous "soft credits" [*créditos blandos*] that were [used to] prepar[e] the city for the World Cup, all while people disappeared. The military junta decided to do something that would have a really strong impact on society. They used the World Cup to cover up the aberrations and the barbarities that were happening. So they organized a facelift [*una lavada de cara*] for all the places where it would take place. In Buenos Aires, here in the capital, there weren't enough hotels to accommodate all the tourism that was going to come. So they decided to organize this hotel and received the money in the form of a credit through an arm of the National Development Bank.

As he spoke, Lacunza pointed out the paradox of the hotel's construction—at once a luxury destination for an influx of tourists and a symbol of authoritarian opulence in a nation under siege.

In 1982 Argentina's military launched an unpopular and ultimately unsuccessful attempt to invade the British-controlled Falkland Islands (Islas Malvinas) off the southern coast of South America. Argentina had asserted its claim on the archipelago since the 1830s but was defeated in this effort. After Argentina surrendered in the Falklands War, as this invasion came to be known, Argentina's internal political divisions and rising popular resistance led the military junta to cede its power to democracy. In 1983 Raúl Alfonsín was elected president—a critical moment for the country but a change that meant little for Iurcovich, who continued to enjoy political favors and economic perks.[9] Over the years, the Bauen Corporation never paid back the principal on its original state-sponsored loan. As Lacunza explained (and a series of documents confirm), the start-up loan "was never repaid. Not a peso, nothing. It's all a lie. They say they paid, [but] they didn't pay anything."

Evidence of fraudulent business deals, money laundering, and the willful ignorance of state officials remained inside the Hotel Bauen, even decades later. In the cooperative's administrative offices, for example, workers dedicated an entire closet to storing hundreds of identical letters from the city

23

1.1 Stacks of overdue tax notifications to the Hotel Bauen from the city of Buenos Aires. Photo by the author.

government. Stacks of green-and-white envelopes were stamped "UNPAID TAXES," a persistent reminder of their former boss's shady business dealings (see figure 1.1). When I asked a longtime worker about the letters, he mentioned that the hotel had originally been incorporated as a consortium (i.e., as a condominium association rather than a commercial hotel) as a tax dodge: each hotel room was registered individually with the government. "It's so crazy here," he noted as he went back to work.

Multinational Capital and Precarious Work

24   In its heyday the Hotel Bauen and its sister property, the Bauen Suites (constructed around the corner in 1982), had hundreds of employees. Workers remembered a bustling hub of activity: "At first," recalled Matías, who was

hired in 1993, there was a lot of work. "I remember, in 1997, it was like a city because we had everything here inside. We had the hospitality part, the bar. There was a clothing store. There was a hair salon on the first floor." Matías remembered that the "movement of people" through the Hotel Bauen was "impressive." But as an employee, he was isolated to his post and restricted from "walk[ing] around to the different places" in the hotel. Alberto, whose tenure began in the 1990s as well, confirmed, "Salons were booked nearly Monday to Monday. There was a really good sales team. . . . There was a lot of product being delivered, lots of controls. . . . We worked long hours. . . . [W]e were there Saturday and Sunday; you didn't get a day off."

During this time the original owners of the hotel began to move their real estate assets. Lacunza explained what members of the cooperative learned when they set out to investigate their former boss:

> We had the opportunity to see some of the mortgages that they [the owners] made in a really sketchy way [*de una manera bastante dudosa*]. The hotel was here [in Buenos Aires], but the loans were made in provinces like Misiones [hundreds of miles away]. And even with a mortgaged hotel, the hotel changed its registered name [*razón social*], simulating sales. I don't know what it's like in the United States. I figure it's similar to here. If you have something mortgaged, you can't sell it. Well, they sold it five times, minimum. In reality, they changed the registered name and kept it.

Archival research by workers, lawyers, and academics backs up Lacunza's description of events. In 1997 the Bauen Corporation sold the property to a Chilean firm called Solari, which had no experience managing hotels and made exactly one payment on its purchase in the four years it retained management. An article published by members of the cooperative years later recounted how Solari let the hotel fall into disrepair, "initiat[ing] a process of emptying [the hotel], laying off workers, and then declaring bankruptcy" (Pierucci and Tonarelli 2014, 150).

Work in the Hotel Bauen became increasingly precarious during those years.[10] The owners were cutting corners in a regulatory context that was increasingly lax. During the 1990s, conservative political administrations modified a series of laws to facilitate a more flexible labor regime, increasing the length of the workweek, reducing salary requirements, and allowing contract work without social guarantees.[11] On why the owners would change the business's registered name, Lacunza speculated, "If you ask me why they would change the name, it's because it was a strategy: first, so that the workers would lose their seniority . . . and also so that everything that had to do with debt and the state would be diluted." Given that the original loan had been financed by a state agency that no longer existed, Lacunza thought the owners may have used the multiple sales to cover their tracks, obscuring the long-forgotten origins of their debt.[12]

With fewer regulatory barriers, Solari subcontracted parts of the hotel to third-party firms, effectively firing longtime employees and rehiring them without seniority or job protections. Few employees were spared. Alberto, who worked in event planning and catering, described, "The first privatizations were here: it was the bar and food service. [But] we held on to the breakfast service . . . [along with] the restaurant and the disco."

Others told me how certain jobs became more task intensive in this period. One person who worked in the lobby explained how three jobs (concierge, receptionist, and cashier) were rolled into one position. As they witnessed these changes, employees felt pressure to adapt; Alberto said that if they expressed their discontent, managers would ask, "Do you want to keep working here?" Their options were clear: "Either you stay here in the Bauen, or we fire you and you can look for work someplace else." According to a different former employee, the private owners took a systematic approach in which workers were "worn down" over time. When confronted with these options to accept the new working conditions or move on, one member described a common response: "What am I going to do? I am forty-five or fifty years old. Where will I go?"

Bankruptcy and Crisis

By 2000 the Hotel Bauen was in crisis. The tower had not received much-needed infrastructural investments, sales were plummeting, and employees were being laid off in droves. Those who remained saw bankruptcy on the horizon. Not only was the management canceling future reservations, but employees were being paid a fraction of their salary. "When you went to get paid, they [the managers] would tell you, 'Look, I'll pay you half,'" one employee remembered. It offended many who had been working full-time for less pay, no seniority, and now no paychecks. Alberto described the deterioration's effect on the staff: "It was belittling. . . . I think that is the biggest realization for a person who has lived in the middle class all their life—without activism, without anything—to see so much mistreatment around you." The erosion of their job quality may have made them feel helpless in the moment, but as Alberto pointed out, it also spurred workers to develop a political consciousness of labor rights.

These were contentious days, you may recall. Callao Avenue—the street that runs in front of the Hotel Bauen—was a regular pathway for protesters marching toward Congress and other government ministries to make their demands known. Years later, as protesters continued to weave through the streets of Buenos Aires, members of the BAUEN Cooperative could often be seen standing on the mezzanine roof overlooking the street, waving and cheering in solidarity with pro-labor organizations, groups of unemployed workers, and social movements mobilizing for human rights. But in 2001 employees observed the mobilizations from inside the hotel, worried about the economy and the future of their jobs.

Inés was working as a housekeeper in these last months of the original Hotel Bauen. With very few overnight guests left, she would watch protesters marching past the towering hotel, hear their chants, and occasionally smell the tires they burned on street corners as the smoke wafted upward. Inés remembered: "The last day that we worked here under a boss, it was December 28. We looked outside, and there was a march protesting the *corralito, cacerolazo*.[13] It was incredible. In all my life, I have never seen that number of people. You couldn't see any space in the street. . . . It was filled with people. . . . The mobilizations were incredible [and] very sad."

During that time the owners of the Hotel Bauen declared bankruptcy, and its title was transferred from the Chilean firm to a third corporation, Mercoteles, that had formed in 2001. Later on, when former employees and advocates probed these transactions, they would find that Mercoteles's *only* registered economic activity was the purchase of the hotel just five days after its formation. In addition, Mercoteles was registered under the name of the son of Marcelo Iurcovich, the original owner of the Bauen Corporation. Based on these findings, the cooperative would later argue in court that Mercoteles was a shell company used to transfer assets back to the original owners of the property, the Iurcovich family.[14]

On December 28, 2001, the hotel closed. The seventy workers who remained were finally fired. And in the streets popular mobilizations continued as people protested the deepening economic and political crisis. These protests did not erupt out of nowhere. They were the culmination of social unrest that accompanied rising unemployment in the late 1990s (see Svampa and Pereyra 2003). In 2001 the middle class joined with the unemployed to decry the economic policies and political leaders who had made this mess. Shouting the slogan "Out with them all!" (*¡Que se vayan todos!*), Argentines told the world that the exclusion and inequality they were experiencing were unjust.

Néstor Kirchner's election to the presidency in 2003 helped restore some stability to the country. Yet it could not heal the wounds from the 2001–2002 crisis.[15] After the country defaulted on its sovereign debt, Argentines continued to struggle with high levels of unemployment and poverty while openly questioning the legitimacy of the laws and policies that had allowed such a crisis to occur. Meanwhile, the Hotel Bauen was boarded up and plastered with posters and graffiti. Its erstwhile owners removed items of value—mattresses, linens, and electronics—from the building. Former employees repeatedly called the trustee appointed by the court to monitor the property during the bankruptcy negotiations, to alert them to the clandestine lootings. But the once grand hotel was left in shambles.

"Occupy, Resist, Produce"

After losing their jobs, Hotel Bauen's workers initially went their separate ways. Some found temporary jobs or decided to retire, while others joined the swollen ranks of the unemployed (by 2002 over 22 percent of Argentina's population was out of work).[16] As weeks and months passed, some former Bauen employees began to uncover irregularities with their previous employment. Lacunza noted, as Gisela did in the introduction, "Since [the hotel closed], we discovered that a lot of the contributions that they [the owners] deducted from our salaries had not been made. Lots of people who were close to retirement had problems with them because when they went to do their retirement paperwork, they found that they had not made the contributions. . . . It was theft." Employees still hoping they would receive the pay they had been owed for the last months of the hotel's operation were crushed. Now there was no retirement money either.

Planning the Occupation

Concerned former Bauen employees started to meet to discuss their options for restitution. Alberto remembered, "I went to some of the meetings they organized at first . . . to see if we could contract a lawyer, if we could pull together some money. It was all really disorganized. The truth is, there weren't any professionals who wanted to work for free. Finding a lawyer who wanted to work for free? Forget it!" Eventually the group connected with organizers from the National Movement of Recuperated Businesses (MNER), which had been helping others in similar circumstances occupy their former workplaces. The Bauen workers began to consider joining the movement, mobilizing under the slogan "Occupy, resist, produce." Doing so could help them gain leverage with the hotel's former owners. It also offered a road map to reclaiming lost jobs. Alberto described this period of possibility and discovery:

> What we tried to do at first was follow the slogan of the movement.... It gave us the push we needed to go in. It's like I told you, after all the abuse and everything that the workers dealt with, there were a lot of people in the meetings who didn't want to go to the trouble of occupying this.... But it's fine because, like I said, if you don't have activist experience [*militancia*], if you don't have political action or an ideology, you can't organize a group.... Really, what happened was the movement [MNER] structured all of this, and we were encouraged to go to factories, to see other recuperated factories, to talk with the compañeros.

During these meetings former Bauen employees visited other worker-recuperated businesses around the city of Buenos Aires. They went, for instance, to Chilavert, a graphics factory in the Nueva Pompeya neighborhood, and to IMPA (Industrias Metalúrgicas y Plásticas Argentina; Metallurgical and Plastic Industries of Argentina), a metallurgical factory in the Almagro neighborhood.[17] Alberto explained what they learned from these worker cooperatives:

> The message was that they were all strong, they endured . . . that's why the slogan was "Occupy, resist, and produce." These were three words that were really time-consuming, because the occupation was long, the resistance was long, and only *then* could you produce.... We had to fight, and everything they were teaching us, that we were seeing, was that as a group you could do many things, but you always needed to try to get support. It is not enough to raise your hand and say, "Okay, sure, we can do it," and afterward only one person shows up. If we were going to do something, we all would do it. And this was something that helped create the group; it gave us the tools . . . the training for the cooperative.

After months of deliberation and practical preparations, the group decided to occupy the hotel.

It was March 23, 2003, when former Bauen employees entered the abandoned tower. The workers were soon joined by activists from the MNER, neighborhood assemblies, and leftist organizations. Notably missing was the gastronomy union, which had previously represented workers in the Hotel Bauen but did not support the occupation.[18]

When the police arrived on the scene, the workers explained their situation. Pilar remembered, "We told them that [we weren't intruders]; we wanted to stay here because we realized that they [the owners] were looting it. And we wanted to keep working. Then the journalists started to come. . . . Everyone started to come, and there were a lot of people." Bolstered by this social support, the group took up 24/7 residence to stake their claim on the hotel. To collect money for food and supplies, some members did piecework and took informal jobs, while others panhandled for spare change on a busy street corner nearby.

Right away, the group began to negotiate with the bankruptcy judge, who soon granted them temporary custody of the hotel. Founding member Tito recalled, "We started to fix everything that we could." Former housekeeper Inés told me about the dirty job they faced: "After having been closed for a year and a half . . . there were eighteen floors that needed to be organized and cleaned. . . . The truth is that everything was really dirty, filled with bugs. There were compañeros who were affected by this. They had skin problems because there were so many fleas. There were a lot of spiders. . . . It was totally abandoned."

For nearly a year and a half, political negotiations dragged on as workers struggled to make ends meet. Tito remembered, at that time, "We said, 'We are going to open it.' The politicians . . . and judges dragged their feet [*pie de plomo*], [but] our stomachs did not. So we moved forward."[19] The group decided, again, to take action: this time, to start operating the hotel, with or without official approval.

Joining a Movement

When workers occupied the property, the Hotel Bauen joined the growing ranks of worker-recuperated businesses in Argentina. In the years that followed, it even became an icon of the movement, largely due to its location (in downtown Buenos Aires), size (a conference hotel that could support many jobs), business activities (hospitality), and organizing efforts, which I describe in chapter 6. Worker-recuperated businesses initially emerged in Argentina in the years leading up to the 2001 economic crisis. The contracting labor market squeezing the employees of the Hotel Bauen was devastating to workers of all stripes. Companies closed their doors. Jobs and capital moved offshore. Employers abandoned their responsibilities, from making good on paychecks to adequately contributing to retirement funds. In this context of political critique and social discontent, groups of workers occupied their former workplaces as a last-ditch effort to keep afloat.[20] These were not well-organized activists or incendiary revolutionaries. They were just people facing extreme necessity in hard times.

Converting a conventional business into a worker cooperative involves a reimprinting process in which workers draw on the economic, political, and technical resources around them to reimagine and transform their organizations. In the wake of the 2001 crisis, some Argentines adopted an activist approach to job creation based on widespread critiques of the unfettered capitalism that had devastated the working class. They framed this reimprinting as a fight for better jobs and more equitable workplaces. External actors provided their expertise too. Social movement organizations like the MNER guided workers as they formed cooperatives.[21] Through these exchanges workers became increasingly informed about the organizing principle of self-management (*autogestión*) and the history of cooperativism in Latin America. Although worker cooperatives have long existed throughout the region, worker-recuperated businesses took part in a "new cooperativism," adopting a horizontal organization, democratic values, and a connection to community in a way that set them apart from traditional cooperatives.[22]

Occupation movements were another source of templates for change.[23] Like other occupations, workers broke the law by violating private property rights when they staked a claim on their former workplaces. But in a fascinating departure, those founding worker co-ops like the BAUEN Cooperative actively "framed their claims as fundamentally a desire to have the law enforced" and "appealed to the government to *uphold* other laws which . . . question the owner's right to the land/factory in the first place and suggest that the workers had a valid legal claim to own it instead" (Brabazon 2016, 24–25).[24] Thus, at the Hotel Bauen, the initial occupation was touted by workers as an attempt to safeguard assets, ensure that bankruptcy laws were enforced, and recuperate unpaid wages and stolen retirement funds. That the nascent collective used the law in this unconventional way created another vector of activism, highlighting uneven enforcement and undermining the legitimacy of the laws in the process.

Despite (or perhaps because of) this approach, most worker-recuperated businesses have become enmeshed in prolonged legal battles to authorize their use of private property and gain control over the means of production. As illegal occupants, they struggle to secure organizational legitimacy, political recognition, and much-needed financing. Although they form new business entities as cooperatives, many worker-recuperated sites undergo long periods of chronic underproduction, financial precarity, and organizational uncertainty. And yet they persist.

In 2018, 384 worker-recuperated businesses were operating in Argentina. According to a survey conducted by the Open Faculty at the University of

31

Buenos Aires, these included everything from metallurgical factories (steel, auto parts, etc.) and meatpacking plants to schools, restaurants, and hotels (Ruggeri 2016). These companies may employ only a small percentage of Argentina's total working population, but their symbolic influence has been substantial, demonstrating that work can become a "site of struggle," a crucible for "innovative alternatives for reorganizing productive life," and a model for other workers around the globe (Vieta 2010, 296; see also Fernández Álvarez 2016; Itzigsohn and Rebón 2015; and Palomino 2003).[25]

The Hotel Bauen's founding, foundering, and occupation are closely intertwined with watershed political and economic moments in Argentina's recent history. It opened under—and with the help of—the military dictatorship. It closed during the economic and social crisis in 2001. And it was reconstructed as working Argentines took matters into their own hands. Now we must ask: *How* did these workers reopen the hotel?

Aufbauen (German): To Rebuild, to Reconstruct

The Hotel Bauen's second founding moment was shaped by deep economic crisis, demands for workers' rights, and burgeoning social movements. But years later, at first glance, the worker-run Bauen still looked a lot like a conventional hotel: work was divided into sectors and organized by managers who coordinated schedules and oversaw daily routines. So, what made it different? In the BAUEN Cooperative, the highest authority was not a boss or general manager. It was the Workers Assembly, which included all members of the cooperative and made decisions via a sort of direct democracy (one person, one vote).[26] Within this democratic workplace, workers demonstrated the feasibility of organizational change by rebuilding a hierarchy, rewriting the rules, and formalizing their operations—in short, by creating a people's hotel.

Buenos Aires, a National Business
Soon after occupying the tower, the group formed a worker cooperative. Lacunza explained, "We thought it was the most democratic form because you have a voice and you have a vote. You can debate and then vote." Having agreed on a structure for their new organization, however, the founders struggled to align their values.[27] Inés hinted that at the outset some people in the group "wanted to run this like a normal hotel." Primo detailed the debate: "At first, this was really divided . . . because there were people who wanted to outsource the work [*tercerizarlo*]." In other words, they wanted to contract people who were not full members of the cooperative. Clearly, Primo was on the side of worker

management. He immediately pointed out the contradiction: "It's like saying, 'Yes, we took [occupied] the entire hotel, but we are outsourcing the sectors.' [So] are we against outsourcing unless we are the ones who manage it?"

These heated debates ultimately came with a handful of resignations. The group's first attempt at organizing, under the banner of the Callao Cooperative (for the street on which the Hotel Bauen stands), disbanded. The remaining members made a second attempt, forming a new cooperative. They decided to call it BAUEN, keeping the original name but infusing it with new meaning as an acronym for Buenos Aires, a National Business (Buenos Aires, una Empresa Nacional). This marked the beginning of a reimprinting process informed by the organization's previous life. The name ultimately became symbolic of this organizational transformation as the original title was resignified under worker control. Years later, a plaque commemorating the formation of the BAUEN Cooperative remained proudly on display in the hotel's lobby (see figure 1.2).

In the BAUEN Cooperative, Primo's preferred structure ultimately prevailed. Rather than outsource certain sectors or managerial roles to nonmembers, "We opted for the . . . proposal to manage this by ourselves." In choosing the vision of an organization managed and staffed by its members, the BAUEN Cooperative institutionalized formal equality in the workplace. A decade later one of the founding members would describe the guiding principles to new members in an orientation: "In a company where you work in a relation of dependence, you work for someone else. In a worker cooperative, you are part of the cooperative, you are a member-owner of the cooperative, and everyone is equal to their compañeros beyond any position or situation that may come up here." The cooperative structure remained a formal equalizer: BAUEN's worker-owners shared in the equity and liability of the firm regardless of their position, past experience, tenure, age, or other differences.

Six months after its formation, the BAUEN Cooperative held its first formal assembly. Thirty founding members elected an administrative council made up of a president, a secretary, a treasurer, two alternates, and a trustee. The inaugural council then began the long process of learning how to run a cooperative in Argentina.

In these early days, meetings were called spontaneously. Many lacked formal documentation, and so we do not have attendance lists, written notes, or records of the decisions made. (Figure 1.3 shows formally documented meetings held in the BAUEN Cooperative.) By law, cooperatives are required to hold an annual "ordinary assembly" to review and approve the previous year's financials and the organizational "memory" statement. Any other

1.2 A member points to a plaque installed in the lobby commemorating the formation of the cooperative. Photo by Lavaca Collective.

meetings are called "extraordinary assemblies." According to the accounts of longtime workers, however, it is clear that members were meeting frequently, even if the gatherings were not formally documented.[28]

The steep learning curve for how to run a cooperative hotel was smoothed a bit by members' relationships with labor activists and other cooperatives. From those networks, the cooperative hired a consultant to help teach its members the legal and organizational requirements. Pilar, elected secretary in 2006, recalled that the consultant had "worked with a lot of cooperatives." When she took the position, "he taught me how to put together the books, where I should take them so we didn't have legal problems." Importantly for our purposes, Pilar also learned the basic requirements for running a meeting and carefully recording minutes in a specific type of tall black ledger. Over a decade later, these musty files were tucked into a floor-to-ceiling

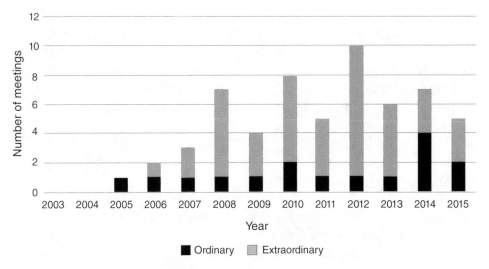

1.3 Assemblies per year in the BAUEN cooperative, 2003–2015. Graph by the author.

safe alongside the membership ledger and founding documents—a sort of BAUEN Cooperative archive. These pages and my extensive conversations with the co-op's founding members offer insight into these early days.

Like their explicit rejection of precarious work, members crafted their new initiative as an explicit rejection of the old way—working *bajo patrón* (under a boss).[29] Tito was elected president shortly after the cooperative's formation in 2003, nearly a quarter century after he set foot in the hotel for the first time. In 1980, when his then-employer decided to relocate its factory, Tito had become an unemployed father with young children. When he saw an ad for a doorman at what he called "an international hotel," he assumed his limited English would be a barrier, but he applied anyway. Soon Tito was hired to work an entry-level position in the lobby (see figure 1.4). "They gave me the opportunity," Tito remembered. "So I started to study the language [English]. I worked first as a doorman and then moved to work as the night concierge and receptionist. After that, like the history of the country, everything became precarious. The role of concierge disappeared, and the receptionist started to also work at the register." Tito would observe nearly two decades of changes before being fired from the hotel.

The onetime doorman eventually became a vocal advocate of efforts to recuperate his longtime workplace. He attended the initial organizing meetings, participated in the occupation, and helped establish the new cooperative.

1.4 Lobby and entrance to the Piano Bar in the Hotel Bauen, 2014.
Photo by Agencia TAO/Nadia Amad.

In an interview with an Argentine news collective in 2005, Tito already
sounded reflective: "There are people who have the idea that a cooperative is
like a pseudo-business." Here he pointed to the fact that despite their organizational form, worker cooperatives could run like conventional businesses.
He cautioned against this perspective. "If you don't address this [possibility],"
he warned, "you are just going to become another rat exploiting your compañeros, enriching yourself with two cars or with whatever you withhold." The
possibility that the hotel might revert to exploitative ways of doing business,
Tito fretted, "could be awoken" at any moment. Just a couple years in, Tito was
clearly aware that reconstructing the Hotel Bauen would require a full-on organizational transformation: "I know that it is going to be difficult. This is one of
the things that keeps me up at night."

36 Transformation is, in some ways, harder than forging something wholly
new. The legacy of the former organization of work and authority in the hotel
loomed over the cooperative's efforts during its early years. To avoid replicat-

ing familiar workplace practices, members of the cooperative attempted to make these shadow structures visible, to bring attention to implicit patterns etched into the hotel and its operations. This was sometimes complicated by factors that quite literally structured the workplace. For instance, research on hotel design shows how the built environment intentionally hides certain types of labor, like housekeeping. As David Brody (2016, 3) explains, "The connection between design and the concealment of housekeepers' work is particularly significant, since it is design that manipulates our perceptions about what does or does not occur at a hotel." In occupying the downtown hotel, members of the BAUEN Cooperative operated in a workspace that had been intentionally crafted to segregate workers from customers—and from each other. While they couldn't change physical layout of the hotel, they could reimagine how workers could move throughout the space. Forming a cooperative thus entailed not only changing the organizational structure and practices but remapping the building itself.

Building a Hierarchy

Aside from filling the elected positions required by law, the cooperative began with very little internal structure. Carmen, a founder, spoke about how the workers created a handwritten chart to indicate who was available at different times of day. Members started by working in positions where they had previous experience, assisting others and gradually learning about the other jobs needed to run the place. She remembered, "In the old Bauen, I worked in housekeeping. But in the new BAUEN [Cooperative], I have done everything. Other than maintenance, I have done everything. It is not that I haven't done any maintenance. I bring the tools and support the ladder for my compañeros so that we can get the work done faster." As Carmen described, an egalitarian ethos was developing in the cooperative as members chipped in and functioned with very little task differentiation.

Things began to change when the cooperative prepared to reopen the hotel. In 2004 after hosting a series of groups and small-scale events, the cooperative debated opening a street-side café to create a steady source of income. Council members meticulously detailed the scope of the investment. Starting the café would require not only all of the cooperative's small savings but additional contributions from the workers. Members voted to move the plan forward, and after a couple months of construction, they inaugurated the Utopia Café. Meeting minutes described the occasion as monumental proof "that self-management is possible since the founding members donated their paychecks to make the investment."

37

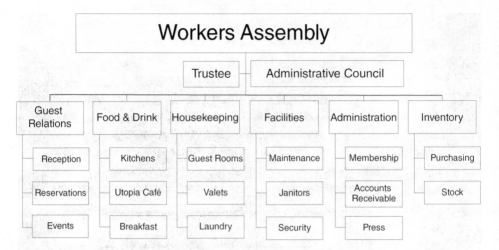

Workers Assembly

Trustee — Administrative Council

Guest Relations	Food & Drink	Housekeeping	Facilities	Administration	Inventory
Reception	Kitchens	Guest Rooms	Maintenance	Membership	Purchasing
Reservations	Utopia Café	Valets	Janitors	Accounts Receivable	Stock
Events	Breakfast	Laundry	Security	Press	

1.5 Organizational structure of the BAUEN Cooperative, 2015. Chart by the author.

With the opening of the café, the cooperative transitioned from a largely horizontal organization to one with formalized work sectors. Meeting minutes documented the steady buildup of a division of labor and hierarchy, job by job.[30] The cooperative continually looked to other recuperated businesses for guidance. Inés pointed out, for instance, "We had the model of Zanon," a recuperated tile factory. "For us, Zanon was . . . Wow! Look at how they have so many people working! They came here and spent hours with us on the organizational part of the cooperative." As the cooperative prepared to host overnight guests, the administrative council continued to add new sectors: members in maintenance and in housekeeping prepared the facilities for guests. One worker was asked to run the laundry, and the treasurer was tapped to create the administration group. Council members created and assigned managers to sales, events, and eventually purchasing. By 2015 the cooperative had eighteen work sectors coordinated by managers (*encargados*) appointed by the administrative council and informally approved by members in the sector (see figure 1.5).

Operating the Hotel Bauen required countless routine decisions around the clock. Managers held the power to hire or remove members from their sectors (but not from the cooperative as a whole). They organized work schedules and oversaw daily operations and customer interactions. Workers in each sector, however, maintained decision-making power over their routines. For example, receptionists oversaw billing processes, managed keys, and served as the first point of contact with customers in the lobby. Waiters and cooks decided what menu to serve in the café and how to handle diners.

And event coordinators met with clients to plan parties, meetings, and multiday conferences independently. This cut down on some of the decisions that otherwise might have hamstrung the full membership.

Sectors operated as semiautonomous groups, some of which were tightly knit and highly coordinated, while others had more internal divisions and higher turnover. For problems that exceeded a single sector or involved disciplinary actions, the administrative council coordinated decision-making. Council members signed off on budgets, approved payments, and oversaw major repairs in the facilities. They also controlled the membership: hiring and firing workers, reviewing disciplinary problems, and imposing sanctions when needed. Thus, routine decisions were made by workers, managers, and council members, and major decisions were reserved for the Workers Assembly, the cooperative's highest authority.

Over the next ten years, the BAUEN Cooperative would gradually expand from approximately 30 founding members to its peak of nearly 160 members in 2013.[31] As work and coordination increased across sectors, the administrative council was also expanded.[32] Inés remembered that the early months and years were a "really insecure" time "for all of us" founders: turnover was high, and salaries were unstable. To illustrate, she referred to a former Bauen employee who "was in the cooperative but left. A lot of people left. They didn't believe that it would be able to continue."

Despite this instability, the cooperative needed dedicated members, so the founders decided to prioritize hiring former Bauen employees and their relatives. Over time, however, this preferential hiring became a source of internal debate.[33] Alejandro, who started working in the cooperative a decade after the hotel reopened for business, thought that the resulting proliferation of familial ties created problems: "To me, it is counterproductive for the cooperative to have so many people who are the 'sons of' or 'friends of' or 'parents of' because . . . what happens? You have a conflict with someone, and the conflict is not personal, but it ends up involving more people who are from that faction [*bando*] or the other." Another member almost furtively explained that she had a "condemned last name" due to the behaviors of some family members who had previously worked in the cooperative.

Despite his opinions about familial networks in the cooperative, Alejandro was a product of these hiring practices. The oldest son of a cooperative founder, he nonetheless chafed at the policy: "They should hire people as it is done here in Argentina, which is by a person's résumé." He articulated his desire for more bureaucracy in the hiring process, explaining to me, "They [job candidates] should come, leave their résumé with their labor market experience, and be hired on that basis." In his opinion, the actual process in the cooperative was more haphazard. One member might say, "Dude, I need someone to work the register," and another would respond, "I'll bring my brother."

Regardless of the ever-evolving debates over hiring practices, when new workers joined the cooperative, they became full and equal members. Given the administrative work required to incorporate new members, the cooperative eventually established a three-month probationary period before a worker could integrate as a full member. But to avoid preemptive disenfranchisement and disengagement, the cooperative eventually decided that even during their probationary periods, new members would be allowed to attend meetings and vote.

Rewriting the Rules

As the cooperative grew, members decided they needed a "tool of conduct" within the hotel. In his capacity as president, in 2004 Tito proposed developing a set of internal regulations (*reglamento interno*) like those the private owners had used. The secretary disagreed with the motion, stating on the record that "our group is totally distinct from the relations of dependence" that define work under a boss. For this reason, he proposed that the cooperative's rules be "linked to our articles of incorporation [*estatuto social*] and [developed] according to our internal needs." In other words, the secretary wanted to explicitly tie rules to values. The council members agreed, and the draft document was circulated to the membership, who debated and ultimately approved the rulebook in the first formal assembly of 2005.[34]

Old copies of the rulebook—long, detailed, and written in dense and formalized language—were stacked in a corner of the member office during my fieldwork in 2015. By then, the document, which had not been modified since its initial approval, was just a relic of the co-op's founding days. Many of the policies had been written in the abstract, outlining possible positions and responsibilities and general rules regarding operations, scheduling, and sanctions before the hotel had fully reopened for business. In the following decade, different administrative councils had attempted to update this centralized rulebook, but more pressing issues related to their survival—threats of eviction, legal challenges, seasonal downturns, and interpersonal disputes—always took precedence.

In 2010, for example, a young woman named Celia was elected to serve as secretary. Organized and energetic, Celia set out to revise the handbook with suggestions from the group, but it never came up for a vote. Two years later, a new administrative council revisited the idea, circulating a draft that had been revised to reflect many policies and practices that had been adopted over the years. The original version of the rulebook had listed the cooperative's principal social and economic objectives: managing its finances, providing insurance, paying a living wage, and prioritizing the hiring of ex-Bauen workers and their family members. In the revised document, the workers removed stipulations about preferential hiring and included details about expanded benefits (retirement, maternity leave and breastfeeding support, family crises, and emergency loans) and the creation of coordinators who would oversee groups of sector managers (now called *responsables* instead of *jefes*) in closely connected sectors. As in past years, there was a fair amount of internal momentum to align the written rules with existing practices, but the final document was never approved by the assembly. These revision efforts unfortunately coincided with a series of contentious leadership changes, and the bureaucratic task was again pushed to the side.

Although seemingly insignificant, what happened to this internal rulebook offers insight into the difficult process of rulemaking in a cooperative fighting for survival. When times were tough, workers in the BAUEN Cooperative prioritized the practice of democracy in everyday interactions over prescribing rules for a still-precarious but democratic workplace. This *selective formalization* was a theme that I would continue to document throughout my investigation of workplace practices in the hotel. In the absence of a single rulebook, the cooperative created and approved ad hoc policies to guide work and membership duties. Decisions that required collective debate were clearly outlined in the cooperative's statutes, and this document was shared with new members. To fill in the gaps, the administrative council took on the task of creating workplace policies that did not require a full vote by the Workers Assembly—things like policies for attendance, scheduling, and overtime. Indeed, many of the rules written into the modified (but still-unapproved) rulebook had been individually discussed among members, approved by the administrative council, and then implemented in the cooperative (see figure 1.6).

To enforce these ad hoc rules, the cooperative developed an internal system of sanctions. Managers and security personnel would submit memos to report issues—from tardiness to scheduling changes to interpersonal problems—to the member office. This system became easier when the cooperative updated its technology, replacing the manual punch cards with a biometric fingerprint reader. When I asked explicitly about the device, a former council member stated blatantly, "The [original] system produced corruption." The issue with the punch cards, he explained, was that people had

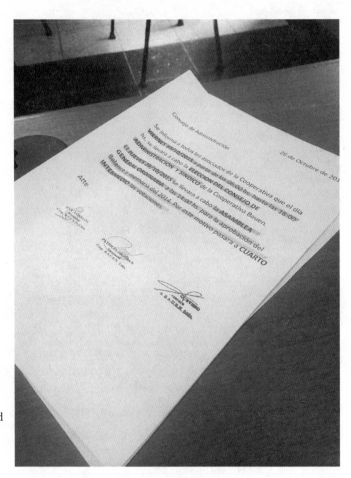

1.6 A memo signed by the administrative council. Photo by the author.

been clocking each other in and out for shifts. The new device had solved the problem: "With your finger, there's no way that you are not yourself."

With these more accurate and impersonal data, workers in the member office could log in to the system to view the number of times a person had been late to work over a given period. For people with "excessive" tardiness (a number that was never clearly defined for me), they would notify the council, which would then apply the appropriate sanction. The council members often referenced the files maintained in the member office, which included not only initial hiring documents but also details on any sanction a member had received during their time in the cooperative. First offenses warranted a written warning, and the council members could vote to suspend repeat violators from work without pay (for a period of three to fifteen days, depending on the previous violations). Multiple members told me over the years that the only offense deemed unforgivable in the cooperative was theft. This was reiterated in a new member orientation I attended: "The only thing that we don't pardon is theft," one council member announced. "We can pardon anything else. Or, rather, it's a discussion. But not theft because it's not the same." Members of the cooperative had the right to appeal any decision, but theft would result in immediate termination.

Formalizing Operations

In addition to establishing internal rules, the BAUEN Cooperative also formalized its operations and finances. As a conference hotel, the cooperative offered rooms to overnight guests, rented ballrooms for events, and provided catering and table service in the Utopia Café. These revenue streams were subject to sales and hospitality taxes, so the cooperative used its ties to social movement organizations to consult with third-party accountants and auditors to review its finances and organize the payment of back taxes owed to the Federal Administration of Public Income (AFIP). A council member explained:

> During the early years, we . . . had to decide if we were going to pay taxes or not, [and] in that moment, we said no, not to pay, to put it all to salaries, because there was a lot of need among the compañeros who had big families, so they had to bring home a paycheck at the end of the month. So that led to not paying, but at some point the tax collectors who [work with] AFIP brought these taxes to our attention, that we would have to pay that tax along with all the interest, so . . . we decided to pay the debt. . . . It's worth saying that at the outset we didn't have a good understanding of how to manage the issue, and we know much more today.

Paying back taxes from the early days of the cooperative exemplified the progressive effort to adopt more standardized business practices. With the help of contracted accountants, the cooperative also started to more closely track its income and expenditures through an electronic register system. Now managing its cash flow, the growing cooperative was able to independently finance much of its operations, invest in its infrastructure, and ultimately provide a reliable income for its workers.

The BAUEN Cooperative's increasing formalization was also a response to its ongoing legal challenges. Recall that the group never won the legal right to use the facilities. So the cooperative developed strategies to fend off threats levied by the private owners and political antagonists, which I describe in more detail in chapter 6.[35] For example, the cooperative worked with city inspectors to meet health and safety codes (although it technically could not pass the inspections without the title to the property). Council members participated in cooperative management training programs with national organizations, proudly displaying their certificates on the wall of the administrative council's modest office as a testament to the cooperative's legitimacy. Without a political or legal resolution, however, the BAUEN Cooperative was unable to access traditional lines of credit or financing for capital investment, adding additional pressure for the business to formalize its operations and finances while remaining nimble and responsive to contingencies.[36]

Democratic Transparency

Most workplaces tend to share very little information with their employees, while others do so selectively, often with the aim of increasing worker productivity and buy-in.[37] The BAUEN Cooperative had different goals from the very start. Indeed, members sought to establish democratic transparency: "an informational environment that is just and democratic in that it enables individuals to protect their interests and, collectively, to control the organizations that affect their lives" (Fung 2013, 184).[38] Transparency was seen as critical to implementing workplace democracy: if members didn't understand the hotel's operations and finances, they couldn't meaningfully participate in decision-making.

From its inception the BAUEN Cooperative adopted policies and practices designed to make information widely available. Much of this was coordinated by the trustee, an officer elected to oversee operations, finances, and inventory; ensure democratic practices; and mediate conflicts in the workplace. As the trustee explained jokingly in a meeting in 2015, "Who knows how many cups of coffee we sell in the lobby every day? You don't? I do!" To encourage transparency, members of the cooperative kept both physical and electronic records not only of its inventory and sales but also of its room and event reservations. Information sharing in the moment was often made possible by hotel-management software. Through this technology members with login credentials could access real-time information about events, occupancy rates, inventory levels, and billing. Tasked with ensuring the scrupulous documentation of the cooperative's operations, the trustee reviewed these data as well.

Council members adopted other initiatives to share information broadly. "One of our objectives and achievements has been to increase transparency," Matías explained as we sat in his office one summer day. As I mentioned earlier, Argentine cooperatives are required by law to hold at least one formal assembly each year. But full-group meetings became more and more predictable. For example, by 2015 the administrative council was holding quarterly meetings to provide regular financial snapshots and open a forum for questions. During one meeting I observed council members spend nearly an hour sharing detailed financial information and answering questions, even reporting the exact amount of money in each of the cooperative's bank accounts as of noon that day. As the meeting went on, one council member announced that the cooperative would be able to increase members' salaries. Attendees clapped and smiled, then proceeded to discuss the specific size and source of the proposed raise. "Previous councils didn't do this every three months," one member explained to me later. "They held [formal] meetings once a year to approve the budget. . . . But now we are doing this every three months because I think that when you present everything at once, you are going to lose something, and you might forget things." That is, more frequent assemblies ensured more members could access information quickly, meeting a key accessibility goal for the cooperative.

Later on, a council member describing this open-book policy emphasized that even this was in response to previous ways of working in the old Hotel Bauen: "We have to have as much clarity as possible in case the compañeros want to come [and look]." Elected leaders even used my presence as a researcher to defend the organization's commitment to democratic transparency.

One day after lunch, Pilar invited me to a meeting in housekeeping. I followed her up the stairs and took a seat in a corner of the small housekeeping office. Pilar opened the meeting by announcing an upcoming election in the cooperative. The conversation then segued into workers' right to information. She assured the housekeepers that, in administration, "nothing is hidden" from them. To my surprise, Pilar paused mid-thought and pointed at me. "Remember her?" she asked the group. "She sees the good, the bad, and the ugly!" She went on to explain that I was observing not only this meeting but *everything* the council was doing, a testament to their openness.

The BAUEN Cooperative practiced democratic transparency by making information available, proportional, accessible, and actionable for its members.[39] It was a far cry from the practices in conventional hotels, where, as researchers like Rachel Sherman (2007) have documented, managers frequently control information and limit informal communication among employees and between employees and guests. The openness certainly did not mean that all members of the BAUEN Cooperative could access information in the same way (if at all) or knew all the same things at the same time. When Pilar said "nothing is hidden," she underlined the organization's explicit commitment to democratic transparency rather than its perfect execution.

All this historical context is necessary if we are to understand the emergence of worker-recuperated businesses in Argentina and the organizational transformation that workers initiated when they occupied the Hotel Bauen. Organizations are usually studied as stable entities that are shaped by the technical, political, and cultural resources available to founders when they are formed. But unlike most organizations, a worker-recuperated business has *two* clear founding moments: one at the creation of the original, privately owned firm and a second during its conversion into a worker cooperative. The process of reimprinting, I argue, is critical for understanding organizational change. As I showed in this chapter, members of the BAUEN Cooperative did not reorganize work in a vacuum; they drew on their available resources, including their analysis of former workplace practices, coordination with experienced helpers from social movement groups and recuperated businesses, and the expertise of professionals and leaders in cooperative management as they restructured the hotel under worker control.

Reimprinting the cooperative, in other words, was directly motivated by workers' critiques of the "old" Bauen. Even in their choice of names, the group embraced their connections to the past by resignifying rather than replacing the word *bauen*. Workers immediately rejected proposals to recreate precarious jobs, instead founding the BAUEN Cooperative on the premise that all workers would be full-time member-owners. Extended efforts to write new rules for the cooperative were distinguished from the punitive policies of the former workplace, and members held a deep resistance to codifying the practices of workplace democracy, focusing again and again on issues of survival over prescriptive policies. And though the cooperative established divisions of labor and hierarchies of authority to run the hotel, they did so with careful attention to maintaining transparency and equality, the polestars of democratic decision-making.

Ultimately, this story of organizational change is critical to making sense of the equality project that I detail in the coming chapters. Understandings of equality are closely tied to local determinations about which inequalities are unjust. The cooperative's efforts to promote more egalitarian relations thus hinged on this reimprinting process, illuminating a collective history that deeply informed members' interpretation of problems and promises for change at work.

Imagine a government that assigns almost everyone a superior whom they must obey. Although superiors give most inferiors a routine to follow, there is no rule of law. Order may be arbitrary and can change at any time, without prior notice or opportunity to appeal. Superiors are unaccountable to those they order around. They are neither elected nor removable by their inferiors. Inferiors have no right to complain in court about how they are being treated, except in a few narrowly defined cases. They also have no right to be consulted about the orders they are given.

—ELIZABETH ANDERSON, *Private Government*

2   Democracy at Work

On a cool afternoon in May 2015, members of the BAUEN Cooperative set aside their daily tasks to attend a meeting of the Workers Assembly, one of the five official full-group meetings they would hold that year. In preparation, members set up round banquet tables and chairs in an empty ballroom above the auditorium. Unlike in standard event preparations, which involved tables covered in carefully pressed linens and centerpieces, the furniture in the room was noticeably scattered and bare. After lunch nearly seventy members—a little over half of the cooperative—convened to address a three-point agenda.

People and groups at all levels of the cooperative made decisions all the time, but the most important and contested issues were decided democratically in the Workers Assembly, the cooperative's highest authority. Lasting almost three hours, the May meeting I attended was first and foremost informational. The council members tasked with facilitating the meeting had spent the week busily preparing to share operational and financial information, and two different votes were on the agenda. Like all of the cooperative's assemblies, the day's meeting also provided a forum for members to make sense of their collective activities by engaging in what Francesca Polletta (2002, 7) calls "deliberative talk," discussing the reasoning behind their opinions with the goal of "not unanimity so much as discourse."[1] Not long into the meeting, it felt as if it took on a life of its own. "Do you like watching us fight?" a member joked as I craned my neck to follow the spirited debates that ping-ponged across the ballroom.

Political equality—a system in which each member of a group has equal influence—is fundamental to democracy.[2] But this rarely extends into the workplace. We don't often think about our workplace as a system of government.[3] In fact, Elizabeth Anderson (2017) argues that most contemporary workplaces operate like communist dictatorships. As she describes in the epigraph to this chapter, inferiors have no say over the decisions that affect their daily lives. But it is no stretch of the imagination when we realize that "inferiors" are workers and "superiors" are bosses. For some, the very idea that our workplaces are authoritarian—"pervasively governing our lives, often to a far greater degree of control than the state" (Anderson 2017, 40)—is deeply unsettling. But since the Industrial Revolution, employers have held the legal authority to govern their employees.

Workers in the BAUEN Cooperative, in contrast, were not governed by an arbitrary or unaccountable power. Members of the cooperative had a voice in an organization that was accountable to their interests. Democratic decision-making was thus an important component of the BAUEN Cooperative's equality project, providing an opportunity for workers to distribute organizational power in ways that meaningfully shaped their participation at work. A series of formal policies enshrined political equality in the cooperative's organizational structure, starting with the fact that all workers were full and equal owners with equal votes in the Workers Assembly. This signals a key equality-producing process. Rather than extracting value from another person's labor (how Karl Marx famously defined exploitation), the process of *inclusion* integrates people into their contributions to a group by leveling fundamental power differences between workers and business owners. Yet policies are not necessarily the same as practices: a cooperative's formal efforts to distribute power do not automatically ensure fair member participation.

48

To examine how over a hundred hospitality workers practiced democracy at work, I conducted many hours of observation and careful notetaking in meetings as well as research in archives dating back to the cooperative's formation. These sources showed me that the collective authority, the Workers Assembly, did much more than rubber-stamp decisions made by managers and elected officers. While formal polices distributed power, the cooperative confronted ongoing challenges as it worked to ensure member participation. My analysis of two of the most important functions of the Workers Assembly—elections and appeals—reveals how decision-making was just one facet of participation for the cooperative's member-owners. This engagement extended into informal workplace dynamics—particularly information passed outside formal channels of communication—through which members negotiated the meanings of equality and fairness in the cooperative. Instead of undermining managerial authority or amplifying uncertainty, these informal dynamics helped to disseminate power among the group and ultimately safeguard democracy at work.

Worker Cooperatives in Theory and Practice

A rich body of social science research has examined democratic participation in workplaces around the globe.[4] Observing the wave of collectives, cooperatives, and communes that emerged in the United States during the 1960s, Joyce Rothschild defined cooperatives as "collectivist organizations" that explicitly rejected bureaucracy.[5] In theory, bureaucracies are impersonal and hierarchical organizations populated by participants who follow rules and make decisions to achieve practical ends (employing what Max Weber [1946] called "instrumental rationality").[6] Collectivist organizations, in contrast, distribute authority, adopt minimal rules, prioritize social relationships, and apply principles of democratic participation.

Instead of relying on static classifications of organizational type (as either bureaucratic or collectivist), Katherine Chen (2009) more recently called for a focus on specific organizing practices and outcomes. In her study of the organization behind the Burning Man arts festival, Chen shows, for example, how the organizers develop sufficient formalization and coordination to plan a large-scale event while also maintaining accountability to members' interests. By negotiating tendencies to under- or overorganize, Chen writes, organizations can become *enabling structures* that participants can use to realize their collective goals and values.

49

In practice, many organizations are hybrids that mix and match bureaucratic and collectivist goals and practices. Research on worker cooperatives, for example, finds that many blend social values and participatory practices with formal rules and hierarchies to ensure fairness, efficiency, and stability.[7] These rules are often flexible and open to members' modifications and interpretations over time. Likewise, conventional businesses can adopt collectivist practices.[8] From the growth of team-based work to the adoption of participation as a management strategy, corporate workplaces have leveraged the benefits of including employees in production and decision-making.[9] In some sectors of the economy—particularly among technology and financial service firms—businesses have even explicitly sought to form flat organizations, throwing out formal bureaucratic practices in favor of participatory ones.[10]

Founded on values of democracy and equality, the BAUEN Cooperative combined collectivist and bureaucratic practices in its equality project. As I described in chapter 1, the workers who occupied the Hotel Bauen created formal rules and established a hierarchy of positions to coordinate hospitality work in their newly formed cooperative. To broadly distribute organizational power, workers codified political equality and participatory democracy into their earliest rules.[11] Understanding how power is distributed involves not just analyzing the formal policies and practices, however. It must also include a deep look at the informal relations that unfold at work.[12]

Decision-making is a key feature of organizations. But groups also engage in *sensemaking* to account for themselves and their workplace practices.[13] Informal relations are highly consequential in this regard, offering a forum for members to identify patterns of meaning in the organizing practices they develop over time.[14] These informal dynamics can have varying effects. For example, when groups lack a structure to pursue their goals, they often privilege informal relationships and emphasize friendship ties in ways that can lead them to underplay problems and inequalities, stifle participation, and thus reduce organizational accountability.[15] In contrast, organizations that overorganize can risk ignoring, suppressing, or co-opting informal relations. Left unchecked, rigid managerial regimes may encourage people to violate rules or allow people to shore up their personal authority in exchange for gifts or favors.[16] In such circumstances, people in positions of authority can even shut down informal relations or manipulate members' commitment as a means of coercive control.[17]

It's time to consider how collective authority—in both decision-making and sensemaking—operated in the BAUEN Cooperative. My analysis of-

2.1 Basic power structure of conventional and cooperative organizations. Chart by the author.

More power ⇕ **Less power**

Owners / Managers / Employees

Conventional organization

Worker-owners / Council members / Managers

Cooperative organization

fers insights into both the role of workplace democracy in the cooperative's equality project and the challenges the workers confronted as they distributed organizational power. Creating a context in which each member has an equal vote and an equal voice is no simple task. Yet a close look at elections and appeals in the cooperative highlights the ways that members engaged in and made sense of these practices.

Democratic Decision-Making and the Problems of Participation

Una voz, un voto—one voice, one vote—was a phrase I heard repeatedly during my research in the Hotel Bauen. It referred explicitly to how political equality was formalized in the hotel. Decisions were made by majority vote, whether in sector meetings, council meetings, or the Workers Assembly. This resulted in an inverted power structure (see figure 2.1). Rather than an owner, boss, or CEO at the top of the organizational hierarchy, the group held the ultimate authority.

Although the cooperative was structured by political equality, members were keenly aware of its limitations. After I had worked with Francisco for a couple of weeks, he told me, "In the cooperative we are all equal," before he paused to correct himself. "We're not actually equal, but we have the same rights and the same responsibilities." Francisco's reflection echoes a long history of debates about the meanings of equality and participation.[18] To operate democratically, the BAUEN Cooperative needed to cultivate a culture that was open to debate and deliberation. Fair treatment, however, required not only formal policies to broadly distribute power but also collective efforts to ensure certain opinions and voices were not amplified over others.[19]

Another member, Daniel, told me that the cooperative was "very democratic" and that "all members have the right to their opinion. Whether they have knowledge or not, their opinion is always valid." To him, the Workers Assembly was "a space where everyone can sit down together, and we can give [an issue] fair treatment." Yet over the years, the cooperative had been

51

forced to address a series of logistical issues that impacted members' ability to actually participate in meetings. Given the nature of work in the hotel, meeting attendance was not mandatory; customer-facing jobs could simply not be left for hours to attend a meeting. In sectors like the café, kitchen, and reception, at least one person remained on duty so that others could participate. Before I was invited to join closed-door meetings, I often stayed with these remaining members, learning what had transpired when others returned after the Workers Assembly adjourned.

The cooperative also tried to minimize the effect of outside commitments on member participation. Small-group meetings were scheduled during each shift, and assemblies usually took place when the morning and afternoon shifts overlapped so that they didn't consume workers' free time. Meetings were announced in advance, both by word of mouth and on printed signs posted where members clocked in and out for their shifts. On the day of a scheduled assembly, I noticed that some members took their breaks earlier than usual to pick up their children from school so they could return in time.[20] Council members also placed reminder calls to each sector fifteen minutes before the scheduled start in an effort to increase attendance.

Despite attempts to address logistical issues, actual participation in meetings and assemblies was notably uneven. In their role as facilitators, a handful of council members would guide the group through an agenda. But in contrast to highly formalized meetings with well-defined speaking rules, the assemblies I attended were loud and dynamic affairs with people coming and going, occasional interruptions, and side conversations among groups of coworkers. Yerba maté tea regularly circulated throughout the room as members spoke extemporaneously, sometimes interrupting the speaker with questions or clarifications. I noticed time and again that charismatic and longtime members of the cooperative—many of whom had held leadership positions—were among the most vocal and willing to take the floor, ask questions, offer opinions, and call for votes (see figure 2.2).

Given the size of the group (approximately 130 members in 2015), members often had to literally speak up in order to be heard. Belén, a longtime member, described participation in meetings this way: "Sometimes it's [like] the law of the jungle. . . . The person who yells the loudest wins. It's like Tarzan, you see? Yell more, win." Older men were frequently and literally louder than others. But the interactions during meetings seemed generally rooted in mutual respect. In a cooperative of this size, members may have had to speak loudly, even yell, but discussions and debates rarely devolved into actual arguments.

2.2 Workers meet for an assembly in the Hotel Bauen. Photo by Martin Barzilai/Sub Cooperative.

According to some founding members of the cooperative, the norms of participation had changed noticeably over the years. Many recalled early meetings as unruly events, often ending in loud, passionate fights. "There are things that, well, we have learned . . . we [used to] yell," one member reminisced. "We left the assemblies upset. It's like we started to become aware that we had statutes, that we had to respect the rules, that we couldn't mistreat each other in an assembly." Unlike the meetings I observed, BAUEN founders characterized the earliest meetings as hostile and stressful affairs. After being accused of mismanaging her sector in a meeting soon after the hotel reopened for business, one member described, "I got up, and I wanted to punch—excuse my language—I wanted to beat the shit out of him [her accuser]." She remembered wanting to say, "What is wrong with you that you would talk to me like this?" Through that experience she realized there were things she shouldn't say or do in assemblies. Reflecting on those early meetings, she noted: "We were learning to see those things you shouldn't do. Because then we modeled respect among the compañeros who came after us."

53

Democratic Trade-Offs: Participation and Conflict

According to longtime members, the BAUEN Cooperative had come a long way in cultivating an egalitarian ethos that permeated democratic deliberation in meetings. This mutual respect was not simply imposed but had to be actively maintained and encouraged. Despite the changes that members recounted, when I talked with people about meeting participation, the fear of interpersonal conflict continued to shade their willingness to speak up.

Francisco, a longtime member who was serving as trustee, described how his participation had changed over time: "If we were to compare 2005 and 2010, we have changed a lot. The cooperative has grown a lot. Before, it was as if you were kind of . . . you were a little scared to talk because . . . It's like any job. You're afraid to open up, to have an opinion, to say something [and then find out] the next week that you've been fired. Because I didn't know what it [a cooperative] was, I really didn't know how to work in a cooperative." Francisco attributed his initial hesitation to talk—something he thought was common in conventional workplaces—to a lack of understanding about his rights within the cooperative. According to the organization's statutes, members could be fired only after a series of documented violations, and any decision could be appealed to the Workers Assembly as a whole. Francisco implied that once he learned that he could express his opinion without jeopardizing his job, he started to speak up.

Other members intimated, however, that a fear of retribution was an ongoing barrier to participation. Martín said matter-of-factly, "Supposedly we are all equal. We aren't equal. There are people who . . . think you have opinions that are contrary to them. They mark you. . . . It shouldn't be like that. . . . We are in a democracy, not under military rule! . . . So in order to maintain my job, I don't say anything. I do what lots of people do. I'm not the only one."

Skeptical about the cooperative's efforts to practice equality, Martín compared the workplace democracy of the cooperative with "military rule." Like Elizabeth Anderson's (2017) argument that workplaces are private governments, Martín drew connections between Argentina's recent history under military dictatorship and authoritarian relations that left workers with very little power over their jobs. He pointed specifically to possible interpersonal conflict with elected officers ("they") as preventing him from feeling that he could freely express his ideas and opinions. Regardless of formal rules and protections, the informal organization of work left some to worry that their coworkers could punish them for their disagreements. To Martín, retaining his job was simply more important than fully participating in the cooperative's deliberative gatherings.

In groups of all sizes, interpersonal issues will emerge. But members of the BAUEN Cooperative were acutely aware of the stakes of becoming embroiled in a workplace conflict. Another member put this clearly: "Imagine if you lost your job! It would be really tough because there are a lot of people who don't have the ability to go out and find a job easily. The labor market here in Argentina is difficult. Imagine this for people who don't have degrees or a certain level of cultural competence. It makes it really complicated. There is a lot of fear of saying something and then being fired. So they just don't say anything." For many working for subsistence wages, the prospect of losing a job over a disagreement was simply untenable. Both inside and outside of meetings, I observed that hesitation around speaking up was inflected by status differences: members who did not have the experience, connections, or credentials of longer-term colleagues might avoid expressing contrary opinions for fear of retribution.

Participation and Class Discrimination
Individual characteristics and circumstances could impede participation, too. A lengthy commute could make an hours-long meeting decidedly unappealing and keep members from arguing a point. An impression that nothing important happened in the meetings could discourage attendance. And something as simple as a lack of numerical literacy could lead attendees to avoid contributing to a deliberation.

On a December morning I met Alejandro in the Utopia Café to work the morning shift. Five days a week, he left his house in the province of Buenos Aires at 5:30 a.m. for his two-hour commute to the hotel. When he arrived, he changed into his uniform—a pressed white oxford shirt, black slacks, and a black vest (waiters were jokingly called *pinguinos*, or penguins)—and then worked a nine-hour shift as a cashier. Around 10 a.m., after the morning rush died down, we took a break at a small table in the back of the café. I had met Alejandro nine months earlier during his first week of work in the cooperative. Since then, we had checked in with each other almost weekly as we each learned the ropes.

Balancing a small cup of coffee, I asked, "What do you think about the assemblies and meetings that we have with everyone?" Alejandro replied thoughtfully, "I have conflicting opinions. On one hand, it's really good that there is democracy. But on the other hand, there is a lot of talk but very little being said. You will be there [in a meeting] for three hours, and no one *says* anything. We will have talked about a lot of stupid things but not about anything concrete for the cooperative. I never hear anyone talk about important issues [like] about the profits [or] where to invest." This is a problem scholars have long traced to underorganizing: in the absence of formal structures, collective efforts can dissipate into "endless meetings" (Polletta 2002).[21]

The most recent meeting Alejandro and I both attended had taken place two weeks before this conversation. It was the annual general assembly in which members reviewed financial and operational statements and voted to approve or reject them. Alejandro recalled it as the first meeting that had dealt with any "important issues." To his mind, debates over interpersonal conflicts and disciplinary decisions—"stupid things"—dominated most meetings and stole attention from more "businesslike" issues of profits and investments.[22]

Other members also noted that full participation could be hard if people lacked certain *capacidades*, or abilities, especially in relation to the hotel's finances. Martín said, "In the assembly we don't only deal with disciplinary situations but also with how the money is spent. How can I say this? They can throw numbers at us, but there are a lot of people who don't understand them. They don't have the ability. . . . Unless you are talking about a [pay] raise, no one cares." He implied that some members—particularly those who had not finished high school—might be ill equipped to make collective decisions simply because they did not understand the numbers. Throughout my fieldwork I heard a handful of members comment that certain coworkers showed up to meetings only when a possible raise was on the agenda. They suggested that those members only paid attention to finances if they stood to benefit personally.

During my observations, however, I frequently saw newer members and those with no formal business training ask keen questions and seek out financial information to better understand the cooperative's operational challenges. The general assembly that Alejandro mentioned was a case in point. That afternoon, the ballroom–turned–meeting room was packed full of members, with over a hundred people in attendance. After summarizing the cooperative's financial position, council members opened the floor to questions.

Amid regular voices—longtime members and founders who probed for details—a series of newly hired housekeepers asked questions. When one woman took the floor, she qualified her question, saying, "Granted, there is a lot that I don't understand." I jotted down her comment—I had also been confused by the same line item she queried. Council members and administrators responded with a detailed answer, and the housekeeper nodded, seemingly satisfied with the response. After the meeting I realized that, like me, some members of the administrative council also noticed who asked questions during the meeting. As they reconvened in their office, the council members spoke positively about members' participation, especially that of the relatively new housekeepers who had read the materials and spoken up.

In fact, the widespread engagement at the meeting that day suggested something very different from the self-serving participation that some of the workers hinted drove their coworkers. Members might still have been conflict averse or nervous to speak up, but the atmosphere that day had been one of openness, inclusion, and effort to ensure that members were fully prepared to vote on the annual reports.

I also spoke with members who openly challenged the idea that class differences prohibited full participation in the cooperative. One Saturday afternoon I met with Belén, who opted to work on the weekend so she could take Sunday and Monday off to be with her young children. The lobbies were unusually quiet as members worked busily behind-the-scenes to prepare for a 150-person event that evening. Over a cup of tea, Belén disagreed with the interpretation that average members could not understand how the hotel operated. "It's not difficult for people to understand, but maybe they don't talk [in meetings]; maybe they think, 'Well, I'm not educated.' But they have household expenses, and they get it. Maybe they just don't say it out loud." By relating the cooperative's operations to household finances, Belén rejected the logic that financial decisions be reserved for trained experts. Even people without formal training, she proposed, could regularly and without fanfare coordinate complex operations.

These conversations, even when people shared different opinions, generally confirmed that members of the cooperative were aware that distributing power also required broad participation, regardless of peoples' tenure, position, education, or past experience. Still, participation in formal meetings and assemblies was uneven. Beyond very practical constraints, members identified conflict avoidance and class discrimination as major barriers to democratic participating. In doing so, they also pointed to the salience of informal workplace dynamics—spaces where actual practices might diverge from formal policies.

Elections and the Meaning of Fairness

As the highest decision-making body, the BAUEN Cooperative's Workers Assembly held the collective authority to create rules, decide on appeals, and grant and revoke authority from its members. Full participation was more of an ideal than a reality, except when it came to the biannual election of the administrative council.[23] By 2015 the council had grown to include nine

57

members, who were selected by the entire membership to enforce the cooperative's rules and oversee the hotel's everyday operations.

For members of the BAUEN Cooperative, 2015 was filled with important elections. In June and July, mayoral and gubernatorial elections were held in the city and province of Buenos Aires, two critical positions affecting the population in and around the capital city (that is, a third of the country's population). Shortly afterward, in October and November, a hotly contested race saw conservative businessman-turned-politician Mauricio Macri win the presidency of Argentina. And to top off the election season, the cooperative's internal elections for the administrative council were slated to take place in November.

The night before the vote, Pilar couldn't sleep. A founding member of the cooperative, she had served as its president for two years, pouring her time and energy into the work. As in previous elections, Pilar and her fellow council members were being challenged by a slate of coworkers who had also decided to run.[24] On the day of the vote, Pilar arrived at work at 7 a.m., tired and ready for the campaign to be over. Voting ran from 6 a.m. to 6 p.m. to accommodate workers on the morning, afternoon, and overnight shifts. She cast her ballot first thing and then stationed herself in an upstairs office well away from the makeshift voting booths. At 6 p.m. volunteers counted the votes as a small crowd convened. I heard over the din of excitement that the incumbent council had won, sixty-eight to forty-four, with one abstention—nearly the entire membership voted.[25]

Each and every election was an important turning point for the cooperative. Not only did the results determine jobs and responsibilities for those running for office, but they also endorsed a vision that leaders would use to chart their collective future. Pilar's and her fellow council members' vision had been validated.

The BAUEN Cooperative formalized political equality in its rules and policies: each member had an equal vote cast on election day. But in the weeks leading up to the vote, I observed members of the cooperative worry about whether workplace democracy would be fair *in practice*. The equality project involved following rules for elections as well as addressing cultural norms around electoral politics.

The members' concerns made sense: in Argentina, political machines had held significant power in poor and working-class neighborhoods for a very long time.[26] This system of electoral politics is known as *clientelism*. Clientelist relationships hinge on exchanges between patrons (politicians) and clients (voters), mediated by organizations. For everyday Argentines, this means that neighborhood brokers dole out resources like food, medicine, or even access to welfare subsidies and workfare plans in exchange for political support. It is no stretch that in the BAUEN Cooperative, such patronage was a familiar way to participate in elections. But this reliance on informal relations created concerns about the organization's collective well-being. Would members vote in the interest of the business? Would they be swayed by favors and friends? During the election season, I found that members of the cooperative exposed and addressed influences on democratic processes in a surprising way: *through rumors.*

Doing Democracy around the Watercooler

Rumors—those tantalizing, informal, and unverified claims that circulate among social groups—are often referred to as the "watercooler effect" at work (see DiFonzo 2008).[27] When people lack verified information or mistrust their lines of formal communication, rumors can fill in the gaps and create solidarity, as members trust information passed from one another over official sources. Rumors are also important indicators of authority, affecting who can speak, what they say, and how much credence their words are given. A lot of the research on rumors treats them as potentially destructive to social cohesion and effective organization, yet in my fieldwork little about listening to and passing along information through these informal channels was petty or inconsequential. As I explore in the following sections, the trade in rumors helped members negotiate friendship, favoritism, and clientelism, all of which were issues they worried might pose a threat to free and fair elections.

Friendship and Favoritism

In the weeks leading up to the internal vote, members of the cooperative organized and publicized the upcoming election. The trustee, who oversaw and ensured transparency in the democratic process, coordinated a great deal, including organizing informational meetings and soliciting candidates, among other initiatives. Council members, meanwhile, submitted their candidacies and then held meetings to educate recently hired members about the voting process.

One afternoon, two council members joined a handful of people who worked in custodial services as they packed into a small, windowless office in the hotel's basement. Surrounded by lockers and cleaning supplies, Pilar checked in to make sure that everyone understood the cooperative's electoral process. She used a sample ballot to demonstrate how to properly cast a vote, and another council member likened it to voting in state elections—the box

59

would be closed, it would be secret, and they could choose only one candidate for each position.

In addition to these how-to talks, council members informed how members should *think* about their votes. In another meeting I attended with a group of workers, one said bluntly, "People need to vote for people who have the capacity to manage the hotel, not based on affinity or friendship," adding that favoritism "will only create problems." This fretting about members possibly supporting candidates based on personal ties instead of qualifications came up frequently.[28] In another sector meeting, a council member commented, "We didn't form our slate based on friendship, we aren't friends. . . . [T]his isn't a soccer team, it's a responsibility."

The BAUEN Cooperative had detailed, formal policies to ensure procedural democracy. But the motivations, loyalties, and logics of voting in practice were dispersed and adapted through the informal organization of work. So it wasn't only council members who talked through hopes and concerns about the elections; this topic came up in interviews and conversations I participated in across work sectors.

Remember, 2015 was packed with elections in Argentina. On the day of the national election, some weeks before the cooperative's internal vote, members working the afternoon shift gathered anxiously at the reception desk, waiting for the polls to close. It had been a slow shift since Election Day is a national holiday there. Between checking the occasional guest in or out of the hotel, members had time to debate the election's possible outcomes as they sipped yerba maté behind the reception desk. At one point, a young waitress named Rita walked across the lobby from the café to get change for a large bill. As the cashier changed the bill, Rita asked who the receptionists were voting for in the cooperative's upcoming election. In a joking way, a receptionist named Paola—a middle-aged woman with a motherly tone—said that Rita "had" to vote her stepbrother, Enzo, who was running for the council. Rita retorted that, at work, Enzo wasn't her family but Conejito (little rabbit), his nickname in the cooperative.[29] As we laughed at her tone, Paola chided the waitress that she needed to vote for Enzo anyway.

This routine interaction illustrated how family ties could influence voting behavior within the cooperative. Rita resisted any obligation to vote for Enzo and clarified her allegiances by referring to him not by a term of familial endearment but by a nickname understood specifically within the cooperative. In response, Paola insisted that Rita's loyalties *should* lie with her relative, regardless, perhaps, of what she saw as best for the cooperative.

60

The hand-wringing about favoritism did not, of course, necessarily reflect how people actually voted. As one member assured the group in a meeting, "When people go to the ballot box, nobody knows what happens." Still, tension existed between personal and collective interests, raising a perennial question about workplace democracy: in whose interest will members vote?

From Favoritism to Clientelism

Whether favoritism mattered or not, there were more explicit and potentially destructive ways that informal workplace dynamics threatened to undermine free and fair elections. In the weeks before the election, rumors started to circulate that some candidates were making promises in order to lock in votes. As I sat in the lunchroom, one worker shared a rumor they had heard: a candidate had allegedly promised someone that if they were elected, they would transfer that person to work in reception. I listened as another member reported their own bit of hearsay: a different candidate had supposedly been promising that mothers would not have to work on weekends. The group burst out laughing at the suggestion that the women in housekeeping could automatically have the time off. Pointing to the practical problems this would create, one member retorted, "I guess Luli"—the only childless housekeeper—"will have to do all the work on the weekends!"

The rumor mill was busy over the following weeks. Days after I heard these rumors at lunch, Romina came to me with a disgusted look on her face. She shared a similar rumor that was two people removed but still worrisome for her. A candidate had supposedly promised housekeepers they would get paid AR$200 more each month, along with an hour-and-a-half-long break during their shifts (see figure 2.3). Having once worked as a housekeeper herself, Romina thought the promise was not only unethical but blatantly untenable: "If the girls in the morning take an hour-and-a-half break, the people who work the afternoon would just be left with more work to do!" Once candidates started promising breaks, Romina feared it would set off a "vicious cycle" of promises that would threaten the cooperative's ability to run a hotel and ultimately risk bankrupting the business.

When some of the rumors made it to the administrative council, council members were troubled by the claims that their opponents were promising favors for votes. In one of their weekly meetings, the group agreed among themselves that they weren't going to make any promises they couldn't keep and that they "weren't going to invent anything." The council members then shared this position with members in the sector meetings.

2.3 Housekeepers on break in the staff kitchen. Photo by Martin Barzilai/Sub Cooperative.

During a meeting in housekeeping before the election, for example, Pilar reflected on her previous term in office and said that although she had worked hard to improve the cooperative, she wasn't going to promise things that the council should not decide unilaterally. "This isn't like a national election where people give you something to vote. This is a cooperative, and you need to vote for who will run it best." It would be easy to be swayed, Pilar said seriously, but the housekeepers needed to vote "according to their conscience."

Beyond concerns over friendship and favoritism, Pilar explicitly addressed the system of clientelism, in which people could expect to receive food or favors in exchange for their political support. These clientelist relationships might be common in the members' neighborhoods, she acknowledged, but in the cooperative, Pilar again reiterated, the members needed to prioritize the group as a whole.

Proponents of workplace democracy often point to the possibility of a spillover effect wherein people who learn the value of democratic participation, fair voting, and deliberation in the workplace become more engaged citizens in other areas of life.[30] The negotiations of fairness in the BAUEN Cooperative suggest that this process goes both ways: the democratic and electoral norms in politics also shape how people do democracy at work. In the BAUEN Cooperative, members confronted norms of clientelism as they sought to resignify democratic participation around ideas of fairness, autonomy, and the collective good.

Concerns about the misuse of power in swaying the elections were also directed at current members of the administrative council. For example, a rumor circulated that new members were being pressured to vote for the incumbent council. In one iteration, a longtime member named Dolores told a new member, Selina, that because a particular council member had hired her, she owed them the respect of her vote (*por agredacimiento de trabajo*). When word got back to the council member, she went directly to assure Selina that she should vote "according to her conscience" and that the votes were secret ("at the hour of voting, no one will know what happens"). No matter what Dolores allegedly said, this incumbent was adamant about fairness.

Even after the election concluded that year, I continued to document rumors that questioned and evaluated the inner workings of the BAUEN Cooperative's democratic process. When I spoke with Alejandro nearly a month after the vote, I was surprised to hear him bring up another election rumor:

> In the weeks before the elections, a lot of new people were hired to join the cooperative, and those people were really associated with the [incumbents], because they had hired them. In reality, they [the new members] shouldn't have voted. I don't know what the statutes say, but they should revise them. But I think that it's nonsense that someone who joined two weeks earlier should be able to vote. These people voted, but they voted because they told them, "Vote for me," and that's how they won. I'm telling you the truth! Fifteen or so people joined the cooperative, and that's how they won the elections.

Alejandro took issue with the cooperative's policy that all members were immediately vested with the right to an equal vote. This political equality, he explained, was ripe for reevaluation because it seemed obvious that the newcomers would vote for the council members who hired them. Alejandro took his reasoning a step further, telling me that not only did new members' votes determine the elections, but the incumbents had purposefully upped hiring in the weeks before the election to increase their votes.

63

Belén, who had previously run for a position on the council, said much the same: "The people who won, it was thanks to the new members.... In the statutes it says that you have to have at least two years' tenure in the cooperative to run for office. If you have to have two years to run for office, you shouldn't have the right to vote [immediately]. I think the two requirements should be equal." Like Alejandro, Belén attributed the incumbent council's electoral victory to a surge in new members, then linked her explanation to a proposal to change the cooperative's voting rules.

These rumors could certainly be interpreted as members making sense of an electoral defeat. They could even be seen as potentially undermining the legitimacy of the election or tearing at the social cohesion among members. In this case, however, the rumors clearly motivated members to evaluate the organizational policies central to their workplace democracy; in this case, who was eligible to vote and hold office. Alejandro was not familiar with the statutes, but Belén had returned to the cooperative's formal rules and proposed specific policy changes in order to, as she put it, align the two policies she saw as incongruent.

It is important to note that rumors are not necessarily false. By definition, rumors are *unverified* information circulated through informal networks. They certainly could be true. After hearing rumors that the election outcome was unfair or even rigged, I dug into the organization's records to verify whether hiring had ramped up before the November election. It hadn't. By late November 2015, the cooperative had a net increase of only nine members (seventy were hired, and sixty-one left voluntarily or were fired) over 2014. During the last quarter of 2015, the administrative council both hired and fired the fewest members all year (thirteen and ten, respectively) (see figure 2.4). Given that the incumbent council had won by over twenty votes, it seemed to me that new members' votes could not have changed the outcome.

Organizational records effectively dispelled this specific rumor, but I came to understand that the members were not actively seeking to address the rumors themselves. Instead, they initiated discussion and deliberation over the *organizational issue* raised by the rumors. Alejandro and Belén, then, discussed possible changes to voting policy that would address their concern about new members as a voting bloc. Rumors about friendship, favoritism, and clientelism in a variety of forms—from promising more pay, longer breaks, or new job opportunities to activating implicit debts for providing new members their jobs—spurred debates over the meaning of free and fair elections.

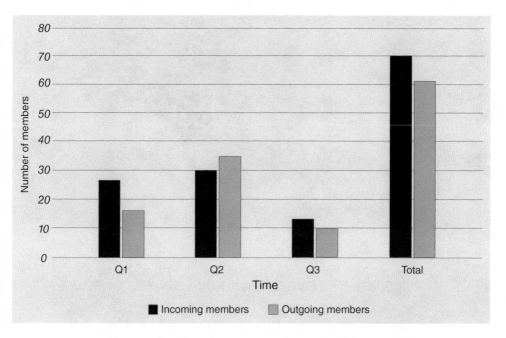

2.4 Net member growth in the BAUEN Cooperative, 2015. Graph by the author.

Deliberation and the Appeals Process

The elected administrative council was accountable to the entire group. In addition to overseeing the day-to-day operations of the hotel, the council regularly called on the Workers Assembly to share information and vote on issues impacting the cooperative. More than just a symbolic entity, the Workers Assembly held the highest authority. With the signatures of 10 percent of the cooperative (in 2015 twelve people), members could convene the assembly to address any issue or evaluate any decision made by a coworker, supervisor, or elected council member. As Daniel explained, "Assemblies are always called to address a specific management issue, [something] that is important to be discussed among everyone, or for a sanction that results from a disciplinary infraction if that member wants to say, in front of everyone, 'Che, I think the sanction you gave me is unfair, I am calling an assembly for [you to decide] if the administrative council was right or not.'" Workers could use their collective authority to check their elected leaders—whether it be to uphold their decisions or reverse them.

Meeting minutes provide a historical record of all the appeals made in the BAUEN Cooperative from its inception. These documents confirmed that

65

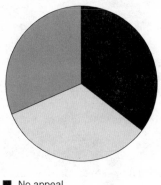

2.5 Decisions made by
the Workers Assembly,
2003–2015. Graph by the
author.

■ No appeal
☐ Appeal: Overturned
▨ Appeal: Upheld

appealing decisions was not uncommon. Of the fifty-seven formal assemblies documented in the cooperative's meeting minutes, thirty-four were called by members to appeal a decision. In exactly half (seventeen) of those appeals, members voted to uphold the existing decisions; in the other half, the decisions were overturned (see figure 2.5). The vast majority of these appeals (thirty-one of thirty-four) regarded suspending or excluding a member for a disciplinary infraction, such as excessive tardiness or mishandling money.

Two appeals that took place during my fieldwork illustrate the ways that formal and informal dynamics impacted efforts to disseminate power in the BAUEN Cooperative.

Saved by the Assembly

Administrative work was predictable and consistent. Every month, members completed the same tasks: on Fridays, they finalized payroll; on the fifteenth and thirtieth, they paid the bills; each week, they updated the listings in the inventory-management software; and each day, they processed credit card payments and filed invoices and receipts. In a narrow office on the third floor, the four members of the administration sector would sit at their desks turned inward to face each other. They often chatted while they worked, laughing and sharing yerba maté throughout the day.

Meetings and assemblies broke this predictable routine. On a Thursday, Sabrina locked the office door behind her and followed her coworkers down the stairs to the auditorium for a meeting of the Workers Assembly. Mem-

66

2.6 Auditorium in the Hotel Bauen. Photo by BAUEN Cooperative.

bers were convening to decide the fate of a compañero's membership in the cooperative and their source of livelihood.

A month before, José, a founder of the cooperative, had been fired following an altercation with a guest. Citing previous disciplinary problems, the administrative council had deliberated on the case, with the secretary recording in the minutes that the council members had "tak[en] into account his participation from the first hour of the struggle for recuperation" but ultimately decided that "[José's] incidents are each time more frequent and more serious, putting at risk the efforts of all the members." Following the disciplinary rules, the council members voted unanimously to fire José. In turn, he decided to appeal the decision, collecting and submitting the requisite signatures to request an assembly.

On the day of the meeting, around 3:30 in the afternoon, workers filed into the auditorium and recorded their attendance by signing a large black ledger (see figure 2.6). With sixty-two members present (just over the required quorum of half the membership), the meeting began. A council member stood on the stage and read five reports written by people who had witnessed the incident. From different points of view, the reports described a busy Sunday afternoon when José allegedly came in on his day off, drunk. After he created

67

a commotion in the lobby, the reports continued, a guest complained to the receptionists. José then tried to sleep in one of the rooms in the hotel without permission. Once the reports had been read, the council member relayed the council's decision before inviting José onto the stage to present his appeal.

Standing just over five feet tall, José was a thin, dark-haired man who had previously worked in maintenance. I was used to seeing him in work clothes—faded canvas pants and a long-sleeved button-up shirt. But on the day of his appeal, he had ironed his slightly worn jeans, greased back his hair, and carefully cleaned his white sneakers. When he took the stage, he spoke in a low voice. Looking out to the audience, José highlighted his twelve years of participation in the cooperative and apologized for his actions that day. Modest and direct, he said that he wanted to keep working in the hotel and asked the group to consider his plea.

After he took his seat, the group cast their votes one by one in a back room and then returned to their faded red velvet seats to await the results. Volunteers counted the ballots and then reported that the group had reversed the council's decision by an almost two-to-one majority (forty-one to twenty-one). Two members then proposed that although José would not be excluded from the cooperative, he should not be absolved for his misconduct. Those present then took a second vote, unanimously approving a twenty-one-day sanction and agreeing not to pay him for the days between his suspension and the appeal. The meeting closed about 6 p.m. As we filtered back to work, I heard a member say that José had been "saved" by the assembly.

In the following days, members of the cooperative continued to discuss the vote informally. Some were surprised or disappointed by the outcome, saying that the cooperative had missed an opportunity to oust a member who didn't work hard. In his appeal, after all, José had not denied what had happened, explained his behavior, or offered much of an apology. By all accounts the administrative council had implemented the formal rules fairly, given that, as the meeting minutes recorded, José's behavior was "putting all the efforts of the members at risk."

Complaints about the (mis)use of the appeals process were common as I talked to members about the Workers Assembly. One rainy day, Emiliano told me: "There are a lot of assemblies where people have been fired, they collect signatures to review their situation. . . . [T]he person was fired simply because they don't follow the rules that they should, the internal rules. So the administrative council fires them. When the person affected doesn't think it's fair, for whatever reason, they collect signatures, and when they collect 10 or 15 percent of the total, they call an assembly to review the case."

"Does this happen a lot?" I asked.

"Yeah, it happens a lot. And lots of times, it's justified. But lots of times, it's not."

Emiliano signaled an important tension: some members felt that people abused their right to an assembly. Martín agreed that appeals were "a nuisance," commenting, "For me, they don't work." He continued, "Here there are people who have two or three opportunities, [even though] they don't work. . . . [T]hey drink and take drugs. . . . [T]here are people here who take advantage of their right to call an assembly."

In other conversations, however, workers emphasized the value of giving people a second chance. Following José's appeal, Alberto and I walked back to work from the auditorium. Before we parted, the longtime member revealed that he had voted to overturn the council's decision. "Where would he find another job?" "What would his daughter do?" Alberto had worked with José for years, and he knew that he was struggling with addiction. Addiction was not a personal failing, Alberto reminded me, but a disease. He hoped that saving José's job would give his compañero the support he needed to stay sober. These details had not been shared publicly in the meeting, but as I spoke with people about the vote, I learned that many had considered the appeal in the context of José's well-being and family.

In short, through José's appeal, members of the cooperative also had an opportunity to assess the fairness of this particular implementation of the rules. Most of these deliberations took place in informal chats about members' thoughts and opinions. To Alberto, the assembly's vote was the right decision for the cooperative: taking care of a founding member.

Discipline and Punish

A second appeal during my fieldwork involved a woman named Carina. Also a founder of the cooperative, Carina had been working in sales as an event planner when the administrative council suspended her for fifteen days without pay. Meeting minutes recorded the justification for the decision: following a large event hosted in the hotel, Carina had accused members in her sector of making sales that benefited them personally. In fact, she had formally called their integrity into question, and the council had solicited explanations from the three people she identified. Each denied the accusations and explained that Carina's rumors had discredited their work and created "arbitrary suspicion" in their work sector.

Council members investigated the event further but found no evidence of wrongdoing. After all was said and done, the administrative council

69

determined that Carina had levied false accusations. Their meeting minutes documenting the decision underscored the gravity of this infraction: working together required mutual respect and solidarity among members of the cooperative, but "spreading absurd and unsubstantiated accusations" created distress and discord. Thus, Carina received a sanction, which she chose to appeal.

I was working at the reception desk when Carina appeared one afternoon. A middle-aged woman with short salt-and-pepper hair, Carina usually wore pressed navy slacks and a blazer at work. That day, she wore a raincoat, which signaled to me that she wasn't there to work. Marco, a receptionist, explained to a new member that Carina was "organizing her appeal." And it worked. Just over a month later, an assembly was held to consider her situation.

In the weeks between Carina's suspension and her appeal, members working in sales and reservations chatted within their shared office about what they thought of the situation and how they might vote. Ruben had worked closely with Carina for over a year. He often referred to her as *vieja*, a term of endearment he used because, he explained, she was "like a mother to him." He told me that, in addition to the most recent suspension, Carina had had previous problems. The year before, he remembered, she had booked a political event without consulting her coworkers or the council members. After the event took place, some members organized a meeting to discuss the event and Carina's unilateral decision to host the group. I could not find a description of this debate in the meeting minutes, but Ruben remembered the meeting this way: things had not turned out well for Carina, and only five people (including him) had "defended" her.

Carina's history of interpersonal problems came up in other conversations. As an event planner, her job required coordinating with many different people across the hotel. But she was known to some for creating conflict. "Carina fights with custodial services, she fights with billing, she fights with audiovisual," one member told me, rattling off her past frictions in the hotel.

As the assembly approached, Ruben was dreading it to the point that he considered not attending. He told me that, this time, Carina had implicated him personally by accusing him of wrongdoing.

"Were you involved?" I asked.

Ruben assured me that he had done nothing wrong, though he didn't claim to be perfect. He had received his share of disciplinary infractions—mostly for tardiness and unexcused absences.

Days later, Ruben (after ultimately deciding to attend) and I went to the assembly after lunch. As workers streamed into the room, I noticed that Carina was not there. The meeting began as usual with the treasurer sharing updates on the cooperative's finances before moving on to Carina's appeal. The council president immediately addressed her conspicuous absence: Carina was having a medical issue. As if she knew the justification would be questioned, she held up a doctor's note so everyone in the room could see it as evidence.

As with José's appeal, a council member proceeded to read the reports and open the floor to deliberation. But without Carina's explanation for her appeal, members turned from evaluating the most recent suspension to airing their grievances. One member who worked in the kitchen said that Carina was overcharging clients for catering, and a coworker affirmed it as true. Another woman said that she had "made a mess out of budgets" and that her poor management affected the people who worked in billing. And, as the president had anticipated, a member insisted that Carina's absence from her own appeal showed that "she clearly didn't care about the assembly." Those members working in the member office who oversaw scheduling and human resources quickly assured the group that the doctor's note was valid, but this was met with unsatisfied grumbling.

Eventually the trustee brought the deliberations back to Carina's appeal and organized the members to vote. Ultimately, the sanction was upheld, again by a two-to-one vote (forty-one to twenty-one). Unlike José, who was saved by the assembly, Carina was not only sanctioned but further punished as a result of her appeal. Having witnessed the collective dissatisfaction with her performance, the council members decided to move Carina to work in a different sector in an attempt to resolve the brewing issues.

In the BAUEN Cooperative, elected officers on the administrative council enforced its rules and policies and were accountable to the group as a whole, formalized in the Workers Assembly as the collective's highest decision-making body. The appeals process in the BAUEN Cooperative was a testament to the active authority of the Workers Assembly. Rather than simply signing off on managerial decisions, members regularly evaluated and sometimes overturned them. The Workers Assembly, in contrast to the administrative council, exercised far greater discretion and retained ultimate authority to reflect on and account for personal considerations and value judgments—in other words, to determine the *fair* application of the rules.

These appeals also provided insight into how informal workplace dynamics shaped democratic decision-making. After being fired for his infraction, José was "saved" by the assembly. His appeal prompted members to consider issues of fairness and justice both before and after the meeting, and the group voted to make an exception to the rule on the basis of informal information sharing. Signaling the importance of both bureaucratic and collectivist organizing practices in this endeavor, one member explained that some people voted "according to the facts," while others voted "from the heart."

Carina's case, in contrast, signaled how interpersonal conflicts and shared grievances could sway collective decision-making. She had been suspended for spreading rumors, accusing her coworkers, and undermining the solidarity needed to run a cooperative. When the issue was brought before the group, the assembly not only upheld the penalty but made it harsher. Past offenses and interpersonal issues were important in both cases, yet they also show how democratic deliberation was borne out in meetings that reinterpreted and enforced the rules on the books.

Formal rules and policies were critically important to the BAUEN Cooperative's equality project. They secured political equality in the organization's governance and provided a foundation for the ongoing practice of workplace democracy. Members of the BAUEN Cooperative were acutely aware of the importance and challenges of participating. The cooperative took steps to encourage broad-based participation, but status differences and life outside the workplace ensured that full and consistent engagement was more of an ideal than a reality.

Efforts to broadly distribute power among members cannot be reduced to formal policies or participation in meetings. The deliberations that were so central to the cooperative occurred both within and *beyond* meetings. In all areas of working life, idle talk constituted an alternative form of workplace participation. Around the proverbial watercooler, members regularly passed information outside formal channels of communication. Some of these rumors were certainly trivial, but others were consequential, prompting members to question the legitimacy of formal policies and the authority of elected officers. In this way, informal communication constituted an additional layer of accountability that helped members uphold and enact their democratic goals and values in the cooperative.

The formal and informal avenues of participation help us better understand how democracy is implemented at work. But these decision-making practices tell us little about how members actually engaged in the management of the hotel. The next chapter delves into how members of the BAUEN Cooperative negotiated the provision of hospitality service in cooperation.

We live by the clients, from their satisfaction, to provide them an experience . . . so that when they come to stay, they are comfortable. . . . You have to respect that you are living by [providing] service."

—ROMINA, member of the BAUEN Cooperative

A lot of times you put on the shirt of a company to protect your job, but here it's literal: when we want to put on the shirt, it's because it's a cooperative; it's all of ours.

—DANIEL, member of the BAUEN Cooperative

3   Hospitality in Cooperation

When new members were hired to work in the Hotel Bauen, they not only learned the job and met their coworkers but also got a crash course on how to work in cooperation. On a Tuesday afternoon in 2015, I joined a group of about twenty new members in a small conference room for an orientation. Their different uniforms signaled their positions: receptionists and waiters wore black slacks and white oxford shirts with a pale blue *B* embroidered on their lapels. Housekeepers and custodians wore matching pants and smocked tops that looked like hospital scrubs. And those working backstage in the kitchens and stockrooms wore BAUEN T-shirts drawn from an accumulation of overstocks squirreled away over the past decade. As the orientation began, members of the administrative council welcomed us and then dimmed the lights to show a documentary about this unique workplace.[1]

To the tune of tango music, subtitles scrolled across the screen, announcing that we would be learning about "the experience of workers without a boss." The screen filled with faces by now familiar to me—longtime members of the cooperative participating in meetings, setting tables, cleaning guest rooms, and attending rallies. In other hotels, employee orientations focus on policies, expectations, and the dictates of corporate culture. In the BAUEN Cooperative, the orientation showcased how work here *differed* from work in those conventional hotels.

A council member named Daniel stopped the video midway through, explaining, "What I want to explain to you very synthetically today is what a worker cooperative is and what the differences are between a worker cooperative and a traditional business." He defined a worker cooperative—"a company managed by a group of workers"—and then emphasized, "we are not in a relation of dependence. We are not working for a boss, a director, or a businessman who is the owner of this company. No, we work for ourselves. We organize according to what the [Workers] Assembly decides." All twenty of the new members, in other words, were joining not as employees but as equal owners, working for themselves and each other (see chapter 2). "We are all equal here," Pilar, then president of the cooperative, stressed that no one in the group should "feel excluded, or like someone is more than someone else."

Equality projects like this involve organizational practices to broadly distribute power and resources and also efforts to transform how people understand their productive labor. New worker-owners at the Hotel Bauen were immediately voting members, or *asociados*. But the BAUEN Cooperative's members more frequently called each other *compañeros*, a term that literally means "those who share bread" (*compartir el pan*) and is commonly used by activists to signal relations of status equality.[2] In this chapter I delve into the journey of becoming a compañero in the BAUEN Cooperative, showing how members received a democratic (re)education by learning about what a cooperative is and does and then embracing a new vision of cowork and organizational interaction.

Service Work and Self-Management

First, we need to zoom out to consider broader issues of commitment and participation in hospitality work. Conventional hotels around the globe clearly rely on their employees to provide services to guests. Workers, managers, and customers collaborate to produce interactive hospitality experiences, often engaging in what Arlie Russell Hochschild (2012) famously dubbed *emotional labor*, managing their own feelings to make others feel attended to, cared for, and considered.[3] At the same time, in conventional workplaces, manager-worker relations are frequently antagonistic. By virtue of their different relationships to the means of production, workers and owners belong to different classes and have competing interests. Scholars have thus focused on managers' attempts to control service encounters in ways that can exploit workers' selfhood and alienate them from their emotions.[4] They have also explored how service workers respond, not passively, but through consent and resistance.

In her study of luxury hotels in the United States, Rachel Sherman examines how management structures impact the production of service. Sherman (2007, 100) details a managerial regime characterized by what she calls "flexible informality," with a flexible division of labor, strong community, and weak authority structures, where "workers themselves basically ran the hotel." In this context of weak and contingent authority, workers engage in *lateral management*, regulating each other and sometimes challenging their managers.

Everyday operations in the Hotel Bauen looked very similar to the flexible informality Sherman describes. In cooperatives, members participate in both democratic governance and everyday management. The BAUEN Cooperative's members divided labor into work sectors while allowing flexibility both across tasks and between sectors (see chapter 1). In this participatory workplace, members took on the responsibility of training each other and overseeing everyday work practices. The cooperative also constructed a hierarchy of authority, with management positions in each work sector and on the administrative council. But this authority was contingent and revocable, always subject to the will of the entire group in the Workers Assembly.

In other words, the BAUEN Cooperative was guided by the idea of *autogestión*, or self-management. Certainly, hospitality experts identify a form of self-management—defined as personal integrity, time management, adaptability, and self-development—as a core competency for workers in conventional hotels.[5] Many of these practices center on an individualist approach closely tied to neoliberal ideologies that emphasize efficiency, prioritize market responsiveness, and ultimately encourage workers to develop their own personal brands and link their contributions to personal career goals.[6] This is not the same as autogestión, a concept that has a long history in factory occupations and labor movements around the globe.[7] In his impressive study of worker-recuperated businesses in Argentina, Marcelo Vieta (2019, 6) defines autogestión as a collective effort to "self-constitute and self-direct production and economic life while attempting to minimize the intrusive mediation of free markets, hierarchical organization, or state and union bureaucracies."[8] Autogestión, then, refers to not only a set of practices but also their potential to bring about social change. The BAUEN Cooperative explicitly embraced the idea of autogestión in this sense, promoting meaningful participation and worker autonomy as central to its collective endeavor. Again and again, the cooperative paired efforts to change workplace relations with a politics of transformation that encouraged members to question the meaning of paid work more broadly.[9]

Members of the cooperative became compañeros through their participation in the everyday management of the Hotel Bauen. As I worked alongside them, I saw that members were responsible for not only self-directing their own work but also collaborating with their coworkers to ensure they provided good service. This was not an idealistic, whistle-while-you-work scene. For members working long hours, the system of lateral management could be both empowering and burdensome. As equal owners in a cooperative workplace, members assumed added responsibility by participating in shared governance (described in chapter 2) *and* lateral management. As a result, most members saw themselves as engaged in *more than a job*, but the "more" meant investing extra attention and effort to help, train, and sometimes even surveil their compañeros.[10] In short, the process of becoming a compañero was intimately connected with the collective construction of what Joan Acker (1990) calls an ideal worker, one who was self-motivated, committed to the collective, and steeped in a political consciousness about their work.

Becoming a Compañero

Becoming a compañero in the BAUEN Cooperative involved a hands-on education in participatory democracy. Formal orientations like the one I described in the opening of this chapter introduced new members to the cooperative's structure, identity, and history. But this training extended into the workday. Adrian, a young man in his twenties, painted a picture of a staff that learned by doing:

> The folks on the council get the new members and show them a video and give them the statutes and explain to them the steps to follow. But in general, it's your fellow compañero who is orienting you: "Look, in this case, we do this; in that case, we do that." . . . For example, if you are new

and I am your simple compañero. I'm not on the council, I'm not from the member office. I will explain to you more or less—from my experience, obviously—what the steps are, the sanctions. I can tell you these things from a more direct relationship.

Over nearly a year working in the BAUEN Cooperative, I observed members teaching and learning about the cooperative firsthand through both on-the-job training and their interactive participation in lateral management.

Teaching Cooperative Hospitality

Yanela joined the cooperative at the beginning of 2015. Just nineteen years old, she had graduated from high school and had held a series of relatively short-lived service jobs. Most recently, she had worked full-time in a tiny kiosk in a downtown subway station, with just enough space for one person to sit at the register. Yanela had goals: she was studying English (a sought-after skill for service workers) and preparing to enter a local police academy. Yanela met Pilar as she passed, like other commuters, through the busy subway stop, pausing at the kiosk to buy a snack or pay a bill. In their brief encounters, Pilar was impressed by Yanela's proficiency with the computer system and one day introduced the idea of applying for a job at the hotel. Eager for a change of scene and a different schedule, Yanela submitted her résumé and was soon hired to work the afternoon shift in reception at the Hotel Bauen.

Nothing about this path into the cooperative was unusual. Most new members came via referrals, whether through family connections and friendship networks or weak ties like the one Yanela and Pilar had formed. Others had no connections to the cooperative but dropped off their résumés for consideration as part of their job search. When a position needed to be filled, workers in the member office would call prospective candidates to see if they were still interested. Much to my surprise, some even had no idea that the hotel was a worker-recuperated business before they were hired, and many had little experience with cooperatives or even hospitality work. For example, a neighbor who happened to work at the Hotel Bauen recommended Pachu for an opening as a valet. Years later, he laughed when he recounted to me what happened: "I didn't even know it was a cooperative. . . . I just needed a job!"

I had learned about the Hotel Bauen as a student interested in cooperatives. So I initially assumed that folks who worked there were drawn by its contentious beginnings and cooperative ethos, as I had been. But over the course of my fieldwork, I was struck by how few members reported that they

3.1 Reception desk with cashier window in the background.
Photo by BAUEN Cooperative.

had sought out jobs in the cooperative because it was a worker-recuperated business. Rafi, who had lived and worked with groups of unemployed workers (*piqueteros*) in La Matanza before joining the cooperative, was an exception. One day over lunch, he told me he had looked for work in the Hotel Bauen because "I was tired of passing out [welfare] plans. . . . I wanted to show that work could actually be done differently."[11] Rafi was familiar with social activism, political organizing, and worker cooperatives, and he brought that experience to the workplace. Others who didn't share Rafi's activist background had more to learn as they became members of this co-operative workplace.

Yanela arrived early for her first day of work. She first met with two long-time workers in the member office, who helped her fill out her employment paperwork in their light-filled office on the third floor.[12] Yanela then changed into a white button-down shirt and black slacks, paired with her own thick platform shoes that had been trendy in Buenos Aires the summer before. By chance, Yanela and I started working in reception around the same time. Together, we spent our first weeks on the job getting to know our coworkers and learning our sector's work routines (see figure 3.1).

All of the cooperative's founding members had previously worked as *hoteleros*—waiters, receptionists, valets, and housekeepers—in the privately owned Hotel Bauen and other hotels across the city. But as the cooperative articulated different hiring priorities and the group grew, new members brought less prior experience in hospitality. Inés and Primo, both founding members, chatted about this important shift. "When we occupied this," Primo said, pointing to the walls around him, "we were all hotel workers." He went on, "Today not everyone is. . . . Now [people join] because they are [someone's] cousin or nephew. . . . It's not that I'm against these people, but what I want to tell you is that these people didn't choose to work in food service and hospitality, but rather they came because they left their job or didn't have any work." Inés agreed, observing how this had affected the cooperative's ability to provide service: "Before . . . we knew that the most important way to attract customers was the way you treated them. . . . [I]f you treat them poorly, [if] you don't answer them, if you don't attend to them, the client will leave, and it will travel mouth-to-mouth. [They will say,] 'Look, the Bauen doesn't have good service, listen to what happened in the Bauen . . .'" Ultimately, new workers' lack of prior experience meant that members would need to teach them how to work in a cooperative *and* how to provide service at the same time.

Inés, once the head housekeeper, shared that she regularly told her housekeepers that they were learning something new: "Girls, girls, this is training [*enseñanza*]." She explained:

> Because they all started without knowing, without experience. This was training. If you take it, then tomorrow you can work in any hotel . . . but they will suffer because the treatment is different. Here it's more like a family. . . . [We say,] "Do this, don't do that." . . . They can go to other hotels to work, but they aren't going to be treated the same. . . . There are girls who went to other hotels who came back and told me, "The truth is you were right." It's nothing like working in a cooperative. It's fine, you earn more . . . but the work is tense, nervous.

Although she still set standards and taught housekeepers how to clean, Inés noted how the culture of the cooperative was more relaxed than in capitalist workplaces.

Inés and I spoke for an hour that day and continued to chat for months to come. Like others, she regularly referenced her experience working in conventional hotels, including the Hotel Bauen when it was under private management: "When we were working under a boss, we had a head housekeeper who did this," she said, dragging her finger across the top of her desk. "And she watched to see if there was any dust left on her finger." The contrast, Inés

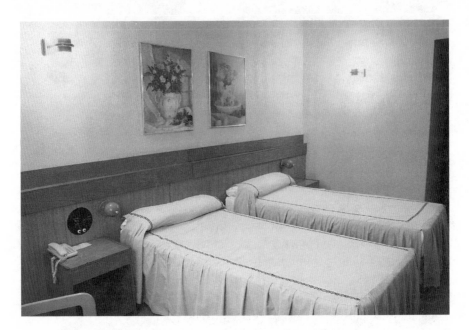

3.2 A double room in the Hotel Bauen. Photo by BAUEN Cooperative.

explained, was between stringent managerial oversight and the more personal and constructive approach taken in the cooperative: "The treatment is different," she assured me.

Training in the BAUEN Cooperative was an informal and collaborative effort. Having worked in a handful of different positions, Adrian described it as a "chain": "[Members] passed things down to me, and then I've been teaching them to other people. That's our method of work, our system. We have all been trained, and then we eventually become the trainers." Others I spoke with used the same term; at one point, when discussing the importance of teaching incoming members how the organization operated, Alberto asserted, "We aren't workers; we are trainers."

When Yanela and I started in reception, we worked closely with a woman named Cecilia, who detailed our daily tasks, introduced us to coworkers, and showed us around the facilities, from the break room and bathrooms to the various ballrooms and guest rooms (see figures 3.2 and 3.3). Cecilia was a founding member of the cooperative and had been the manager in reception for over a year at that point. She was well versed in the interconnected work in the "front of house," where reservations, event planning, and reception coordinated closely. During our first shifts, she coached us through the

3.3 An executive double room in the Hotel Bauen. Photo by BAUEN Cooperative.

check-in process, taught us how to use the computer system, and made sure we knew the basic guest schedule. After I successfully checked in a group of guests on my own, I reminded them off-script that dinner would be served in the restaurant. Cecilia beamed: "See, isn't it easy?"

The on-the-job training that Yanela and I received was paired with encouragement to rethink our understanding of work itself. Just a week after we started, Cecilia hurried us from our post at the reception desk to a small first-floor conference room where members of the administrative council were passing out copies of the cooperative's bylaws. During this orientation the council members fielded questions about our rights and responsibilities as official members of the cooperative.[13]

Pilar, the president, emphasized that new members needed to "change their thinking" to work without a boss. She then opened the meeting for discussion. The people around me began to spontaneously share reflections from their first weeks working in the hotel. "I never even cleaned my own room!" joked a woman who had joined in housekeeping. She went on, "I know it's easy to say this, but it's a really big responsibility to be self-sufficient. Here it's about 'self' . . . self-sufficient, self-managed, and self-taught." Yanela then raised her hand to share a story from earlier in our shift. A woman had

Hospitality in Cooperation

called the front desk after hearing a rumor that the cooperative had closed. The caller explained that she had fond memories of the hotel and had always been treated well there. Yanela assured her that the cooperative was still open for business and then encouraged all of us to provide good service to earn repeat clients. Finishing with a proud smile, Yanela enjoyed applause from the others attending the orientation.

In the BAUEN Cooperative, providing good service not only was important for the business's survival but also signaled solidarity with its customers. As such, the emphasis was less on deference and doting attention to guests and more on how good service could promote the cooperative's reputation and cultivate customer loyalty.

Running a conference hotel that regularly hosted events and provided lodging to overnight guests, members of the BAUEN Cooperative were acutely aware of the importance and challenges of providing good service. "Service work is fundamental for me because . . . we are a cooperative," said Romina, who had interacted with guests in her work as a housekeeper. "We live by the clients, from their satisfaction, to provide them an experience . . . so that when they come to stay, they are comfortable." Being part of a cooperative was important to many, yet they knew that only a portion of customers chose to stay there because it was run by the workers. "Many of them aren't interested [in the cooperative]," another member pointed out. "If the guest is paying . . . they don't care about your struggle. . . . You have to respect that you are living by [providing] service." So, at the same time that the cooperative regularly hosted activists and social organizations, members agreed that their social mission should not affect their standards.

As in most hotels, receptionists were frequently the first line of customer contact, checking guests in and out and addressing questions and issues throughout their stays. In addition to teaching us the logistics of the front desk, Cecilia also coached us on how to interact with customers. Yanela was friendly and energetic, eagerly taking up her post from 1:30 p.m. to 9:30 p.m., Wednesday through Sunday. When customers approached her, she smiled and listened to their questions and requests, often asking them to wait while she quietly asked more seasoned members where things were located or how to respond. Yanela was quick to pick things up and rarely had to ask for guidance twice. Still, whether owing to her age or her lack of formal training, she sometimes struggled to perform professionally.

One day while Yanela was learning to process payments, she giggled at an inside joke with a coworker as she counted change for a customer. Afterward, Yanela retreated from the desk to get her giggles out. Cecilia, having

82

observed the customer interaction, pointedly asked what was so funny. As Yanela explained the joke, Cecilia became serious and made direct eye contact. "You have to be really respectful and serious with customers who come here. It would have been bad if Francisco [the trustee] had seen that. You need to always be professional."

In this and other instances, Cecilia monitored and provided feedback on our service interactions. But managers like Cecilia had only weak authority in their sectors. They coordinated scheduling, set flexible work tasks, and advanced disciplinary complaints to the administrative council. But they also worked alongside their coworkers in shifts, participated equally in meetings and assemblies, and regularly discussed their decisions with others. Cecilia's mention of Francisco, the elected trustee who oversaw transparency and accountability, subtly reinforced her point. She signaled to Yanela that *multiple* authorities kept an eye on her work (and everyone else's). On any given day, Francisco flitted from sector to sector to check occupancy levels and observe members in reception and the café, discuss upcoming events with members in reservations and event planning, touch base with housekeepers and valets preparing rooms, and oversee ongoing maintenance and repair projects. This managerial labor was shared by many members, who participated in a lateral rather than strictly hierarchical system of oversight.

Lateral Management

Whether experienced as hoteleros or new to the hospitality business, members worked together to provide service *in cooperation* and under the watchful eyes of their fellow workers. Similar to workers in conventional hotels that adopted a more flexible and informal managerial regime, those in the BAUEN Cooperative oversaw their service work together. This lateral management wasn't just a by-product of weak authority or the lack of rules. It was an intentional outcome of the cooperative's emphasis on participatory democracy and autogestión. More than a job requirement, the emphasis on and practice of lateral management changed interpersonal dynamics, distributed managerial power, and resignified the meaning of paid work.

Among coworkers, this mutual oversight was often framed, as previously mentioned, as *training*. Managers provided guidance, but coworkers were just as important for instilling the formal tasks and tempos of different jobs. In reception Cecilia wasn't the only person offering us advice on how to deal with customers and insights into the informal rules of work. Jesús, who had worked the afternoon shift in reception for over two years, confidently taught us how to use the electronic reservation system, access occupancy charts, identify

83

who was checking in or out, and create reports. When we struggled with directing calls from the main phone line at the front desk, Jesús placed practice calls to us from another line so we could memorize the internal transfer codes and rehearse responses to common questions.

As I rotated positions to get a broad view of work in the cooperative, I found a similar approach to training carried across sectors. In administration the manager taught newer members how to update spreadsheets and file documents, while coworkers chimed in with advice and feedback based on their own on-the-job experiences. In housekeeping the department head coordinated schedules and assigned floors, while housekeepers taught each other the cleaning standards and provided support by working in pairs.

As equal owners in a cooperative workplace, members assumed the added responsibility of participating in shared governance *and* lateral management. Those in customer-facing roles not only had to manage their service interactions with customers but also with their coworkers. I regularly observed members providing feedback to and checking in with each other after difficult service encounters, engaging in what Hochschild (2012) calls "collective emotional labor." In short, emotional labor in the cooperative was not only an individual requirement but also a group accomplishment.[14]

For many, the labor of managing one another could be a source of frustration. During the period I worked in reception, for example, a woman named Luisina rotated into the section from the laundry (see chapter 5 for more on job rotation). Luisina was not new to the cooperative, but she struggled during her first shifts at the reception desk. After a particularly busy evening, longtime receptionist Felipe complained about his difficulties training her. He told me that the night before, about 10 p.m., a leftist political group called La Cámpora had contacted the cooperative because lodging elsewhere had fallen through. At the last minute, the receptionists accepted its reservation for fifty-two people. As Felipe scrambled to check them all in, he felt Luisina was less than helpful—she asked too many questions, he complained, and even interrupted when he was talking with customers. Visibly perturbed, Felipe confided to me that Luisina did not even have basic computer skills, lamenting, "She doesn't even know how to cut and paste!"

Training and lateral management resulted in co-op members engaging in even more emotional labor with both clients and coworkers. Some members, like Felipe, resented coworkers who seemed to need more support than others. In response, the cooperative looked for ways to reduce the labor of managing each other. For example, over the years, I observed the cooperative adopt new technologies to depersonalize some of this oversight. During my third period of fieldwork in the hotel, I noticed that the manual time clock that members had used to clock in and out of their shifts had been replaced by a biometric fingerprint reader. As I explained in chapter 1, when I asked about the device, a worker explained that there were occasional issues with members clocking in for coworkers who were running late. Instead of relying on hearsay or personal reports of such behavior, he explained, the technology helped increase personal accountability, streamline work processes, and ultimately reduce conflicts over attendance.

In addition to the biometric reader, other technologies were installed to increase surveillance. For example, after a spurt of petty thefts in the lobby, the cooperative purchased security cameras to monitor the public spaces of the lobby and café as well as cash registers and stairwells to track any suspicious movement. Members had an uneasy relationship with these security cameras. One afternoon while I was working in reception, Yanela pulled out her cell phone to check her text messages during a lull in foot traffic through the lobby. When he noticed her openly looking at her phone, Jesús pointed out the pair of cameras installed in reception—one directed at the register and another at the front desk. We could be watched, he warned, so we should never use our cell phones or drink yerba maté in their purview.

I later learned that the cameras ran 24/7 and the recordings were saved for a time in case the cooperative needed to review any footage. In council meetings the elected officers would sometimes use this film to resolve questions about who worked when or to track movements in the public spaces of the hotel. When I asked people about the cameras, many members agreed with this transparency in principle. Especially in contexts where members handled cash, most thought that the cameras were, to some extent, necessary. But as Jesus's advice to Yanela hints, members were nonetheless wary of the cameras and devised ways to avoid being filmed.

The reception desk and register were always visible—to both customers and cameras—with the exception of an area behind a large safe that offered a respite from this visibility. The safe was likely an impressive technology in its day, but by the time I worked in reception, it looked like a relic from the past. Sandro, who also worked in reception, assured me that the safe was functional. Guests could enter from the lobby via a buzzer-operated door to store their valuables (like "a lot of money or cocaine," he joked). Far more commonly, though, the outdated safe provided workers a shield from public view. In the dark corner, tucked away from public view, workers arranged a watercooler and a small table and chairs where they stored their personal items, shared yerba maté, and took breaks without interruption.

85

Ultimately, collective efforts at lateral management bordered on surveillance. As part of their responsibilities in the cooperative, members were called on to help their fellow compañeros by providing on-the-job training, emotional support, and feedback to ensure they provided good service. Because this placed extra burdens on workers, over the years the cooperative adopted technologies to depersonalize these demands and ensure rule following without interpersonal oversight. While workers widely agreed that the technologies helped streamline their work and ensure transparency and safety, the devices also exacerbated their uneasy sense of being under constant surveillance.

The Ideal (Self-Managed) Worker

Working in the Hotel Bauen was different from a conventional job, whether members were voting in the Workers Assembly or participating in the everyday operations of the hotel. These expectations—collectively constructed and culturally sustained—provided a working blueprint for what a "good member" of the BAUEN Cooperative looked like. Scholars have identified how organizations construct such ideal workers and measure individuals against abstract images and expectations. In many workplaces, for example, the ideal worker is unencumbered by personal issues and family life, able to work long hours, and dedicated to their job above other priorities. Given the perennial demands for care work that are most often fulfilled by women, these norms clearly favor men.[15]

The expectations bound up in an ideal worker matter for a variety of reasons, affecting how organizations fill jobs and positions of authority, the rules and policies written to define those roles, and the expectations and evaluation of the person in that job.[16] In the BAUEN Cooperative, I found that the ideal self-managed worker had three main characteristics: they were self-motivated in their daily tasks, were deeply committed to the collective, and had developed a political consciousness about the meaning and value of work in cooperation, modifying their political orientation and social values accordingly.

The Motivation to Self-Manage

Self-motivation was a key characteristic that defined the ideal worker in the BAUEN Cooperative. Francisco, whom we met earlier in this chapter, was a prime example. He was always on the move and rarely sat down, even during meetings. He was also constantly shifting roles and contributing to different sectors in the cooperative. If I spotted him wearing a customer-service uniform in the morning, it was just as likely he'd be wearing a set of work clothes to pitch in on a repair job by afternoon.

Francisco joined the BAUEN Cooperative in March 2005 through a family member's referral. He started working in custodial services, cleaning and setting up ballrooms for events. Three years later, he moved to work as a waiter and then cashier in the Utopia Café. He had no experience in food service at the time, so he learned the ropes from coworkers. A year later, he became a shift manager, overseeing the small team that served coffee and classic *porteño* dishes throughout the day.[17] Eager to contribute to the cooperative, Francisco decided to run for an elected office. The first time he ran for trustee, he lost. Undeterred, he ran again and was elected two years later.

On his work history in the hotel, Francisco told me, "I have won within the cooperative . . . those times of learning to use the billing system, I made friends." He laughed and continued, "I made enemies, but I have more friends than enemies. It was a little bit like I had to convince my compañeros of my thinking and what I was aiming for [*hacia dónde yo apuntaba*]. Many understood me, and that's why I am where I am today. If not, I wouldn't be here."

Working in the cooperative included long hours and attention that went beyond simply showing up for his shift.[18] Francisco explained:

I have a bunch of things that I produce and do in one sector. It would be good if there were other compañeros who did that. It is going to be difficult because you have to put in the effort [*ponerle ganas*]. I see that there are compañeros who come [to work] and don't put in the effort. I don't take it out on them, but it bothers me a little when I come at 6 a.m. and leave at midnight. And it doesn't have to be like that. You always have a little time for your cooperative. It's *your* cooperative. What happens if I didn't stay extra hours and I take all your money? They will call me a thief. So [I tell them] to stay, be concerned, and get a little bit more involved [*quedate, preocupate y . . . esmérate*] in the cooperative and collaborate a little. What we want to achieve here is for the compañeros to get involved in the system. [We want them] to see what a bank statement is, what a balance sheet is . . . because when someone learns to read a report, they can understand anything. [When they don't], it's because they don't want to.

Like the founders and other elected officers, Francisco thought that although there were ample opportunities to participate, the problem was motivation.

In the BAUEN Cooperative, showing up for work was about more than physical presence. Each worker-owner was expected to seek out tasks throughout the workday, making the most of their time to build the cooperative

87

3.4 A member cleans the floors in the entrance to the Hotel Bauen. Photo by Nicolas Parodi/ANCCOM.

through customer service and coworker training. Affirmations of self-motivation circulated throughout the workday. For example, Inés described Ester as "dedicated" to her work. Ester had held many different jobs in the cooperative, but Inés remembered that when Ester was manager of the laundry, she would volunteer to help guests with their personal laundry (a service that wasn't formally offered) in addition to washing their sheets and towels. She was also meticulous—known for making sure linens were bleached and perfumed properly—and communicated well. In other words, she had the self-motivation of an ideal worker-owner.

Julio described another member, José Luis, in similar terms, calling him "a tremendous worker" before elaborating:

> He does his job. He doesn't ask you for more than what he does. He shines the floors. He does it every morning. Have you noticed that this floor is always waxed? . . . He is there every day Monday through Saturday doing the same thing. He cleans the sidewalk, [and] he removes all the grime. . . . He cleans here and there [pointing to different spots], always the same. He does it well, and he is watchful [*celoso*] over his work. If you step on a spot where he has just cleaned, he will move you. Lots of people think he's crazy—[they say,] "That's insane!"—but he is a guy that. . . . To me, he is the best worker . . . the best model [*exponente*] that this cooperative has. He is the example of a person who does their job well.

To Julio, José Luis demonstrated his self-motivation at work through an attention to detail that others sometimes considered excessive (see figure 3.4).

Some members thrived with the autonomy of self-management, but others found it challenging. For Sabrina, learning her roles and self-managing

88

in the cooperative took time. When she joined in 2004 on the recommendation of family members who worked in the hotel, she started as a waitress in the café: "[At first] there were a lot of things that I didn't understand because I came from a capitalist system . . . working under a boss, working a shift, and then just going home. And here this doesn't happen. So in the beginning, it's hard to learn [self-management]. But after a while, you adapt and begin to like it." Over the years, her job here took on greater meaning beyond cashing a paycheck. Sabrina not only gained extensive experience in hotel management but set her own schedule, controlled her daily work routines, and felt relaxed in a workplace where she felt like she didn't have to worry about arbitrary mandates from higher-ups.

The opposite of self-motivation—laziness (*vagancia*)—was widely described as detrimental to the cooperative. Julio, who had described José Luis, identified this as a major challenge at work: "For example, there are people who are so lazy that they leave things until they become a problem [*ya se hizo carne el problema*]. So every silly thing [*pavada*] becomes a problem. And they even complain about the work, although they do nothing in comparison to [José Luis]." A self-motivated worker like José Luis took the initiative to identify tasks *before* they became problems; others, Julio implied, dragged the whole thing down.

Pilar also felt there were certain members who never seemed to learn how to self-manage: "You have to explain something to them over and over and over again, but they still won't do it unless you tell them to." As Pilar pointed out, some people seemed to respond only to managerial oversight. When such instances arose, fellow members would use these occasions to clarify the expectations of the cooperative: rather than waiting for someone else to tell you what to do, self-managed workers needed to be self-motivated to work hard for the well-being of their collective endeavor.

Commitment and Collectivism

The ideal member of the BAUEN Cooperative was also deeply committed to the organization beyond their individual interests. Commitment involved caring about the business, expressing loyalty to it, and actively participating by providing feedback, debating ideas, and including others in decision-making.

The important role of commitment is a common finding in research on collectivist organizations and intentional communities. In her study of communes in the United States, Rosabeth Moss Kanter (1972) breaks down commitment, writing that it entails an *instrumental* tie as well as *affective* and *moral* connections that generate meaningful social relationships and reinforce

3.5 A member wears the cooperative's T-shirt. Photo by Lavaca Collective.

the norms and values of group membership. In worker cooperatives, members invest in the organization not only because it is the source of their economic livelihood (instrumental commitment) but also because they develop personal attachments to the group. Each of these are critical to developing a "we-feeling" that maintains group cohesion and supports solidarity (Kanter 1968, 509).

In conventional workplaces where employees hold no ownership stake, managers sometimes try to cultivate feelings of "psychological ownership" in which workers feel a deep and personal investment in the organization.[19] In other words, they try to stoke commitment without actually including workers in the payoff. In worker cooperatives, by contrast, individual feelings of ownership are reinforced by workers' actual equity stake in the business, which bolsters the sense of commitment.[20]

Throughout my fieldwork, members of the BAUEN Cooperative made it clear that work in this context required a commitment well beyond a normal day job. In one orientation Pilar urged, "As new members who are coming into the cooperative, I would like you to really put on the T-shirt [*lleven la camiseta*]" (see figure 3.5). This phrase—regularly used in meetings and emblazoned on flyers and T-shirts—signaled the shared expectations of membership. Joining the cooperative meant working a job *and* developing loyalty and commitment to the group.

The idea of "putting on the shirt" was a soccer reference (*refutbolera*), Daniel acknowledged. But unlike other jobs, the council member explained, joining a cooperative "offers the real opportunity for everyone to actually be part of a company and put on a shirt that is their own," he said. "A lot of times you put on the shirt of a company to protect your job, but here it's literal: when we want to put on the shirt, it's because it's a cooperative, it's all of ours." As Daniel emphasized, commitment to the cooperative was more than symbolic; it was rooted in a genuine ownership stake ("the shirt is your own"; the business is "all of ours").

Members demonstrated this commitment by emphasizing the well-being of the collective as a whole, especially by volunteering to work jobs across different sectors. As one member commented to me, "If I have to clean, I'll clean. . . . [M]ostly I have no problems in any sector where they send me. If you work, you're not going to have any problems, even if they send you to . . . sweep the whole street, you are going to do it." Again, the incentive was not financial. Nor was it about career advancement in the traditional sense. Adrian, a younger member working in administration, outlined the collectivist ethos behind his commitment to the cooperative in this way: "The incentive has to be your own. . . . Let me give you an example. In reception I was paid nearly the same as [I am now]. Why would I change jobs if I'll be paid the same? . . . If a person thinks of things progressively, [then] yes, I'll go, I'll learn, and I'll improve with the experience that I'll have tomorrow. The incentive has to be born from yourself to want to learn, to want to be in a better place." Here Adrian is describing the importance of an internal shift by which he and others moved from thinking about jobs from an individual perspective to developing a deeper motivation to contribute—one rooted in an affective commitment and self-driven loyalty.

The commitment members felt was both sustainable and sustaining. As Sabrina put it, "I always considered that to be in a cooperative is a choice. . . . Today I choose to be here, in addition to the obvious ways it supports me financially."

Political Consciousness
The last aspect of an ideal worker in the BAUEN Cooperative was a deep understanding of their work as a political act. During her tenure as president, Pilar worked in a sunny office tucked away from the bustle of customers and events. Pilar, you'll recall, was one of the original Bauen employees who broke into the shuttered hotel and occupied it. She remembered how activists, neighborhood organizations, and other groups came to support them

that memorable day—and how, at the time, these demonstrations of support caught her off guard: "I had never volunteered for a political party or anything like that. . . . I didn't understand what [activism] was."

Pilar remembered back to when the Hotel Bauen operated under private ownership and conventional management. She got her first job in 1994 as a housekeeper at the then-four-star Hotel Bauen. She was a new mother who needed a job to support her family. "I started at zero," she confided. "The truth is that I didn't understand anything because it's not the same to make a bed at your house as to do so in a hotel. It's totally different."

Pilar learned the daily tasks and routines of a housekeeper, yet she had a hard time adapting to the impersonal workplace. As one of nearly four hundred workers—housekeepers, waiters, administrators, and event personnel—operating the adjoining Hotel Bauen and Bauen Suites at the time, she said that she "felt like [she] was a number, not even a name." She went on, "It was like I was watching a movie about prisoners, who brought their little metal trays [to eat]. I would sit down, and they would give us food, two courses, dessert . . . all on the tray. And when I went to sit down, my coworkers would turn their chairs [away] because I was new and I had to pay my dues [*pagar derecho de piso*]." Despite these challenges Pilar's life was modest and comfortable: she was happily married, her daughter went to private school, and there was usually money to spare at the end of the year. As she described, "We lived in a bubble because . . . in 1994 . . . [Carlos] Menem [was president]. . . . My husband had a car, [and] we were well off. We had a house behind my mother-in-law's, but we were fine. At the end of the year, we would pack up the car and go on vacation in Mar del Plata, on the coast."

This bubble burst when the economic crisis worsened in 2001, an outcome of the political and economic forces that had shaped Argentina throughout the 1990s. Pilar remembered, "The truth is that there was no work. We saw things falling apart. . . . I'm telling you this because it felt like I was living in a ghost country." As I described in chapter 1, while the currency collapsed and protests erupted, Pilar and her coworkers watched as people took to the streets of Buenos Aires, just meters from the Hotel Bauen's doors. But she and her coworkers stayed inside.

Before the 2001 crisis, Pilar admitted that she saw protests as a "nuisance." Marches could—and commonly did—cut off major arteries of the city, stymying the careful choreography of her hour-long daily commute on a series of public buses. But she told me that she experienced a "click"—a moment of greater social awareness—when she joined her former coworkers in occupying and recuperating the hotel. She started to see her past reactions as individualist and self-serving: "Before, when they cut off the road, [I would ask,] 'Why are they blocking the street?'" Now she asked, "What happened?" Occupying the hotel, forming a cooperative, and undertaking an equality project had made her realize the importance of social protest.

In the years since reopening the hotel under worker control, Pilar had become accustomed to organizing events to garner support for the cooperative. With her compañeros, she had also taken to the streets to advocate for groups that had supported them in their moments of need. And, as I explore further in chapter 6, the BAUEN Cooperative integrated activist practices into its everyday work routines, operating like a social movement organization to defend its right to exist. All this changed Pilar's perspective on work itself. Rather than a means to an end, her active participation in the cooperative was politically significant: she was working to create better jobs, a more equal organization, and a society that valued people over profits.

Pilar was not the only member of the cooperative to report such a political awakening. Tito's "click" came after a bubble burst, too. He began in an entry-level job in the Hotel Bauen in 1980, then was promoted to a job in reception that came with reliable tips: "What happened was that I was here for many years. Thanks to the extra income [from tips], I could build my house. But also because of this extra cash, I lived in a bubble. That and the things that I was exposed to here—like selling [tickets] to a tango, a show, a city tour, a hired car. Materially, I did really well. But this also pushed me into a bubble . . . the champagne, the French cologne, the refined taste [*paladar negro*], the foods from here and there . . . a bubble."[21] Tito described having a middle-class income and proximity to luxury. But after losing his job and enduring a series of hardships, he changed the way he understood his work. Tito had been unemployed for some time when he joined his former coworkers to occupy the Hotel Bauen. And he would go on to be elected by his peers to the cooperative's administrative council.

In the leadership role, Tito guided the cooperative through its initial legal struggles, helped build its social legitimacy, and eventually reopened the hotel for business. Like Pilar's, Tito's vision of his work within the walls of the hotel soon reverberated with political implications. In the years that followed, he became a vocal spokesperson for the cooperative, and after serving on the council, he worked in the cooperative's press sector to organize the campaign to expropriate the hotel.

Over the years, I met Tito multiple times in his office to talk about his organizing efforts and his views on the movement of worker-recuperated businesses. He adorned the walls of the small office with photographs of

93

cooperative members alongside posters of his political inspirations: Eva Perón, Hugo Chávez, and Che Guevara. Tito had taken up a self-study of *autogestión*, learning the meanings of worker self-management, the history of workplace occupations around the globe, and the resurgence of the cooperative movement in Latin America. This click was transformational for Tito. The person I came to know during my repeated visits to the Hotel Bauen was a far cry from his description of his past self as a man who valued the refined taste of specialty foods, champagne, and costly cologne.

Developing a political consciousness helped members of the cooperative broaden their thinking about seemingly insulated organizational decisions. It also encouraged them to infuse their work with greater meaning and significance. Members who had experienced a click thought outside the conventional understandings of business. As Pilar commented, "There are people who are redeemable [*rescatables*] and fight to believe in something, and there are others who cut down the dream because they believe that it's not possible." The idea that "another world is possible"—an assertion popularized in 2001 at the World Social Forum in Porto Alegre, Brazil—took on concrete meaning through work in the Hotel Bauen. An ideal member of the cooperative was thus someone who believed in the importance of working in cooperation, not one who was cynical about the process or value of these efforts.

In many ways, the demands of the ideal worker in the BAUEN Cooperative align with similar imperatives in conventional workplaces, particularly those that embrace neoliberal ideologies that view workers as individual entrepreneurs who are expected to constantly develop their skills. As a collective, the BAUEN Cooperative constructed a series of expectations for what it meant to become a compañero and practice self-management. To call someone a compañero literally means they are a person with whom you share bread—it signals a relation of status equality. The ideal compañero was self-motivated, committed, and politically engaged, able to self-direct and show their loyalty and commitment by developing a consciousness about their work as a political act.

Of course, conventional workplaces also demand unpaid, immaterial labor, even screening potential employees based on their passion for their work.[22] But while the practices may be similar, the meaning and purpose of those expectations could not be more different. Autogestión was a guiding principle in the BAUEN Cooperative, making the most of the dual meaning of this neoliberal catchphrase in local parlance. Rather than promoting an individualist approach to work, autogestión emphasizes the transformative value of self-directed production within organizations decoupled from capitalist markets and state institutions. Collective efforts to self-direct production were not designed exclusively to increase worker productivity, reduce turnover, or increase profits amid morally lacking working relationships. Rather, the cooperative embraced autogestión as a way to promote meaningful participation and encourage autonomy as a contribution to the collective whole.

The workplace participation described in this chapter was central to the group's equality project. Beyond creating and enforcing policies to broadly distribute power, the group also sought to transform how people interacted with each other and to reframe the meaning of their work. Lofty ideals like these were grounded in the everyday routines at the Hotel Bauen such that building solidarity was about building skills and competencies, too. Nowhere was this more evident than in the practice of rotating jobs.

In utopia . . . who takes out the garbage?
—ROSABETH MOSS KANTER, *Commitment and Community*

4   Rotating Opportunity

"The cooperative does things that don't coincide with the [real] world," Daniel said one evening in an office in the Hotel Bauen. A self-described night owl, Daniel was often hard to find before the lunch hour but would stay late into the night coordinating events or catching up with his responsibilities in sales. He learned about the Hotel Bauen through his work as an activist in the cooperative movement and later as an advocate for worker-recuperated businesses. After several years he decided to officially join the BAUEN Cooperative and work full-time in the hotel.

Though he worked in sales when we met, he had held several positions in press and event management, as well as serving on two administrative councils. He described his work as part of a system of job rotation: "[I am] on the administrative council, but if there is a change in [the] council, we can end up in another place in the cooperative. . . . It's like this is a wheel where no one's future is assured. . . . It's like, in the back of your mind, you know that you don't have privileges, you can do any job. . . . [These are] things that would never happen in more conventional jobs where there is a more fixed class structure. . . . Here everything is absolutely changeable." Job rotation in the BAUEN Cooperative was a radical departure from more conventional job-placement strategies using skills, past experience, or education to match people with positions.[1] Daniel went on, "In a conventional hotel, if someone starts in custodial services, it is difficult to move to administration or management for an infinity of reasons, not just because of their training."

Like Daniel, others identified job rotation as special to the cooperative hotel. Theo went so far as to say that working this way felt like "an upside-down world." He explained the outcome: "A person who has an education might be fixing pipes, a person who is a painter is on the computer, the person . . . who may be much better as a receptionist is collecting trash."

Workplace recuperation, as we've explored so far, involves a second founding moment in which workers reimprint new ideas of how a business can and should run. As members of the BAUEN Cooperative set out to redesign work as part of their equality project, job rotation was a primary focus. Inés, a founder of the cooperative who worked for decades in housekeeping, described the intent: "The idea was that we should all have to do everything: the housekeeper could be the waitress, just as the waitress could be the housekeeper." In the new Hotel Bauen, labor would be understood as a set of practices that could be learned by anyone, regardless of their formal education or past experience.

Redefining who could do what was a meaningful step in establishing more egalitarian relations among members, the heart of an equality project. Yet the informal practice of job rotation created some notable challenges. The BAUEN Cooperative used formal rules to codify other equality-producing practices like democratic decision-making in the workplace (see chapter 2). But over the course of my fieldwork, I discovered that there was no formal policy of job rotation but rather an ad hoc movement of people between work sectors. This *selective* formalization had an important impact on the practice. The resulting internal labor market provided broad job opportunities to members, while at the same time creating uncertainties about who could access these opportunities and when and how this could be done. As Daniel noted at the outset of this chapter, rotation in the cooperative was like a wheel, and although members held stable jobs, no one's future was assured.

97

One of the primary ways that work perpetuates social inequality is by segregating people into different jobs. Occupational segregation occurs through processes that sort people according to gender, race, individual preferences, education, skills, and credentials, which directly impact their pay and future prospects.[2] Once workers are sorted, the built environment of many workplaces often keeps people apart, both workers from customers and workers from each other.[3] This sorting means that many people sense that they are constrained—and, indeed, they may very well be constrained—to a particular job or career trajectory. In contrast, job rotation provides an opportunity for people to *sort themselves*, try out different types of work, and expand their skill set beyond their past experience.

Job rotation was not invented by the BAUEN Cooperative. Formal systems of job rotation were once a feature of many industrial workplaces. For example, in his comparative study of the internal labor markets of two factories in the United States and the United Kingdom, Michael Burawoy (1983) finds that, in one, workers were able to request permanent job transfers or apply for vacant positions based on their seniority.[4] Trade unions have historically played an important role in facilitating these workplace practices. Yet with union decline, this type of opportunity promoted through job rotation is increasingly uncommon, and it has never been the norm in service workplaces.[5]

Practices akin to job rotation are also part of the trend toward flexible specialization. In response to deregulation, technological changes, and international competition, which intensified in the 1980s, management scholars proposed ways to make organizations more responsive to market demands. In particular, systems of just-in-time production require various forms of organizational flexibility as well as efforts to increase worker participation, provide more training, and organize workers into self-directed, cross-functional teams.[6] In her study of garment factories in the United States and Mexico, Jane Collins (2001) identifies this as a shift toward "combination jobs," allowing management to take workers who had once specialized in a given area and—under the cover of terms like *multiskilling* and *cross-training*—make them perform additional tasks without extra pay. After waves of layoffs, Collins notes, the factories that had established combination jobs were able to continue producing the same volume with fewer people. Production may have stayed consistent, but the remaining workers reported extreme stress and exhaustion.

As corporate workplaces have downsized and flattened management hierarchies, some have also adopted temporary job-rotation programs that allow midlevel employees to move through different positions, work under different bosses, and—in theory—gain new skills. In other settings, workers have joined cross-functional teams to oversee complex projects, share knowledge, and make decisions, a trend that Alexandra Kalev (2009, 1598) calls "the most far-reaching effort to transform the organization of work." In different ways, these new work arrangements modified once rigidly segregated divisions of labor at the end of the twentieth century. In doing so, shifts *in* work opened opportunities to restructure inequities perpetuated *at* work (Kelly and Kalev 2006; Smith 1996).

Flexible, team-based work practices vary significantly across organizations.[7] Jane Collins (2003) differentiates the impact of such practices by considering those that follow a "high road" versus a "low road." So-called high-road flexibility involves job enlargement, cross-training, teamwork, and job rotation, practices that require organizational commitment and are most commonly implemented in lean manufacturing and white-collar corporate workplaces.[8] In other organizations, low-road flexibility practices maintain the routinization of daily tasks while expanding contingent and nonstandard employment relations, particularly in low-wage service work. This means increasing workers' responsibilities while dramatically reducing employers' commitments to their workers.

Many hotels take the low road, offering low pay, long and irregular hours, and poor employment conditions.[9] Hotels around the globe recruit temporary and part-time workers—often targeting women, racial and ethnic minorities, and immigrants—to work nonconventional hours, owing to the need for twenty-four-hour staffing even on weekends and holidays. And because customer demand for hotels often fluctuates dramatically, hotels rely on their ability to lay off workers when they are no longer needed. In Buenos Aires, for example, the low season lasts from June to August, the winter months in the Southern Hemisphere.

Collectivist organizations that experiment with job rotation do so not to implement this sort of flexibility but to humanize work processes, disrupt conventional hierarchies of power, and cultivate an appreciation for the organization as a whole.[10] According to a survey conducted by the Open Faculty at the University of Buenos Aires, nearly two-thirds of all worker-recuperated businesses in Argentina have adopted some system of job rotation, may it be to allow members to collaborate on tasks, take on new roles, or work in multiple sectors simultaneously (Ruggeri 2011).

Rotating work has far-reaching effects. In her study of Brukman, a worker-recuperated garment factory in Buenos Aires, María Inés Fernández Álvarez (2016) describes the temporal and spatial implications of the practice. She finds that members shifted from productive to managerial tasks, participated in activist events to support their claim to the property, and blurred the distinction between public and private life by bringing children to work, staying overnight, and mediating domestic disputes. By diversifying work activities, members of the Brukman cooperative also redefined the working day (which extended into evenings and weekends) and working space (not limited to the factory but also including the home and sites of protest). These practices clearly have major implications not only for how we produce goods and services but also for how we interact with others and ultimately what we believe *labor* means in our daily lives.

Studies of occupational integration offer a starting point to consider how organizations can reconfigure job-sorting processes. Much of this research documents the effects of changes in employment law following the passage of the US Civil Rights Act in 1964. As workplace regulation and oversight changed, overall occupational segregation by race and gender declined until 1980 and has been relatively flat since then.[11] Notably, this occupational integration has been highly uneven, and although some workplaces experienced desegregation, these mandates did not spur total integration between working people. In many cases, either occupations were resegregated (i.e., men moved out, and women moved in) or women were concentrated in part-time, lower-wage, or less desirable jobs.[12] More recently, Kevin Stainback and Donald Tomaskovic-Devey (2012) looked at patterns of desegregation at the organizational level. They find that despite external catalysts for change, organizations distribute people across jobs in specific ways that perpetuate racialized and gendered divisions of labor.[13] Occupational segregation, these studies show, is difficult to unravel, and progress toward integration can easily be reversed.

At the outset, rotating jobs in the BAUEN Cooperative was not simply a practical move. It was part of an equality project, a way that workers could access opportunity and contest entrenched patterns of inequality in the workplace. Scholars have identified the process of *opportunity hoarding* as central to the production of inequality.[14] But this pattern of social closure is not unidirectional. People can also share resources with those outside their networks by engaging in *opportunity distribution*. But the questions remain: How did job rotation operate in practice? And how did it evolve over time?

Job Rotation as Re-sorting

In the BAUEN Cooperative, job rotation provided workers an opportunity to engage in what I call *occupational re-sorting*. The practice was closely tied to the overall job security that accompanied working in the cooperative. Not only were all members full-time workers, but after a probationary period, they could not be fired without just cause. Thus, when positions opened, personal situations changed, or interpersonal conflicts arose, existing members could transfer to different sectors. And nearly all of them did: almost every worker I encountered had held more than one position in the cooperative.

The work histories of Cecilia and Emiliano illustrate two pathways through the cooperative hotel. Both had changed jobs frequently and liked the variety that accompanied working with different people, learning new skills, and following new schedules. Some of their moves were lateral, while others involved greater or lesser responsibility. But for both, their previous job had little impact on where they went next.

(Missed) Opportunities: Cecilia's Work History

Cecilia first heard about the Hotel Bauen in her teens when her then-boyfriend worked there under private management. After workers occupied the hotel in 2003, Cecilia joined the group, spending more and more of her free time in the tower. As she explained, "Everything [in the neighborhood] was closed, and so I stayed here. . . . I was so young, and I brought all my things [to live] here . . . and have been here ever since."

Initially Cecilia worked with a group of housekeepers who taught her how to clean. Without industrial cleaning products, a functioning elevator, or even hot water, Cecilia walked the twenty-story tower with buckets of supplies, using brooms and rags to scrub the matted carpets and clear away debris. After months of cleaning, Cecilia transferred to work in the newly reopened staff kitchen. Every day, she woke up early to prepare breakfast and lunch on a tight budget for thirty or forty members. After an interpersonal conflict with a coworker, she asked the administrative council for an opportunity to change sectors, stopping briefly to work in security before an exciting opportunity arose to create a new sector. She explained:

> After a while, the cooperative repaired the telephone lines, and there was the possibility of opening a department of reservations. . . . So I decided to do it, without knowing anything about reservations. I didn't know anything about hospitality. I knew absolutely nothing. But I said, "Well, I can

101

do it." I was twenty-two years old—twenty-one or twenty-two. . . . They gave me a computer, a telephone, and another person worked with me. . . . At first, I picked up the phone with fear, but over time I learned, and I created the department of reservations . . . more or less as I imagined it, based on what I taught myself.

This was about the time Cecilia started to study hospitality at a local college. With her additional training, she and a coworker expanded the sector to include both reservations and event planning. They started with small events because, as Cecilia joked, "We didn't know anything!" She continued, "But over time we learned more and started to get it. With study and practice . . . I learned almost all there is—public relations, sales, reservations, reception, billing, events. I learned it all. I wasn't scared of anything anymore."

Cecilia remembered being happy with her position. She loved organizing beautiful parties, especially *quinceañeras*, and showed me countless photographs of ballrooms she had decorated and set up for events.[15] "I'm really detail oriented," she noted as we scrolled through the images. Wanting every event to be "impeccable," Cecilia taught herself how to fold the napkins into shapes, match the plates with the silverware, and set the tables properly. Before long, reservations and event planning became two of the most important income-generating sectors in the Hotel Bauen.

A couple of years after Cecilia set up the sectors, a newly elected administrative council transferred her to work in reception, which was in need of leadership. Cecilia recalled with a touch of resignation: "After the change in council, well, it's what always happens: the council changes, and they change [our] sectors. It's nothing, so I am here in reception. . . . It's just like that in the hotel, people are passed between sectors. . . . You learn how everything works in the hotel as you change sectors."

Cecelia had offered to share her event photos for this project, so about a week after our first interview, we met in reception, where she was working until her shift ended at 10 p.m. As the files slowly transferred to my computer, we sat at the little table stowed behind the safe drinking *tereré*.[16] She had been thinking about our conversation and wanted to revisit some of the questions I had asked about her previous work experiences. While working in events, she added, she had been offered a job coordinating events at a smaller hotel. It was a serious offer—a good opportunity and "a lot more money." But she liked her job in the Hotel Bauen. She was learning a lot, she was loyal to the cooperative, and she just wasn't ready to leave. Almost immediately after declining this job offer, she was transferred out of events.

Noticeably more relaxed than in our first recorded interview, the rotation Cecilia had initially described as "nothing" now seemed devastating. Cecilia expressed her frustration with the move: "They put me here to give people their room keys," she complained. "This is a job that anyone could do." Quietly, Cecilia reached out to see about the job she'd been offered at the smaller hotel, but it was no longer available. "I missed an opportunity that could have changed my life," she sighed.

Although upset about her rotation, Cecilia liked her coworkers and was good at accommodating schedules to keep reception—a twenty-four-hour sector—running smoothly. Some months later, she decided to run for office and was elected as the trustee of the cooperative. Not only had *she* determined the next step in her career, but Cecilia also became the first woman to hold the position.

"I Learned from My Mistakes": Emiliano's Work History

Like Cecilia, Emiliano reminisced, "I started [here] not knowing anything." It was a slow afternoon in the reservations office—no events to plan, groups to organize, or phone calls to return. I had been eating lunch with Emiliano for about three weeks when I transferred to work in his sector, but before then I'd worked with his girlfriend, Lenora (they met while working in the cooperative). Every day, just before noon, Emiliano would lock his office door and walk from the back lobby to the staff entrance behind the reception desk, where he would wait for Lenora to join him for lunch. Emiliano was shy and soft-spoken around strangers but curious and quirky with his friends and coworkers.

Born and raised in the province of Buenos Aires, Emiliano had graduated from high school with a certificate in electronics repair. His father was a founding member of the cooperative, so when the cooperative reopened the Hotel Bauen in 2005, he thought he might be able to help by repairing the hotel's aging televisions.

"This was my first job, and I started from zero," he reiterated to me. Like other young, single members, Emiliano even moved into the hotel, helping to maintain a presence at the property around the clock. He remembered fondly, "I liked it . . . more than anything because I was in downtown [Buenos Aires], everything was close. I was young, I had money, I lived alone, I couldn't ask for anything else!" There wasn't really much need for electronics repair, so Emiliano worked positions that needed to be filled. His first job was in laundry. "I first went to help out, but then I ended up staying there with my friend because we could cover the work." He then moved to custodial services—"I think it was because we needed people there [in the sector]. The thing is, all of us were rotating, and so when they asked me to move to cleaning, I went along with it." The manager had put out a call for people, and Emiliano, as he recalled, simply answered.

Emiliano continued rotating positions through the hotel, recounting a dizzying work history as he moved to work as a receptionist, as a cashier, and then in reservations, learning the necessary skills along the way. "I learned from my mistakes, like most of my compañeros," he told me. While Cecilia and some others went to college over the years, he continued, "Most of us never studied hospitality or anything like that. It's nice. I actually really like it, and I have learned a lot. And now I'm in a position where I have responsibilities." Despite his lack of labor market experience or prior knowledge of hospitality, Emiliano could gain skills through practice at the Hotel Bauen. Eventually, he was appointed by the administrative council to manage his sector.

Gendered Entry Points

With only a few exceptions, all the people I worked with had rotated jobs internally at the Hotel Bauen. Like Cecilia and Emiliano, most members started in jobs that required intense manual labor—housekeeping, custodial services, valet, or laundry—with a clear sorting by which women were most often initially hired as housekeeping staff, while most men started in custodial services or as valets assisting the housekeepers.[17]

Multiple factors explain these gendered patterns in hiring. First, supply-side factors in the labor market sorted men and women into different application pools. To apply for a job in the BAUEN Cooperative, prospective members (many of whom relied on personal contacts) submitted their names and résumés for consideration. Women applicants who listed experience in cleaning or domestic work were usually forwarded directly to the managers of housekeeping when they had an opening. Second, demand-side factors impacted which sectors integrated which new members. In its first dozen or so years, the cooperative's membership grew steadily, keeping pace with increasing demand in the hotel (see chapter 1). There was occasional turnover as members left for personal reasons, took different jobs, or retired. And because existing members rotated jobs, receiving sectors like housekeeping and custodial services saw more frequent job openings than sectors like administration, events, or the member office—positions that members generally rotated *into*.

This, I discovered, was not an accident. One council member told me that the cooperative intentionally rotated workers out of more physical jobs: "We try to make sure the housekeepers work two or three years, and then we find them a rotation. Today I can tell you that in administration all the women were housekeepers. . . . We try to make sure that the women don't break their backs working or get physically exhausted when it can be avoided. So when those people pass to administration, new housekeepers enter with a long road ahead. They have three years to exploit their bodies and not cause any damage." The physical toll of certain jobs was repeatedly offered as a reason to rotate members—and as a way to explain higher turnover in certain sectors. Inroads into the cooperative were clearly gendered. But once people became members, job rotation offered ongoing opportunities for workers to re-sort themselves.

Redefining Skill

One of the fascinating components of job rotation was the impact of moving from sector to sector. In particular, job rotation prompted many members of the cooperative to question the difference between "skilled" and "unskilled" work. When people are sorted and segregated into certain jobs, these exclusionary processes are supported and justified by shared understandings of different kinds of work. Labels like *skilled* and *unskilled* sometimes reflect differences in a job's complexity or risk. But they are often proxy terms for other factors like prestige or credentials, which are frequently deployed to exclude certain people from certain jobs.[18]

To make sense of this, Paul Attewell (1990) offers the useful distinction between skills that are "achieved" and those that are "ascribed." Things we can learn through education and training are *achieved* skills that are earned, whereas skills that are attributed to groups of people (like women being caring and men being authoritative) are *ascribed* based on social categories. What's more, the seemingly objective evaluation of skill is based on the unequal recognition of certain tasks over others. For example, jobs historically performed by women, like childcare and cleaning, are often coded as unskilled, whereas male-typed jobs, like factory work, are recognized as skillful and thus result in higher status and wages.[19] In the BAUEN Cooperative, members saw all jobs as integral to their collective goal to keep the hotel open for business. If housekeeping is as important as bookkeeping, it begs the question: Is there such a thing as unskilled work?

Plenty of research suggests that job placement is commonly determined by cultural stereotypes rather than technical skills. As mentioned earlier in this chapter, commonsense definitions of what constitutes skilled or unskilled labor shift over time. With the growth of the service sector, for instance,

105

employers around the globe now include "soft" social skills and characteristics like loyalty, enthusiasm, personal presentation, and adaptability among their hiring requirements.[20] Many service jobs look for a certain type of person that fits their model. For example, in her study of professional service firms, Lauren Rivera (2012) reports that hiring agents believe that required job skills can be taught to the best candidates—ostensibly a leveling idea. Yet these evaluators rely on class and cultural indicators to find people who "match" the position or are just "a good fit" (1007–8).[21]

Disrupting entrenched patterns of occupational segregation was critical to the construction of an equality project.[22] Through the practice of job rotation, members of the BAUEN Cooperative redefined skill in two ways: first, by discursively leveling individual ability and, second, by rejecting conventional justifications for occupational mobility.[23]

Leveling Human Capital

In the BAUEN Cooperative, workers attempted to level the occupational playing field by emphasizing the value of practice over the theory that people acquire through formal education or job training. Enzo made this explicit during a weekly council meeting: "We aren't technicians or professionals or degree holders," but on the administrative council, "we value the effort of each person." Speaking as an elected leader, Enzo discursively equalized his fellow members by rejecting conventional markers of human capital like formal education, past job experience, training, and credentials.

The cooperative made job-rotation decisions based on individual and organizational needs instead of training or credentials. Because education often proxies for social class, the practice of generally disregarding people's degrees helped the cooperative disrupt the class hierarchies that so often map onto organizational divisions of labor.

Martín was one of the many members who rotated into an administrative position that would conventionally require a degree. A slight man in his thirties, Martín described his work history over his seven years in the cooperative: "I didn't start here in billing. I started cleaning, and [the council] gave me the opportunity to improve my job. It was good for me because you can't do that in another company. You have to have an education, skills. . . . [I]n another company, they ask for your degree. Here, no."

Aware of the distinctive opportunities they had in the cooperative, members like Martín regularly contrasted the logic of job rotation with the situation in conventional firms. Reflecting on his job rotation over his six years in the cooperative, Adrian explicitly compared the cooperative and a conventional firm: "In a [traditional] company, you die in one position. Unfortunately, you die in one position. But here there are people who never finished elementary school but now are managing important areas of the hotel. Like Francisco. He didn't finish elementary school, but he is in a really important sector. Would a company give you the opportunity to do that if you didn't finish elementary school? Forget it!"

Francisco, whom you met in chapter 3, had started in custodial services and then rotated through a series of positions that taught him more about how the hotel operated. When I worked with him in 2015, Francisco was serving as the trustee of the cooperative, a job that entailed mediating conflicts among members, assisting members in the use of democratic procedures, and overseeing the cooperative's administration and finances. Francisco, however, had not originally aspired to such a position. He was raised in poverty, and when it came to his education, he explained:

> I had the opportunity to study, but for me, it was a waste of time. . . . I could have finished elementary school, but I didn't want to because it's like, I thought that I didn't need to study because . . . I'm smart, I can learn. . . . Today there are compañeros here who have educations, who finished high school, who have a degree, but they don't know what I know. I don't miss anything. I am grateful that I was given the opportunity to learn [in the cooperative], and for me, it's my pride and honor to tell you, "Look, I did this, I did that."

As Francisco's story illustrates, practical experience was valued so highly in the cooperative that even elected positions could be held by members without formal qualifications. To make this possible, Martín, Adrian, and others rejected dominant definitions and assessments of skill in the workplace.

During the time I worked at the Hotel Bauen, I also experienced firsthand the dexterity required to rotate jobs. In each sector I experienced a learning curve: in reception I picked up skills to check guests in and out, ensuring that new guests were assigned clean rooms and that outgoing guests paid their bills. Whereas the rhythm of work in housekeeping and reception was organized around periods of high occupancy, other sectors, like administration and billing, worked on a monthly schedule. Away from the gaze of customers and guests, these workers collected and deposited daily earnings, tracked costs, paid suppliers, and prepared paychecks. Despite these differences members still understood skills to be largely transferrable.

Practical experience and a willingness to learn were deemed especially important characteristics. Indeed, the ideal worker described in chapter 3

107

was first and foremost self-motivated. One council member explained the emphasis on learning in the cooperative: "If someone wants to learn, everyone can." This is not to say that members did not regularly discuss more formal metrics, nor that they discounted education entirely. Indeed, many acknowledged that people with a formal education understood the theory behind the work. Pilar mentioned, "If you are sitting at a desk . . . you have only the theory and not the practice." In the BAUEN Cooperative, you could have practice without theory and gain respect, but the inverse was not true.

Romina's journey through multiple jobs in the hotel was eminently practical. Years before, she had joined the cooperative as a housekeeper before rotating through a series of desk jobs that required her to use technology. She told me that she had the "theory" from taking high school computer classes but had never had a computer at home. As she rotated jobs, she supplemented her formal education with practical experience. She told me, "I taught myself how to use the computer system. This is something that before [when working as a housekeeper], I never would have been able to do." After many years in the cooperative, she ran for and was elected to the administrative council, a role that required her to use a computer every day. In particular, Romina had to learn to use the hotel-management software, which involved multiple interfaces coordinated among reservations, housekeeping, billing, stock, and administration.

One day, Romina and I joined Susi, a seasoned housekeeper, who was teaching a newer member to use the software. They noticed midway through the lesson that room 807 wasn't appearing in the master list of available rooms. Puzzled by the omission, Romina referenced a small notebook where she had long taken notes about the booking system. After trying a couple of things (changing room codes, checking/unchecking boxes), they figured out the problem, and Romina diligently recorded the solution in her notebook. Without formal instruction, the three women problem-solved together, using a process of trial and error to eventually resolve the issue, return room 807 to the master list, and deepen their understanding of the software in the process.

While job rotation centered on the assumption that workers could learn through practice, such efforts at discursively leveling human capital created challenges, particularly as the cooperative added positions of authority. Romina was well aware of these tensions, telling me, "We have created different positions, but there are a lot of problems if you are going to categorize people." She said that it was an "open debate" over what to do with people who had formal training.

Technical, administrative, and infrastructural issues brought these debates into stark relief. For instance, the cooperative held standing contracts with an accountant and a lawyer—both of whom were experts in cooperative administration. "If you aren't a professional, you can contract someone who understands it . . . and learn from that person," one member told me on another occasion. When tasks were beyond the scope of the members' practical knowledge, they would vote to hire professionals who could both do the job and provide training for cooperative members to take up those tasks.

In addition to these standing contracts, the cooperative regularly employed plumbers, electricians, elevator technicians, and other craftspeople to help maintain the aging facilities. But when these technicians did work in the cooperative, members were often suspicious of their intentions and expertise. In an assembly called to discuss investments in the building, for example, the group demanded that a member always oversee the elevator technicians. There had been a series of conflicts with service providers who allegedly billed the cooperative without completing the promised repairs. To build trust and avoid this sort of friction, the cooperative not only oversaw these technicians but also preferred to contract people who came with a referral. This also allowed for more trust and flexibility. For example, the administrative council contracted a young man named Ariel to replace the worn carpet that lined one floor of guest rooms with new tile. As funds became available, the cooperative would buy the tile they could afford (often from the worker-recuperated tile factory Zanon), take blocks of rooms out of commission, and then contact Ariel—the son of a member's family friend—to do the installation (see figure 4.1). He'd return only when the hotel was ready to revamp another set of rooms.

The BAUEN Cooperative regularly negotiated the limits of what jobs and tasks they could do internally. When discussing understaffed sectors, one council member emphasized that she wanted to fill the positions through job rotation, assuring the group that "they didn't need to bring in anyone from the outside." Weeks later, another member countered this perspective, suggesting they needed to bring in "outside people" to fill vacancies. Daniel reminded the group of a former member with previous experience in billing who had "transformed" an important sector and then asserted, "We need a woman with administrative experience who is not too young and not too old, who is willing to work for what we can pay."

You may have noticed that Daniel indicated gender and age in his description of a hypothetical new member. Other studies have explored why companies may seek out middle-aged women in particular: they are more likely than

4.1 Laying new tile in guest rooms on the fourteenth floor of the Hotel Bauen. Photo by the author.

younger people and men to have both labor market experience and the ability to "manage up" from a position of relative powerlessness.[24] As Romina said, how skills and experience motivated hiring was an "open debate"; even in a workplace with opportunities for occupational re-sorting, qualifications, age, and gender influenced determinations about who best matched a given job.

Out of Rotation: An Exception

As with any rule, there were exceptions to the BAUEN Cooperative's general approach to job rotation. Santino had studied tourism and was working with a tourism commission for cooperatives and mutual firms when he met workers from the Hotel Bauen. He described how he ended up in the BAUEN Cooperative: "They were looking for someone in sales; they didn't have anyone, and there was a new administrative council . . . so I came to help a little, and it's been five years since. . . . Lots of people who tell you their history, you are going to see that they have passed through various sectors. But I have really only been in sales."

Obviously, Santino's work history reveals that the cooperative at least occasionally recruited and matched incoming members to jobs that aligned with their previous experience and credentials. Unlike the bulk of members,

110

who joined with little experience in either hospitality or cooperatives, Santino had an abundance of both. Moreover, because of his credentials—in his words, "I'm a tourism expert . . . but I never finished my thesis to receive my university diploma"—he never rotated jobs. Essentially, his professional training and personal preferences took him out of rotation.

During my fieldwork Santino decided to leave the cooperative, citing long hours as his reason for taking another job. Over the five years he had worked full-time in the hotel, I learned, he had also held a second job earning commissions from travel agencies (a contrast with other members' supplemental income streams, which I discuss further in chapter 5). Given his experience, credentials, and extra income, Santino's decision to leave the cooperative can be read as a testament to both his financial stability and his opportunities in the labor market. Overall, he left on good terms, returning occasionally to attend events and catch up with his former compañeros and friends.

Accessing Opportunity

Many of the workplace transformations implemented by the BAUEN Cooperative were codified into policies like those that formally distributed power through democratic decision-making, as I described in chapter 2. The case of job rotation was different.

In lieu of a written policy, job rotation in the BAUEN Cooperative was coordinated by the administrative council, which approved all staffing changes, including hiring, rotation, and firing. The council also worked closely with sector managers and coordinators to rotate members in and out of positions. When I asked who made job-rotation decisions, one member referred to their own experience: "[A council member] came and talked to me. Obviously, they had talked with my manager, and they told me that they were thinking about moving me to administration, and I would get a lot of experience, new understandings, new work skills, new developments."

Job rotation was on the agenda of many weekly meetings of the administrative council that I attended. If the rotations were approved, the council members formalized the decision in a written memo sent to those members who would help with the logistics (setting new schedules and providing the proper uniforms, for example). And of course, as I described in chapter 2, the Workers Assembly could intervene in the council's job-rotation decisions, although this rarely happened, according to meeting minutes.

Through many formal and informal conversations, I discovered that members accessed rotation opportunities in different ways (see table 4.1).

Table 4.1 Reasons Workers Rotated Jobs

INDIVIDUAL	ORGANIZATIONAL
Health issues	Changes in leadership
Interpersonal issues (friendship/conflict)	Interpersonal issues (conflict)
Skill development	Turnover
Scheduling	Understaffing

Some described their active involvement, explicitly asking to change jobs for personal or professional reasons. Other members were singled out when a sector was understaffed or an organizational need arose. Ultimately, job rotation offered many benefits and opportunities to members of the cooperative. But the idealized version of this practice was enmeshed with the problems and challenges of democratic workplace participation. Rosabeth Moss Kanter (1972, 64) points to this perennial issue in the epigraph to this chapter: "In utopia . . . who takes out the garbage?"

The following work history highlights the individual and organizational reasons behind job rotation. Inés, whom you met in previous chapters, worked as a housekeeper in the Hotel Bauen from 1994 until it was shut down by its private owners in 2001. After losing her job, she lived off her meager unemployment check until she received a call from the head housekeeper of the Bauen Suites, the Hotel Bauen's sister property, asking if she wanted to return as a temporary worker. As she explained, "The girls were the same ones we had worked with when we were *bajo patrón* [under a boss]. The two hotels were connected, we all ate together . . . so I knew all the people on the other side."

Inés accepted the position "on the other side" and went to work as an extra in the apartment-style hotel just around the corner from the shuttered Hotel Bauen. She remembered a strict managerial regime: "We weren't allowed to talk among ourselves because things wouldn't be good if we were talking, as if we were plotting something against the other hotel! We were being watched all the time, so we didn't talk among ourselves. No, it was really hard at that time . . . and they didn't want me either. . . . I was always an extra . . . because I was ex-Bauen."

She was still working at the Bauen Suites in 2003 when her former co-workers occupied the adjacent property. She remembered that a friend "called me and said, 'Look, Inés, we are going to take the hotel.' I told her I was working that day, [and she said,] 'I know that you're with us, but please don't open your mouth on the other side!'" Inés felt conflicted. As a single mother with three children, she worried about the uncertainty of joining the nascent cooperative.

Eventually, a former coworker who was occupying the hotel pushed her to pick a side: "She told me, 'You have to decide: come to this side or stay there [in the Bauen Suites], but we really need you here.' So I went home. I talked with my kids and explained that we wouldn't have money coming into the house if I went to help, and they told me, 'If you want to, you should return, mama.' And so I returned here" to the Hotel Bauen.

As a member of the newly formed BAUEN Cooperative, Inés spent twelve years working in housekeeping, eventually assuming the position of head housekeeper before she was ready for a change: "A lot of things that happened were exhausting, I spent a lot of time alone. . . . I was left for many months working alone for twelve hours a day without a replacement, without having a day off, dealing with a lot of internal problems in the sector. The moment came when I decided to change my sector, so I talked with [the president] who said to me, 'Okay, when there's an opportunity, you will change sectors.' And, well, there was an opportunity to move here to administration, and so I passed here." Inés had a cumulative twenty years' experience in housekeeping when she transferred to administration. As she adjusted to the demands of her new job, she felt the effects of the decades of exhaustion. After she fell and broke her foot, Inés was homebound for almost three months. When she returned to her new role, she restarted the process of learning to track expenditures and file paperwork.

Rotating jobs offered Inés a viable way to return to work in a far less physically demanding role. She was able to sit at a desk and be off her feet instead of climbing flights of stairs to access the guest rooms in the twenty-story tower. But her rotation was also challenging. She was unfamiliar with the job requirements, and she didn't know how to use computer programs like Excel. As I described in chapter 3, when members like Inés rotated into jobs without the requisite skills, other workers dedicated more time to training them and sometimes simply picked up the slack. As one member bluntly observed, "It's hard to work with people who don't know what they are doing."

During my stint working in administration, I spent time each day teaching Inés how to make spreadsheets in Excel. As she diligently took notes and practiced on her own, I observed her gain confidence in her new role. In fact, nearly a year after her move, she decided not to rotate again. The administrative council had struggled with a series of staffing and interpersonal conflicts that unfolded in housekeeping. As a potential solution, the council members proposed that Inés return to reorganize the sector—news that didn't surprise Inés but didn't entice her either. She responded that she was "comfortable" in administration and did not want to go back to work as a housekeeper.

Inés's work history illustrates how both individual and organizational motivations impacted job rotation: whereas her first rotation was self-initiated, motivated by her exhaustion and age, the proposed second rotation was prompted by organizational needs. More important, perhaps, Inés turned down the second rotation with no negative repercussions; her decision was respected.

Organizational needs prompting rotations were frequently put forward by council members seeking to address issues like understaffing, turnover, and interpersonal conflict (see table 4.1). Across my interviews with workers, I also documented individual reasons behind rotations, from a desire to gain new skills to requests to accommodate health issues, schedules, and interpersonal dynamics. Crissy, for example, asked to change jobs to ease her commute. When I asked whether she liked the new position, she said that the schedule suited her, and she no longer had to worry about walking alone at night or the extra expense of taking a taxi in order to feel safe getting home. Belén told me about multiple requests she had made to rotate jobs during her tenure in the cooperative. She sought to change positions first to work with a group of people she liked (her *compañeras de siempre*, or lifelong friends) and, later, to accommodate her young children's school schedule: "I said okay [to the job rotation], but I need Sunday and Monday as my days off. . . . I need to be with my kids."

There were also members who reported having explicitly requested a job transfer but never received the opportunity to rotate. Alejandro, whom you met in chapter 2, joined the cooperative as a cashier in the Utopia Café while he was studying business administration at a local college. He worked for a couple of months before he scheduled a meeting with members of the administrative council. He wanted to transfer to a sector where he could directly apply his business acumen. Ten months later, though, he was still working in the café. Alejandro suspected that he had been overlooked for a transfer because of an interpersonal feud. The council members, he suspected, did not like his relative, who was a former cooperative member. But when Alejandro's case came up in a weekly council meeting that I attended, the council members reported that they simply needed reliable cashiers (he had made no errors on the register) and couldn't afford to rotate Alejandro without lining up a capable replacement.

114

New Council, New Jobs

Staffing changes were ongoing throughout my fieldwork, though many concentrated around the election of a new administrative council. It soon became clear to me that job rotation was not just a practical move. It was closely related to issues of trust and loyalty. Across countless conversations multiple people told me that new council members tended to rotate "their people" into key jobs.

I observed this process firsthand when the incumbent council was re-elected in 2015. Within days of their victory, they started considering possible job rotations. At their first meeting of the term, the council members discussed the need to have "people they trusted" in managerial positions. Referencing the outcome of the recent election, one member in the room reminded the group that "forty-three people . . . voted against them," later referring to members who voted for the other slate of candidates as "enemies."

These comments, however, were met with resistance: another council member quickly disagreed with this reasoning, saying that everyone had the right to vote and that individuals' votes were closed and thus should not impact the council members' decisions. Another suggested they needed to be "smart" about whom they rotated: if someone critiqued their management, they should ask that person to help solve the problem rather than create enemies. The group liked this suggestion and moved on to map out the proposed changes on a dry-erase board.

After a series of meetings, the administrative council agreed to rotate a handful of members, mostly based on individual requests. Though this all seemed relatively smooth in my observation, members described more disruptions that had accompanied leadership changes in years past. For example, when recounting their work histories, certain members felt that their personal needs had not been taken into account or that they had been "removed" from jobs during these moments of change, phrasing that hinted that not all job rotations were voluntary.

Rotation as Punishment

Rotating jobs both helped members build skills and supported individual and organizational needs. But it was also used to snuff out interpersonal problems and even punish members based on personal biases. Daniel, whose account of job rotation opened this chapter, acknowledged the conflicting uses of the practice: "We are trying to alter the typical productive structure of modern capitalist society . . . a little bit consciously and sometimes unconsciously.

Do you remember the other day when we talked about [how] if [someone] was upset, they might be moved to another sector?" he asked me. I nodded. "Well, that is perhaps an unconscious way that someone ends up learning another job in another sector, but it happens."

Belén didn't agree that it was an unconscious practice. She thought, rather, that it was a concerning way to handle conflict. She explained, "We can move a compañero who is in a sector because they aren't working out. But first we need to talk with the managers and . . . with each person who is under the managers because sometimes the managers have an affinity with people who work with them. If you don't listen until the last minute, how do you know how to manage people?" To her, job rotation was not always a quick fix because it didn't address the root of the interpersonal problems.

Oftentimes, job rotation occurred after a member received a disciplinary sanction. For example, after Adrian was sanctioned while working as a cashier, he rotated to a different sector. On the move, he explained, "They [the council members] took me out of the sector for a problem that I had [handling money] and sent me to work in security." It sounded fairly routine, yet others suggested that the practice could also be used selectively and punitively. For example, although Theo had asked to transfer to a sector where he could learn how to use a computer, he had been rotated to work in the kitchen. On this particular instance of job rotation, another member observed, "You know Theocito?" He was an excellent waiter, she said, excitedly telling me, "He can carry like ten plates and more cups than I could count!" but "[a council member] got mad at him and sent him to be a cook."

Many individual stories suggested that the practice could be used as both an opportunity and a punishment. Recall the story of Carina in chapter 2, who was rotated to a different job after she brought an appeal before the Workers Assembly. Alejo had a similar experience. During my fieldwork I heard through the grapevine that Alejo had recently rotated jobs because of "problems" with the administrative council. Months later, when we found time for an interview, I carefully asked what had happened.

Born in Paraguay, Alejo had emigrated to Argentina years before to reunite with his mother, who had come to the country for work. At age nineteen he started working at the Hotel Bauen as a valet in housekeeping. It didn't start well. His manager kept him busy all day long and treated him badly. He attributed this mistreatment to being the "*hermano de*" (brother of), suggesting that people did not like him because they had past conflicts with a family member who had once worked in the cooperative. The day Alejo came in to quit, though, a sympathetic member introduced him to the manager of custodial services. Rather than leave, Alejo rotated sectors, eventually working as a janitor, a dishwasher, a *cafetero* making coffee, a waiter, and a cashier before moving again to become a bellhop in the lobby.

One slow holiday, Alejo remembered that he and another member decided to pass the time by running an errand. They ended up stopping at a nearby bar. When they returned to the hotel much later, he was written up for drinking on the job. Alejo knew he had made a mistake and remembered accepting a suspension without pay and being removed from his job in the lobby. He returned to work in custodial services but soon received formal notice that he had been fired for being late to work. This time Alejo felt that the sanction was unfair.

The council members, he explained, had added up all the times he had been late since he joined the cooperative and then used it as grounds to fire him. After speaking with the trustee about his options, he decided to appeal his termination. He then collected enough signatures to call an assembly.

Alejo arrived at his assembly early and scared. In his memory the auditorium seemed disappointingly "filled with *their* [the council's] people." Others eventually joined, but Alejo felt that the meeting was more formal than others. The council members, he recalled, even read his entire disciplinary file in front of the group, something he thought was unprecedented. At first, it seemed as if he wouldn't win his appeal. But a gradual shift in sentiments gave him some hope. When the time came to vote, the members in attendance overturned the council's decision to fire him. Alejo was back at work in custodial services the next day.

It wasn't long, however, before he was transferred again. Without explanation, Alejo was rotated to work in the staff kitchen. The abrupt change was maddening for Alejo, who felt utterly unprepared: "I had never picked up a knife in my life except to feed myself." Still, since starting in the kitchen, he told me, he had learned a lot. He observed that "although they wanted to persecute me," the change had been really good for him: he liked his coworkers and felt more comfortable in his new role.

Many factors help explain why Alejo felt "persecuted" at work. First, he identified family connections as undermining relationships with his coworkers. His age and nationality also may have contributed to his experience of feeling targeted. While Alejo had spent "half of [his] life" in Argentina, Paraguayans experience discrimination in the Argentine labor market, which may have shaped the way he was perceived by coworkers.[25] Whether or not he was actually persecuted, Alejo's work history in the cooperative seems clear evidence of punitive use of job rotation.

Despite his experience and even a chance to return to his hometown (where he would have a job and a place to live with family), Alejo told me he planned to continue working in the cooperative. I asked why he decided to stay, but Alejo could not put his finger on it. He described it as a *sentimiento* (feeling) that what he was doing at the Hotel Bauen and in the cooperative was important.

The complaints and discontent around job rotation ultimately related to its lack of formalization in the workplace. This contrasts with what are considered best practices in restructuring internal labor markets.[26] In the absence of a formalized policy to clarify its purpose and implementation, job rotation was practiced in various ways that corresponded to individual goals and values—including those related to control and punishment.[27] As I have shown, members in the BAUEN Cooperative had the opportunity to rotate jobs to address and accommodate both personal and organizational needs. But because the practice was informal, it was sometimes unclear whether and how members could access the opportunity to rotate and what reasons decision-makers could use to justify or deny a rotation.

Job rotation was central to the BAUEN Cooperative's equality project. Most new members started out working in gender-typed manual jobs, with women generally joining as housekeepers and men as custodians or valets. With time, workers could re-sort themselves by rotating between sectors based on individual and organizational needs. This practice allowed for unprecedented occupational mobility among members of the BAUEN Cooperative, yet it also fell victim to selective formalization. With no clear policy to determine how jobs were or were not made available, some members felt frustrated and overlooked. In this opaque process, others even felt penalized and punished, left with little control over their contributions to the cooperative.

Many of the jobs in the Hotel Bauen could be classified as "low-skilled." They did not require professional credentials (like doctors or lawyers) or extensive training and experience (like plumbers and electricians). Definitions of who is skilled or unskilled matter because they influence the process by which some people are sorted into certain jobs over others. This chapter offered insights into how members of the BAUEN Cooperative disrupted entrenched patterns of occupational segregation by redefining the meaning of skilled work. This was key to its equality project. Prompted by job-rotation practices, workers explicitly questioned status distinctions based on education, credentials, and past work experience, and this allowed the cooperative to promote more egalitarian relations among its members. This points to another way that equality is produced organizationally: through *symbolic leveling*, the process of discursively emphasizing individuals' equivalent ability to participate in decision-making, learn new skills, and contribute value to a group.

Redefining skill can only go so far in creating relational equality without addressing material conditions in the workplace. That members of the cooperative received the same base pay regardless of their position was critical to facilitating job rotation. As one member made clear, it did not bother him to change positions because "we all make the same amount of money." How did the BAUEN Cooperative navigate difference while equalizing pay? We turn to this next.

Time is money.
—BENJAMIN FRANKLIN,
Advice to a Young Tradesman

5   The Politics of Equal Pay

It is widely accepted that people are paid differently for their work. Managers make more money than their subordinates, people with degrees and certifications make more than those without, and years of accumulated experience usually correspond with better pay. Most of us accept these inequalities as normal, legitimate, and even favorable features of the economy. In fact, capitalism is scaffolded by the idea that inequality and precarity incentivize people to show up, work hard, and stick around. But in stark contrast to most organizations, all members of the BAUEN Cooperative earned the same base pay rate, whether they cleaned the guest rooms, waited tables in the café, handled the administrative work, or held an elected office.

Pay equity, alongside the practices of democratic decision-making and job rotation detailed in chapters 2 and 4, was integral to the BAUEN Cooperative's equality project. Despite the differences in what people brought to the workplace, there was no question about who was valued.[1] Everyone was compensated equally, and this provided a foundation for members to relate to each other on a more equal footing. Of course, market forces still held power within this downtown hotel. Although pay was equal, members of the cooperative barely made minimum wage. "The truth is that the salary isn't enough for us," I was told throughout my fieldwork. "We need a raise."

The BAUEN Cooperative maintained its commitment to equal pay in the context of low-wage service work by creatively developing a system that I call *survival finance*. This idea builds on urban poverty research that has identified the patchwork of economic survival strategies that people develop in response to low-wage work and unreliable access to social safety nets.[2] As we see in this chapter, organizations also develop survival strategies.

At the Hotel Bauen, the system of survival finance leveraged three primary ways that workers benefited from full-time employment: through wages, credit, and time. Compensation, in this framework, involves more than money, though it certainly *starts* with money. In this chapter I first lay out the structure of wages in the BAUEN Cooperative and the ways workers negotiated pay equity as the organization grew over time. Then I investigate the second component of this organization's survival finance: providing workers access to credit internally. Finally, I examine the value of time in calculating member compensation; with low margins, the cooperative nonetheless generated profit, in part because of its creative use of paid time off.

None of these practices is unique to the BAUEN Cooperative. Many employers provide nonwage benefits to workers, from emergency grants and college scholarships to debt assistance, free or discounted food, and support for childcare, adoption, and transportation. Some of these perks are charitable efforts to make up for persistently low wages and a lack of job mobility. For example, Walmart employees who make close to minimum wage can apply for grants from the company's philanthropic arm when they experience disasters or other hardships.[3] Among high-wage workers, companies often use perks as incentives for hiring, morale building, and retention. Employees at Google, to give just one example, have access to free food and snacks, tuition reimbursement, flexible and remote work options, and subsidized transportation.

In contrast to the revocable perks in both the charity and loyalty models, survival finance is a standalone compensation system that not only sheds light on an important part of the BAUEN Cooperative's equality project that

121

addressed categories of value but also helps explain how it survived in the face of market pressures.

The Persistence of Pay Inequality

Difference in pay is perhaps the most well-studied indicator of inequality at work.[4] In workplaces around the globe, women and racial-minority men are more likely than white men to work low-paying jobs. When they do hold equivalent positions and credentials, they earn less money than their white male counterparts. In 2017 in Argentina, men earned nearly a third more than women on average (Gasalla 2017).

Since the 1960s, concern over the wage gap between men and women has risen substantially, resulting in initiatives to address pay inequality. One such attempt was the development of comparable-worth policies, which assess the level of pay for work deemed of equal value.[5] To determine which jobs were undervalued, advocates compared pay rates to the market wages for jobs similar in knowledge, complexity, and responsibility; gaps indicated whether wages were artificially depressed, allowing for targeted antidiscrimination and pro-equity efforts.[6] In the United States, implementation of comparable-worth policies generated debate over the legitimacy of wage gaps, the possibility of determining worth objectively, and the merits of intervention into market-based pay.[7] Ultimately, these policies mostly targeted inequalities in public-sector jobs, although some private-sector firms have set goals for pay equity or have used such policies to settle wage-discrimination claims.[8]

Another approach to address inequality is the adoption of merit-based practices to determine pay raises. In corporate workplaces companies use performance evaluations to provide employee feedback, assess performance, and direct decisions about compensation. Scholars considering such efforts to reward workers based on individual merit insist, however, that these practices simply mask and justify inequality. For example, Emilio Castilla (2008) finds that even in workplaces with formal pay and promotion mechanisms in place, a "performance-reward bias" persists.

From Fair Pay to Equal Pay

As we know intuitively, a certain degree of difference in pay is widely considered legitimate.[9] But in the BAUEN Cooperative, efforts to equalize pay went beyond the call for "equal pay for equal work." *All members* received the same base pay.

In many ways, the cooperative's commitment to equal pay hearkens back to earlier proposals to revalue work and reconfigure wage labor. In the nineteenth century, social theorists proposed to replace the money system with a currency based on labor time.[10] Utopian socialists took up the call to abolish money in favor of "labor money" or "time chits" that would directly reflect the time required to produce a commodity. As Nigel Dodd (2016, 342) explains, "The fundamental principle behind labor money is simple: an hour of a person's time is worth exactly the same as an hour of any other person's time." While thoroughly critiqued (Karl Marx [1973, 68] derogatively called advocates "time chitters"), the proposal was adopted by many utopian communities of the time.[11]

The familiar adage that "time is money" is put to work in modern experiments with time banking.[12] In time banks, members exchange goods and services outside the market using time as a community currency.[13] Bartering is a classic noncash exchange. If you need childcare, you can exchange vegetables you have grown for an hour of babysitting. Time banks allow groups of people to move beyond the constraints of simple bilateral bartering, providing goods and services in exchange for credits that participants can use to access other offerings in the bank.

Argentina is no stranger to alternative currencies and time banks. During the 1990s, local exchange systems developed as neighbors arranged markets that eventually developed into barter clubs (called *clubes de trueque*), exchanging food, clothes, crafts, health services, and training. As these groups grew, many moved from using an hours system (like time banking) to issuing notes of credit.[14] By offering alternative currencies to cash, these clubs provided a forum for marginalized populations, the downwardly mobile, and the structurally unemployed to make ends meet in a dismal economy.[15]

During the 2001 economic crisis, participation in these clubs skyrocketed as the government froze bank accounts and devalued the peso, which further restricted access to cash. Existing barter clubs as well as parallel local currencies and government-issued bonds offered a lifeline for many ordinary people. Sitting at her desk in the Hotel Bauen, Pilar thought back to this period and the way the cooperative also relied on bartering during its early days. Eager to show me artifacts of this not-so-distant time, Pilar scrolled through pictures of once common alternative currencies on her desktop computer. When the cooperative could not get money from the traditional bank, she told me, they bartered for goods. Through informal networks of exchange, "we could get everything we needed to make bread."

Wages and Financialization

How work organizations set pay rates is neither natural nor intuitive. Money has been historically treated as a rational instrument in social life. But Viviana Zelizer (1989, 343) challenges this approach, arguing that "we assign different meanings and designate separate uses for particular kinds of monies." In other words, what constitutes wages and how organizations even define compensation result from relations among people.

Three interrelated trends are critical to understanding wages today.[16] First, wages have stagnated dramatically, meaning that although productivity has increased, it has not translated into overall pay increases. Second, money paid as wages has not kept pace with inflation or the rising costs of living. Lisa Adkins (2015) calls the result "indebted laboring," in which a person does not earn enough from paid work to cover the basic costs of subsistence. To make ends meet, workers must take on personal debt.[17] The third trend is that wages now include both money *and* workers' access to credit. Wages are no longer exclusively exchanged for labor power but, as Adkins (2015, 347) explains, for "a right to access trade in the unrealized potential of money." In short, wages have been impacted by what scholars call *financialization*, or the encroachment of finance into other parts of economic life.[18] With wages being financialized, workers can be exploited through their labor, and, at the same time, their wages act as a commodity that can be used by others to generate financial products.[19]

The BAUEN Cooperative stayed true to its original commitment to equal pay throughout its tenure in the Hotel Bauen. Confronting issues including low wages, economic uncertainty, and personal debt, the cooperative developed what I call *survival finance*: a system of total compensation in which members worked for a wage, access to credit, and future time off. Since monetary wages are susceptible to fluctuating inflation and other economic uncertainties, the cooperative's use of credit and the nonmarket exchange of time created alternative avenues for workers to avoid financial exploitation in a subsistence economy.

Wages and Overtime

From its inception in 2003, all members of the BAUEN Cooperative earned the same base pay rate (*el básico*). By 2015 the monthly *básico* was AR$2,750, parceled out through fixed advances at the end of each week (*adelantos*), with the remainder of the salary deposited directly into members' bank accounts at the end of the month.[20]

124

RECIBO ANTICIPO DE RETORNO			
Cooperativa de Trabajo Buenos Aires una Emp. Nac.Ltda Matricula N° 25,801- Av Callao 360 Ciudad de Buenos Aires Tel: 4373-9009 Cuit : XX-XXXXXXXX-X			
Asociado :LAST NAME FIRST NAME Cuit : XX-XXXXXXXX-X		Fecha de ingreso : DATE PAY CYCLE ADDRESS	
Codigo	Conceptos	importes	descuentos
1	Anticipo de Retorno Mensual	$2,750.00	
2	Sector	$0.00	
3	Antiguedad	$385.00	
4	viatico	$450.00	
5	Adicional Fundador	$0.00	
6	Adicional por Caja	$0.00	
7	Categorias: A:B:C:D1:D2	$150.00	
8	Puntualidad	$250.00	
9	Presentismo	$100.00	
10	Adicional por Hijo	$0.00	
11	Adicional varios	$600.00	
12	Monotributo	$390.00	
13	Devolucion	$0.00	
14	Adelantos		-$1,820.00
15	Habitacion		$0.00
16	Monotributo		-$623.00
17	Descuentos Dias		$0.00
18	Celular		$0.00
19	Otros		-$600.00
Total		$5,075.00	-$3,043.00
Neto			$2,032.00
Recibi la suma de pesos:			
Firma asociado			

5.1 Sample pay stub in the BAUEN Cooperative, 2015. Image by the author.

When it first reopened under worker control, the cooperative paid its members by evenly dividing its fluctuating profits. As its financial situation became more stable, the Workers Assembly eventually set a formal base pay rate, which increased over time. The assembly also instituted additional stipends that created some variation in take-home pay. Whereas other worker-recuperated businesses abandoned pay-equity schemes, the BAUEN Cooperative modified its pay structure while maintaining a formal commitment to equality.[21]

A sample monthly pay stub clearly shows the base monthly salary, followed by a series of variable and fixed *pluses* (stipends) based on position, attendance, and status (see figure 5.1). For example, the cooperative categorized positions and allocated stipends based on the extra responsibility required of managers, coordinators, and council members (*categorías:* A:B:C:D1:D2) as well as those who worked with money as cashiers or administrators (*adicional por caja*). For those with longer shifts, members received compensation for the extra hours (*sector*), and all members were rewarded for attendance and punctuality (*puntualidad*). Status distinctions determined other stipends. Seniority was compensated relative to members' tenure in the cooperative, measured in years (*antigüedad*); members with children received a plus for their family status (*adicional por hijo*); and founding members of the cooperative were awarded a small stipend to recognize their sacrifices and commitment (*adicional fundador*). Finally, all members received the same travel stipend (*viático*) to offset the cost of their daily commutes as well as onetime bonuses on their birthday, on Mother's Day or Father's Day (if they were parents), at the birth of a child, before the end-of-year holidays, and at the beginning of the school year (*adicional varios*).

A four-member team working in administration calculated members' take-home pay as well as any deductions from a member's monthly salary. If members stayed overnight in the hotel, for example, the cost of the room was subtracted from that month's pay unless the stay was approved by a manager (*habitación*). Indeed, during my fieldwork members commonly stayed overnight free of charge after working evening events and long hours of overtime. The pay stub also accounted for the monthly employment tax, because in Argentina members of cooperatives are legally registered as self-employed. In this arrangement the cooperative contributed to offset the self-employment tax (*monotributo*). It also deducted pay for any unexcused absences (*descuentos días*), the cost of group cell phone plans (*celular*), and a final category (*otros*) for all other debts to the cooperative, which I delve into later in the chapter.

Beyond a paycheck, members of the BAUEN Cooperative also received the same amount of paid vacation time, which they were required to use during the calendar year, along with profit-sharing benefits common to cooperatives.[22] Twice a year, the treasurer evaluated the cooperative's financial position, proposed a profit-sharing amount to the assembly, and then distributed the bonus to all group members at an equal rate (adjusted for days worked within the six-month period).

These stipends introduced variation into actual take-home salaries, yet these differences in pay were bounded (see table 5.1). Adrian, in his early twenties, worked in administration after holding a series of other jobs in different sectors of the hotel. When I asked him about his salary, he explained, "Well, there are small differences. For example, the *básico* is equal for every-

Table 5.1 Stipends per Month, 2015

CATEGORY	FIXED AMOUNTS	VARIABLE AMOUNTS	
		Lowest	*Highest*
Working with money	$150		
Manager	$350		
Council member	$650		
Founder	$300		
Seniority (by year)		$0	$660
Family (per child in home)	$100		
Attendance (days worked)		$0	$100
Punctuality (days on time)		$0	$250
Miscellaneous		$0	$600

one, and it varies from there based on category. It's not a big difference. If you go to [another] company . . . a worker would earn five grand, and the manager would get seven grand. Here it's not like that." Although members like Adrian seemed comfortable with this variation, stipends could increase take-home pay by over half. The highest-paid member in the cooperative, for instance, would be a founder who held an elected office and worked with money. This member would make AR$1,760 more each month than a new member who did not receive any additions. Still, stipends and all, the salary for full-time work in the BAUEN Cooperative was less than the minimum wage in Argentina. "The salary is not enough," Matías commented. "[Prices] are going up every day. Inflation is getting worse. . . . You leave with AR$1,000, and you can't even pay all your bills."

You may have noted the discrepancy here. While the BAUEN Cooperative had an equal base pay rate, members made different amounts of money based on their role, tenure, and other factors. How did these stipends come about? And how did members of the cooperative reconcile these differences with their commitment to equal pay?

Pay as Incentive
Many of the small variations in pay, I found, were motivated by very practical efforts to incentivize work and were widely viewed as legitimate by workers in the cooperative. Pilar, serving as the cooperative's president in 2015, explained that the compensation system was a way to financially motivate

members to follow basic rules: "The issue is [about] money, your salary. When you know that you are going to lose AR$100, you aren't going to let that happen!" She told me that to incentivize a person to "come [on time] and do it again tomorrow," there has to be a carrot, and you have to be able to withdraw that carrot—as she put it, "You have to take from the side that hurts you the most [*se toma por el lado que más te duele*]."

Despite these small incentives, members still grappled with a common sticking point: the free-rider problem. Free riding occurs when people take advantage of a common resource without contributing their fair share. Belén had worked in the hotel for almost ten years and was often a critical voice in meetings. Candid and direct, Belén said, "Here we all earn the same, and some people just don't work." In cooperatives, free riding often takes the form of members who shirk shared responsibilities, a problem that can result in internal surveillance, the development of a strong group culture, and the selection of like-minded members.[23]

Like Belén, Martín was also concerned about shirking. He had been a member of the cooperative for nearly six years, first working to set up tables and chairs for events before rotating into an office job. One rainy Tuesday I was wrapping up an interview with Emiliano when Martín joined us in the office. As we continued to talk about pay, Martín chimed in, "I think that we also should have differences [in pay] so everyone has a motivation. Because if we all earn the same . . ." He paused. "I don't know. . . . I understand that it is a cooperative, but that's why I think you have to take a leap of faith [*dar un salto*]. . . . There are a lot of people who work and others who don't work; we all know they are here. We all have known for years who works [and] who doesn't work." But as he signaled, they had no way to reward hard workers financially.

Members were clearly committed to the policy of pay equality, yet they also grappled with what they saw as a lack of material incentive in the workplace. For example, Alejandro thought that members should have the opportunity to earn commissions like those he saw in other service workplaces: "I think people in certain sectors should make more, much more." Pointing to members working in sales, Alejandro sounded like the business student he was: "Here in this country, lots of people work on commission. . . . [T]he majority of salespeople have commissions because it's an incentive to keep looking for sales. What happens here [in the hotel] is that . . . people come in to reserve ballrooms or guest rooms, but nobody is worried about going out to look [for customers]."

To Alejandro, it seemed natural that commissions would spur members in sales to go the extra mile to improve the cooperative's revenues. He observed,

128

"Everyone makes reservations by phone. [In other places] they are sending emails every day, and obviously those people have an incentive, like a bonus or a commission that you are paid. You make more if you look for more people." After our conversation he told me he planned to talk to the administrative council about his idea, but he wasn't confident that they would take it seriously: "Here, like, everything is short-sighted, the same salary, the level of sales. Why am I going to worry about anything?"

During my fieldwork in the Hotel Bauen, members like Alejandro repeatedly insinuated that equal pay hurt the organization, even as the group progressively modified the rules. Many of these small changes were motivated by very practical efforts to incentivize work, debates that continued as members evaluated the pay structure and the ways it could be used to improve work in the hotel.

Financial Transparency

Issues related to the cooperative's finances were common topics of conversation in the Hotel Bauen, from banter in the lunchroom to deliberation in formal meetings and assemblies. At many conventional workplaces, discussing pay is discouraged (if not prohibited) whereas every line item of the cooperative's pay structure—from the *básico* to the different *pluses*—was clearly enumerated on members' monthly pay stubs.[24] These ongoing and open deliberations about pay were a testament to the BAUEN Cooperative's commitment to transparency, which I discussed in chapter 1.

Perhaps more important, pay rates were determined collectively in the Workers Assembly, creating a broad understanding of and legitimacy for the wage structure.[25] A council member was quick to point out that no one made unilateral decisions about pay: "The assembly also votes on all this! It's not as if we as a council decide and, well, show up with what we have proposed." A close reading of the cooperative's meeting minutes revealed that the administrative council sometimes applied salary increases immediately that were later approved retroactively by the assembly. For example, in response to an abrupt increase in the cost of transportation and an official increase in the price of goods, the council responded by increasing one of the stipends by AR$200.[26] In its next meeting weeks later, the change was approved by the assembly.

Members discussed the cooperative's finances and pay rates regularly and openly. During one meeting the treasurer gave a quarterly financial report, describing the exact amounts of money in each bank account, profits made from rooms and events, and total money spent on supplies, investments, and utilities. "Because of all the events," he explained to applause, "we have the money to increase salaries." Standing at a dry-erase board in front of the group, the treasurer broke down the salary into its parts and opened the floor to discuss where the increase should be allotted.

Amid a flurry of possible ideas, one member suggested increasing the *básico*, to which the treasurer responded, "We can't touch that," since it would impact their self-employment taxes. People in the meeting listened and nodded. Another council member, Daniel, then reminded the group about the decision's impact on pay equity: "We need to be attentive to the fact that pluses change the salary, and so the differences created need to be taken into account."

Perhaps, someone suggested, the group might increase the stipend for attendance. Celia—a young mother who worked in housekeeping—disagreed: if they did that, her wages would suffer. "When I wake up and my baby is sick," Celia pointed out, "I would just be penalized more for being late or missing work." Another member backed her up, saying that people who took the train or bus (transportation that was sometimes delayed) would also be affected differently by the raise. No decision was made that day. But members had raised important considerations about how the pay increase would be applied later.

Unregulated Pay Variation

Over its organizational life, the BAUEN Cooperative evolved from paying all members equally to adapting its commitment to equal pay through a series of bounded and transparent variations that members approved democratically. Two important sources of variation, however, were left unregulated by these policies and were largely absent from the debates I have described: tips and overtime.

Members of the cooperative rejected simple ideas about equality. Discussions about job requirements illustrated that members were well aware that the actual work done in different sectors varied tremendously. Alejandro put it this way:

> Each sector has its benefits and drawbacks. For example, here [in the bar] you have the benefit of, I don't know, you can eat whenever you want, right? . . . Or if you want to make a coffee, you can make a coffee. You have that perk, but the downside is that now you have to work a lot, and you have to do [this] almost all day. Right now, it's relaxed, but there are times when you are running . . . all over the place. Other sectors have the perk that, I don't know, they can work two hours and then have six hours resting because there is nothing to do.

5.2 A member serves coffee in the Utopia Café. Photo by Emergentes.

Certain jobs within the hotel also offered opportunities to earn tips. As is common in hotels, workers in the front of house frequently received small tips or gifts from customers. Waiters earned tips based on the amount of the bill (it was customary to tip 10 percent or less); valets counted on small cash tips when delivering luggage to guest rooms; and receptionists would add tips to the cost of taxis, tours, and meals they booked for guests (see figure 5.2).

On one occasion while I worked in reception, a German family who spoke very little Spanish made reservations in the hotel. When they checked in late one night, they asked me for help arranging transportation to the airport the next morning. The manager advised me to include a commission in the cost of the car service. Since the car cost AR$230, we agreed to charge the guests AR$320, which would create a commission of just under AR$100 to be shared among the three of us on the clock. This process was by no means standard but varied by how much individual receptionists decided to include in the price. That evening, we left a note for the morning receptionists describing the family, the reservation, and the price we had quoted the guests. The next day, our tip had been left in a labeled envelope in the back of the cash drawer.

Tips also varied across workers within sectors. Longtime members, particularly women, sometimes established acquaintances with regular customers that resulted in tips. For example, one evening, Cecilia, whom you met in chapter 4, was working the register in reception. When a business traveler

The Politics of Equal Pay

checked in, he paid for his room in cash. Cecilia stood behind the glass window counting the bills (AR$1,995). She informed the man that he had overpaid, but he insisted she keep the extra cash for herself. When the customer left, Cecilia told me that he was a "regular" known as a generous tipper as she deposited the exact amount of his bill in the cash drawer, made change for the value of the tip (AR$105), and discreetly tucked the cash into her cleavage.

Small tips and gifts were common in other sectors. Suppliers would bring product samples and gift bags to workers in administration, for instance, and guests left cash tips in their rooms for housekeeping staff on the day they checked out. Perhaps because of this variation, there was no formal policy on how to address tips. I found that in some sectors tips were shared among all members working a given shift, whereas in others they were received and kept individually.

On the whole, a select few workers actually had the opportunity to earn tips. And though members commonly discussed pay rates, I heard far less talk about tips. Before working in administration, Adrian held a job as a valet in the lobby. When I asked about tipping, he remembered, "Friday, Saturday, and Sunday, I worked double shifts from 7 in the morning until 12 at night. From 7 to 4 in the kitchen, and then from 4 to 12 as a valet. The truth is that I did really well because . . . it's a shame to talk about with people who didn't have this . . . but the tips were good. I made almost AR$300 [in tips every weekend]." Adrian was not the only person who noted this advantage. Despite the lack of internal regulation, members of the cooperative were well aware that some people received tips and understood them as an acceptable variation.

But not all tips were considered just a perk of the job. Reviewing meeting minutes from the cooperative's inception, I found that some members had been formally sanctioned for violating the norms of good service by actively or aggressively soliciting tips. One longtime member was suspended by the council for three days after asking for money in exchange for helping a guest open their room door. Notes written about the incident stated that her "only justification" for the interaction was that her help was "at will." On another occasion, a member of the cooperative was fired when it came to light that she had accepted a large tip when booking a ballroom for an event. In this case, the amount of money was deemed far too large to be appropriately considered a tip.

Overtime Work

Overtime work created a second source of unregulated pay differences. At a hotel equipped with a variety of gathering spaces, workers regularly planned events and provided catering for dinners, conferences, and social events that

5.3 A ballroom set up for a party. Photo by BAUEN Cooperative.

required extra labor (see figure 5.3). Outside the schedule of full-time jobs, overtime shifts provided opportunities for members to earn more money on top of their salary. Unlike the limited variation in take-home pay caused by small tips, bigger differences could emerge when members worked overtime.

During the weeks I spent in the lobby, I observed members work their full-time shifts and then return to the hotel later to staff events. Omar, for example, worked the morning shift in reception, arriving just before 6 a.m. and leaving around 2 p.m. to pick up his daughter from school. One night, Omar returned to the hotel to work at a dinner that was scheduled to start at 9 p.m. Before the event began, I asked him about the overtime shift. He explained, "As waiters, we work for three or four hours serving food and then helping with the dishes." The number of waiters depended on the size of the event, he stated with authority: "You need one waiter for every twenty-five people. So, for an event like tonight with a hundred people, there are four of us." He gestured, showing how he could carry five plates of food at once. "Most people when they start can only carry two," he said. "And their arms hurt the next day."

These events required not only seasoned waiters like Omar but kitchen staff, security, cleanup, and coordination. Yet shifts were not evenly distributed among members who wanted to participate. While I was working in

133

food service, I observed a coordinator named Matías manage the overtime shifts. When I probed about the distribution of shifts, he began with a practical explanation: certain people worked more overtime because it overlapped with their current job. For example, waitstaff from the Utopia Café would wait tables during events, and the cooks who coordinated catering covered overtime shifts in the kitchen. To fill other positions, Matías kept a list of people interested in working overtime tacked to a bulletin board in his basement office—about twenty-five members he thought he could count on to show up and stay late.

Unlike the issue of tips, who worked overtime shifts and how much they were paid were ongoing topics of debate. These debates became particularly heated when Matías took his annual vacation, leaving a different group of people in charge. During that time, I was working in an administrative office with Carina, a quiet woman in her forties. The cooperative had hosted a lot of events that week, so Carina created a spreadsheet to list everyone who had worked and how much they had earned. One member stood out: in one week alone, he had made more than anyone else by working as a "supervisor" for multiple events. "Supervisor?" Carina asked hypothetically as she rolled her eyes. She went on to say that Matías was "not going to like this."

When I followed up, she explained that Matías liked to share the shifts among as many people as possible. If you asked to work an event, you would get one eventually. But in Matías's absence, overtime work was hoarded by certain people in the cooperative, with material consequences. A relatively closed group of members was able to rely on these event shifts to supplement their income. Nevertheless, certain people (in this case, Matías) attempted to make overtime shifts available more broadly, something that he did when he returned to work. But like the issues with job rotation described in chapter 4, there were no formal policies in place to distribute overtime when people like Matías were no longer in charge.

The distribution of overtime shifts was not the only sticking point. The cooperative also encountered challenges when it came to determining the *value* of overtime work. "The value of an event shift always creates problems," Matías commented. "Our policy was always to try to pay [the market rate] in catering. . . . For the compañeros who haven't worked overtime, sometimes it seems like a lot. But we really can't pay less because we may need external help, and if we pay less, they won't show up."

Since the cooperative occasionally supplemented its own members with extra help (often recruited from family and friends), Matías believed that the overtime pay rates needed to be comparable to those offered by private companies. During our conversations it was clear that he did not see this as incompatible with the cooperative's commitment to equal pay. He explained, "When you schedule an event, you calculate the value of all the extra shifts and include this in your price." In other words, the *customers* were directly paying the cost of the event shifts, not the cooperative itself.

Overtime shifts that were not related to events, such as covering a standard shift for a coworker, were compensated differently. Rather than what Matías called the "going rate" for event shifts (upward of AR$100 per hour in 2015), overtime in sector work paid just AR$33 per hour. How Matías reconciled these rates points to the different meanings and designations members assigned to their various sources of income.[27] Unlike other financial decisions made in the cooperative, inequality was legitimized by explicitly linking pay rates to market prices that were covered by an external party.

Ultimately, members could make significantly more money each month by working overtime. In fact, some workers actually relied on event overtime work to raise their take-home pay. Carina was a case in point. Her consistent full-time schedule—8 a.m. to 6 p.m. on weekdays—allowed her to pick up overtime work on evenings and weekends. She had worked three events in a row when a tired but pleased Carina told me, "After last night I have enough to pay all my bills." The overtime hours covered her monthly utilities, almost AR$2,000, in addition to her AR$4,500 rent for a one-bedroom apartment near the hotel that she shared with her partner. But she was getting worn out and said that she was thinking about moving: "I just don't want to keep working all the time for a house that I only sleep in," she lamented.

As Carina noted, even in the cooperative, wages were barely enough to keep up with the cost of living in the city of Buenos Aires. Tips and overtime helped some, but not all members could bridge the gap. Without a formal policy to share tips or overtime (especially when certain people, like Matías, were not in charge), the cooperative's informal practices produced new inequalities among members.

Credit and Debt

At the end of each year, the BAUEN Cooperative produced an annual report that included financial statements and a narrative summary about the organization. Once the report was completed, the Workers Assembly reviewed and voted on it before sending it to state agencies to maintain its status as a worker cooperative. Taken together, these reports offer an official history of the organization, highlighting major events, successes, and challenges confronted by the group. The 2008 annual report included a helpful reminder of the second element of the cooperative's survival finance: "This business emerged as a response to the need for jobs for those who had been left on the street by the closure of this hotel. Thus, without capital or access to credit . . . and with much sacrifice and effort, it has satisfied neglected needs." In other words, the Hotel Bauen's closure cut workers off from both wages and the ability to borrow—what scholars call "financialized wages."[28] And the BAUEN Cooperative had restored both. How?

Many of these financial details became clear during the weeks I spent working in administration. As I shadowed members in the sector, filed documents, and became familiar with the swelling archives, I learned more about how the cooperative made, saved, and spent money.

Enzo, the cooperative's elected treasurer at the time, worked in a dark office on the third floor. He spent his days reviewing cash flows, monitoring bank accounts, overseeing spending, and signing checks. Enzo, in his thirties, could often be found wearing large headphones to drown out distractions during the long hours he spent at his computer. One morning, he set his headphones aside to spend an hour with me discussing the cooperative's finances. His assessment of the group and its endeavors aligned with the needs outlined in the 2008 annual report. He explained, "We have disguised [this] worker cooperative as a consumer, credit, and service cooperative. Why? Because everyone in the cooperative understands and realizes that we all have needs."

Enzo described how the cooperative had developed financial practices to reflect its organizational priorities—economic considerations but also social and cultural ones.[29] Formally a worker cooperative—an organization equally owned and operated by its members—the BAUEN Cooperative operated like a hybrid organization, he thought. By issuing personal loans, it mimicked services provided by credit cooperatives, and by providing discounted rates on bulk goods, it operated like a consumer cooperative.

These internal credit mechanisms were crucially important. First, they offered benefits to members left out of conventional wage reports. Second, they introduced an additional relationship into the workplace, one produced not by members' ownership stake in the cooperative but by their debts to it.[30]

Emergency Loans

From its inception, and when it had the resources to do so, the BAUEN Cooperative provided its members access to zero-interest loans. Electronic bookkeeping records documented loans as far back as 2004, when the cooperative started to generate a stable income. Sabrina, who worked in administration, outlined the simple application process: a member needed only "write a memo explaining [their] request and submit it to the administrative council." Anyone who had worked in the hotel for more than six months and who did not have any other debt with the cooperative was eligible for a loan. Though council members formally approved individual requests, "in reality," Sabrina confided, "everyone who asks is given a loan."

Credit can be a financial boon for the issuer, but the BAUEN Cooperative did not benefit financially from this practice. They were zero-interest loans. If anything, the loans reduced the organization's assets by diverting cash from interest-earning savings and repayment on other debts. Rather, loans were provided to support the basic needs of the members. This was made clear in how members repaid the loans. When the administrative council approved a loan, it also determined the payment schedule by considering what the member could afford. As Enzo reported, the cooperative never approved a loan and then said, "Sure, but you have to pay it back in two installments." Rather, council members wanted repayment to be accessible: "Two installments? That amount would be almost half their monthly pay!" Enzo said.

Most loans ranged between AR$1,000 and AR$2,000 and were paid back in monthly installments automatically deducted from members' paychecks. In 2015 there were twenty-eight active loans (sixteen for women, twelve for men), ranging from AR$400 to AR$7,000 each. Few of the cooperative's records stated the reasons for these loans, though occasional handwritten notes remained on original memos. Through those, I learned that everyone who had once lived in the hotel (a practice that ended in 2015) had been offered moving assistance via cooperative loans. Another member received a loan to pay for his daughter's *quinceañera*, which was organized and catered by the cooperative, and still another loan was designated to help with school expenses for a member's children.

Concerned with their ability to address personal emergencies, members discussed ways to expand this credit system. During an assembly I attended in 2015, the council members provided updates on members who had medical problems and needed financial support. In that meeting Omar suggested that the cooperative set aside AR$100,000 for emergencies, to be disbursed in loans at 10 percent interest (far better, he reasoned, than external lenders' 30–40 percent interest on short-term loans). As members considered the proposal, the trustee intervened, proposing that they also discuss improving the donation system.

Supplementing formal loans, the BAUEN Cooperative customarily addressed emergency situations by collecting charitable donations on behalf of specific members.[31] In the lunchroom the trustee would circulate sheets of paper for members to jot down their name and contribution to a given cause. Workers in administration would then deduct the pledged donations from individual paychecks and credit them to the member in need.

Back in the meeting, the trustee suggested that the donation system would be more efficient if members could donate a flat rate—"say, AR$30"—to make it easier to tally. Although the group discussed this and other ideas, this was just the beginning of their deliberations, and they did not vote to enshrine any of these proposals into policy that day.

Omar's Request

Personal loans were rarely a point of contention in the cooperative—as Sabrina commented, "Everyone who asks is given a loan." Members regularly came into administration to request loans, review their repayment schedule, or pay back the principal. But on one occasion an unmet request for a loan offered insight into the ways members made sense of their shared finances.

In October the president of the cooperative called an emergency council meeting. Omar had approached her earlier in the day, distraught. As he explained to Pilar, with whom he had worked since the founding days, he had just discovered that his brother was sick and he needed to send AR$10,000 to his family. Alarmed, Pilar went directly to administration to see about a loan. But she discovered that Omar had already taken out a AR$5,000 loan just two months earlier, plus he was repaying the cooperative for a television he had gotten through a bulk purchase earlier that year.

In the meeting the council members reviewed the loan policy formalized in 2014. It stated that members could request loans up to AR$5,000, they could have only one loan at a time, and all exceptions had to be approved by the assembly. After reviewing the policy, Enzo, the treasurer, was concerned to find out that Omar had not received formal approval to hold two concurrent loans. He attributed this to an oversight, explaining that he had been enforcing the one-loan rule with others. For example, more recently, when a different member requested a second loan, Enzo had made him pay the last two installments on his first loan in order to take out the next. Given Omar's debt to the cooperative, the council was conflicted and looked to past emergencies for precedent regarding how to proceed. In the case of a longtime housekeeper, the council had paid her for the days of work she missed when her husband was hospitalized for cancer treatments. They remembered approving the same exception for a janitor when his child with severe disabilities was experiencing complications. The council members noted that these examples were very different from giving cash in a lump sum, even though others had been paid for days they did not work.

The closest example anyone in the group could remember was Primo. Primo had started working in the Hotel Bauen in the 1990s. After the hotel closed in 2001 and he was laid off, he found a job elsewhere as a custodian, which allowed him to support his family. After his compañeros occupied the Hotel Bauen, he began to stay overnight in the hotel to reduce the hours spent on his long commute home. Years later, Primo recalled the decision to join the cooperative: "Although I had a job, the moment came when I decided to dedicate myself 100 percent to this." But over the years a series of subsequent health problems made it increasingly hard for him to work, and when he needed help covering medical expenses, the cooperative organized a collection. The administrative council then "completed" the donation with a loan so that Primo could cover the AR$5,000 in out-of-pocket medical costs.

After tapping their organizational memory, Pilar suggested they follow this model for Omar. Matías, however, thought it would set a risky precedent. Omar already had debt to the cooperative and now was asking for a large amount of money. "What if other people come asking for more?" Matías asked. "Can the cooperative pay more than that?"

Romina raised a point I would hear again in many council meetings: perhaps they could require receipts "in order to show the members" the justification for Omar's expense. Because of the BAUEN Cooperative's commitment to transparency and to avoid any personal implications of fraud, the council members carefully tracked and documented any discretionary spending.

Amid these suggestions, Pilar was visibly upset. She was both Omar's friend and an elected officer of the cooperative. Months before, I'd noted her reflect that sometimes enforcing the rules could be "painful and ugly." Romina was sympathetic and tried to offer some perspective: "On the other hand, you might end up with a situation that isn't going to serve them [other members] later."

During this extended meeting, another council member brought up that Omar had relatives who also worked in the cooperative. What if *they* took out a loan? Omar's cousin, for example, did not have any debt to the cooperative; she could request a AR$5,000 loan, and the council could match it. Everyone seemed more comfortable with the idea, and in a moment of consensus, the council summoned Omar to explain the solution they had devised.

After the short briefing, Omar erupted in frustration: "My situation isn't like other people's!" He appealed to Pilar, saying that there were people in the cooperative who "deserved the support" and that Pilar "knew what it was like." Other members chimed in, trying to maintain the calm, but Omar rejected their suggestions and stormed out of the room. Pilar burst into tears, while other council members expressed frustration that Omar had seemed to expect the money on demand. Romina was also disturbed by how comfortable Omar was with bending the cooperative's rules. "He knows where to hit you," she told Pilar of his emotional appeal and subtle references to memories of their shared struggles in the early days of the cooperative. Enzo agreed: "He plays [a] psychological game."

The next day, two council members—Romina and Daniel—followed up with Omar. I observed the conversation from the desk I often sat at next to Romina. Omar elaborated that the AR$10,000 he had requested was only *his* part of the emergency expense—his family members had their own obligations; moreover, he actually needed more than he originally thought. When Romina brought up the debts he already had to the cooperative, Omar retorted, "Doesn't the cooperative have millions of pesos in the bank? Is that not true?" If so, "then AR$5,000 [*lucas*] is nothing."

Omar asked emphatically, "Why did we recuperate this source of work if we would have to just go somewhere else for the money [*la gita*]?" Romina countered that Omar was not the only person in the cooperative with problems and needs, and they could not bend the rules. She reiterated that the cooperative required everyone to finish repaying one loan before taking out another. "One member needed money for a surgery, another needed money for a prosthesis . . . everyone had problems," she explained to an unmoved Omar. In the cooperative, she emphasized, no one—not even a founding member—could employ a logic like "my issue is more important than yours."

In the heat of the moment, Daniel tried to deescalate things and calm Omar down. He said that he understood Omar's frustration and that the council was doing everything they could to help. Romina then suggested he request an exception to the one-loan rule in the Workers Assembly scheduled for the next day. But Omar declined, saying he did not want to act poor (*humilde*) in front of everyone. After he left the office, Romina and Daniel looked disturbed. Romina sighed, noting that, by Omar's logic, he would just transfer all the cooperative's money to his own bank account.

As Omar's story demonstrates, the extension of credit in the cooperative workplace could be both a blessing and a curse. On one hand, members could access cash with no interest to help them through times of need.[32] On the other hand, this debt added layers to the web of interdependencies in the workplace. In conventional arrangements, extending credit creates an unequal relationship between debtor and creditor. But in the BAUEN Cooperative, credit was extended by an organization collectively owned by the borrowers themselves, many of whom were linked by long relationships and even familial ties. The council members, of course, were sensitive to the challenges that borrowing could produce. But in the end, Omar declined to take his issue before the Workers Assembly, the only authority that could have made an exception to the rules.

Bulk Buying

In addition to offering loans, the BAUEN Cooperative extended credit to its members in a second way: by providing the opportunity to buy food and household items on short-term credit. Much like the cost-saving strategies of a food co-op, people can access lower prices by coordinating their purchases into bulk orders. Members regularly requested cases of milk, blocks of cheese, meat, and other groceries to be delivered along with the cooperative's weekly supply.

When members wanted to buy goods, they wrote a memo and gave it to the manager of stock, who included the personal requests in her weekly orders. She then passed the memos to members in administration, who tallied up the money spent and deducted it from members' monthly paychecks. The practice not only helped members access lower prices but also spread them out into payments to soften the financial blow. Bulk buying thus benefited members of the cooperative in two ways: by lowering household expenses and by offering a short-term line of credit to defray the full immediate cost of the purchase.

At the end of May, I joined members working in administration in the tedious task of calculating the paycheck deductions. We pulled up chairs to Sabrina's desk to help with the process. Inés read numbers aloud from index cards, and Sabrina entered the values into a spreadsheet to calculate members' take-home pay. Valentín's index card that month announced many deductions, including a loan payment (AR$1,000), three advance paychecks (AR$2,100), a donation (AR$50), and around AR$600 in bulk purchases. As Sabrina entered these values, the calculation deducted a total of AR$3,750 from his final monthly paycheck. Seeing the impact, she made a manual change, typing AR$300 into the formula, instead of the AR$600 in bulk goods he had actually bought.

I asked why Sabrina was discounting his goods, and she explained that she had decided to break the cost into two payments. It was just too much to deduct from one check, she told me. Inés agreed, making a note on his index card so she would remember to account for the leftover AR$300 next month. Even with this ad hoc modification, Valentín would have hardly any take-home pay (*ni un peso*). By allowing members to purchase goods in bulk, the BAUEN Cooperative extended an additional line of credit to its members that was reconciled in their paycheck at the end of the month. Sabrina's modification suggests that this credit was applied (and sometimes informally extended) with attention to its impact on the member's ability to make ends meet. Survival finance was not about increasing financial burdens but making things easier for low-wage workers navigating a rising cost of living.

Time Banking for the Bottom Line

In addition to wages and credit, the third component of survival finance involved earning time: specifically, paid time off from work. Over the years, the BAUEN Cooperative developed an internal time bank. In exchange for working certain events and holidays, members could negotiate with their managers to either earn overtime wages or bank future paid days off (*días a favor*). For example, Matías, one of the event coordinators, sometimes let members bank future vacation days, while Sarita, the kitchen manager, did not have enough people working in her sector to allow for this accumulation and instead preferred to pay overtime wages. In housekeeping the manager would give housekeepers half of an overtime shift (*media extra*) if occupancy was high and the work was exceptionally hard.

For large special events, the cooperative formalized compensation in time. This practice served a dual purpose. First, when the cooperative needed more staff on hand, it could make the long hours of overtime work more attractive by adjusting the ratio of time worked to compensatory time off. Sometimes it might be a one-to-one ratio, but other times workers might earn, say, one and a half hours of paid time off in exchange for one hour of actual overtime work. Second, payment in time effectively delayed the cooperative's largest expense: labor. Doing this could significantly change the financial calculus of an event, making it possible for the cooperative to turn a profit when margins were tight.

The Eighth Annual Tattoo Fest

For many years, the BAUEN Cooperative hosted a three-day festival of tattoo artists who came from far and wide to feature their work in downtown Buenos Aires (see figure 5.4). Members of the cooperative were well-practiced hosts for events ranging from small lunches and receptions to large parties and national press conferences. The Tattoo Fest was larger and longer than

5.4 Banner hanging from the entrance of the Hotel Bauen publicizing the 2015 Tattoo Fest. Photo by BAUEN Cooperative.

most events requiring nearly all the space at the Hotel Bauen. In the hotel's largest ballroom, workers erected stalls in which artists could give tattoos and sell their wares.[33] Smaller ballrooms featured trainings and seminars led by well-known artists as well as live music on Saturday and Sunday nights. Attendees' entry fee (in 2015, AR$100) was valid all weekend, resulting in increased foot traffic through the hotel's lobby and café.

In addition to providing the venue for this large event, the BAUEN Cooperative also sold food and drinks to the many people who came to the attractions. In preparation, workers set up additional registers, created simplified menus, stocked up on supplies, and increased security in the building. As this suggests, the Tattoo Fest also required far more staff than other events—certainly more than Matías's list of twenty-five or so people eager for overtime. In 2015, as in years past, the administrative council incentivized the members by offering all who worked overtime *two* paid days off for each day of work during the festival.

Years of trial and error meant that the Eighth Annual Tattoo Fest went off with very few hitches. Over the long weekend, the Hotel Bauen bustled with activity. Marveling at the scene, one journalist reported, "Can you imagine hundreds of people, young and old, many whom are tattooed to their

143

teeth, with hundreds of kilos of rings in their bodies, and brazenly walking around, filling the entryway of the Hotel Bauen, the same five-star hotel that was born during the military dictatorship?" (Romero 2016).

On the Monday after the event, managers submitted memos documenting the overtime hours to the member office. There, members compiled the information and translated the hours worked into paid time off that would be banked in the master list. While workers in the member office documented the labor money earned in this ad hoc time bank, the trustee reviewed all the income and expenses associated with the festival to produce a summary report (as they did for all large events in the hotel). One afternoon, I sat with the trustee as he finished the report: the cooperative had earned nearly AR$47,000 over the Tattoo Fest weekend. The windfall was made possible by the report's missing line item: labor costs. Put differently, the cooperative turned a profit only because all of the weekend's overtime labor was paid in future time off.

Overworked and Underpaid

By members' accounts, the Tattoo Fest was a success. The organizers were happy, the facilities were adequate, and the cooperative turned a profit. Yet in the days that followed, members complained about the physical toll of overwork. Carina, for example, had worked all three days of the Tattoo Fest and then a late-night dinner on Monday night atop her normal schedule. By Tuesday she was exhausted. As we sat together at her desk around midday, Carina admitted that she was unmotivated to work (*fiaca*). Her feet still hurt so much that she had cried in the night, she confided. And she wasn't alone: earlier that day, as we passed in the stairwell, I asked a member who coordinated the weekend event how he was doing, and he simply responded, "Everything hurts."

Pilar's weekend schedule had also been punishing. On Saturday, she had worked from 8 a.m. to 6 p.m., returning on Sunday at 1 p.m. for the afternoon shift. Because of a minor accident—people messing around (*boludeando*) in the early morning hours—she ended up staying up until nearly 6 a.m. Still in the hotel at sunrise, Pilar grabbed an hour of sleep in an empty guest room before working her normal Monday shift. Like Carina, Pilar was tired but scheduled to work another event on Tuesday evening. Her exhaustion was palpable: throughout the workday she yawned and struggled to find her words when I asked any questions.

144   Although members regularly sought out overtime work, on some occasions these same members resisted pressure to take on extra shifts. Exhaustion and burnout were real struggles for these hospitality workers. One

afternoon, Matías asked whether Pilar could work at an evening event. She needed the cash, she replied, but "my health isn't worth the extra money [*un mango*]." This played into ongoing debates both within the BAUEN Cooperative and with other organizations about whether self-management encouraged self-exploitation (*autoexploitación*).

Overwork is not only about long hours. In what Alison Wynn (2018) terms *everwork*, overwork also results from the accumulation of unpredictable scheduling, constant availability, and extensive face time. Council members were aware of the toll of everwork on the members. "When there are a lot of events, the staff ends up exhausted [*reventado*]," Matías explained. He continued, "It's not just that we work eight or nine hours in our sectors . . . but afterward we have events. Short events go until midnight or 1 a.m., but there are events that start at 6 p.m. and end the next day at 6 a.m. So, imagine you worked nine hours, and you had to work twelve more. You end up worn out [*palmado*]. That's why sometimes we call people from outside, so we don't kill people here." While Matías considered addressing overwork by hiring outside event staff, Alberto discussed other efforts to keep the workday manageable and avoid burnout: "In the hotel people can work twelve-hour shifts. That's when we ask ourselves, 'How many hours are we going to work?' We have tried, whenever possible, to maintain an eight-hour workday for the benefit of the members." Attention to the workday, Alberto made clear, was not just about customers and revenues but also about members' personal needs.

In fact, the council members even considered *reducing* regular shifts to account for the inherent demands of overtime work in the conference hotel. Enzo told me about this proposal, which he thought could be "sustainable for the sectors" while allowing members to "spend that little hour with family": "There has been an idea to reduce the workday and improve wages, because the work here in the cooperative is . . . really demanding [*sacrificado*]. We have to be here for double shifts providing services. It depends on the events we have, but sometimes on the weekends, we are confined here in the hotel. . . . We know that we have to incentivize [this work], and we thought that [reducing the workday] would be one possibility." Despite a widespread sense that overwork was an ongoing problem, members continued to seek out long hours to augment their low wages. A young man named Ronnie came to the administrative council's office one afternoon seeking approval for his overtime request. The previous week, a series of mechanical problems had shut down the passenger elevators in the twenty-story tower. The cooperative had resorted to using the service elevator to ferry guests to

145

their rooms on higher floors. Ronnie volunteered to work as an elevator attendant, making sure that the elevator returned to the lobby and was never put over capacity.

In addition to his normal shift, 6 a.m. to 2 p.m., Ronnie worked a second shift from 2 p.m. to 10 p.m., for a total of nearly sixteen hours a day. The council arranged for him to stay in the hotel overnight, so at least he would not have to make the long commute to his house in the province. Later, when the council members reviewed Ronnie's memo for overtime, Romina suggested they approve only two more days. She worried he might get overtired or neglect his responsibilities at home. When Ronnie came to discuss his schedule, he understood Romina's concerns but insisted that he needed the extra hours: his partner was out of work, and they had two young children.

In addition to economic needs, some members justified overwork as part of their broader commitment to the cooperative. In a service workplace where long hours of overtime were the norm, ideal self-managed workers, as I described in chapter 3, ran the risk of exploiting themselves for the collective good. For example, when I noted late one night after an event that it seemed as if Francisco was always working in the hotel, he responded, "I put all the effort I have into the cooperative. I've dedicated myself more to the cooperative than anything else, and today the cooperative is doing well, so I have to keep maintaining it. I can't let it down." Members worked long hours not only to earn additional wages but also to help keep the cooperative afloat. Alberto explained his long hours of overtime as an "investment" in the cooperative: "So many hours have been invested, hours that someone could have put toward another focus." He went on to explain that in the cooperative "the hours were not being eaten up by an employer, but we are seeing them grow."

The policy of equal pay was a radical step in the BAUEN Cooperative's equality project. In word and deed, the organization valued all members' efforts equally. Over the years, the BAUEN Cooperative creatively navigated its commitment to equal pay, maintaining an equal base salary while introducing some differences to incentivize rule following and discourage free riding.

Responding to member needs in the context of low-wage service work, the cooperative developed a system of survival finance. This set of financial practices served to diversify the forms of compensation to include cash, credit, and time. On top of wages, the cooperative provided short- and long-term credit so that workers could avoid predatory loans. It also improvised an internal time bank to help incentivize long hours and turn profits when margins were tight. The system of survival finance helped both the members and the organization make ends meet. But the cooperative was never free from external pressures, whether from market forces or, as we learn in the next chapter, political actors who would determine its fate.

El Bauen es de todos.
The Bauen belongs to the people.
—BAUEN Cooperative

6   The Activist Workplace

For clients and guests, it might have been easy to forget that the Hotel Bauen stayed open because of a bold act: the illegal occupation of private property. Time and again, I noted the business-as-usual mentality that characterized work in this recuperated business. Members followed predictable routines as they went about their daily tasks, attended to guests, and cycled events through the ballrooms.

In the previous chapters, I detail how workers constructed an equality project *within* the organization, describing the practices the members adopted to facilitate relational equality. Through internal innovations and creative responses to the emergent challenges, members of the BAUEN Cooperative sought to broadly distribute power, opportunities, and resources among themselves. From its inception in 2003 to its closure in 2020, the BAUEN Cooperative appealed for—but never won—the permanent legal right to use the downtown hotel. Now it is time to consider an important lingering question: How, without the title to the property, did the workers run a functioning hotel?

The answer to how and why the BAUEN Cooperative was able to illegally operate the hotel requires a close look at how the equality project extended *beyond* the workplace. To stay open for business, the cooperative had to navigate relationships not only with customers and suppliers but also with police officers, bureaucrats, and politicians. These state actors did not allow the BAUEN Cooperative to survive through simple neglect, a lack of resources, or their own inability to enforce the law. Rather, the Hotel Bauen remained in operation until the closure in 2020 during the global coronavirus pandemic because the state *did not enforce* the law. Through the dramatic highs and lows of the long-running campaign to expropriate the property, state actors engaged in forbearance, allowing the cooperative to survive due to their unwillingness to resolve the situation.[1] At the same time, the campaign for expropriation left an indelible mark on the cooperative itself. In response to the shifting demands of its efforts to legalize the occupation, the BAUEN Cooperative politicized its equality project by integrating social movement practices into its work routines, becoming what I call an *activist workplace*.

A Legal Gray Zone

When members of the newly formed cooperative occupied the Hotel Bauen, the very real possibility of eviction loomed large. Many had witnessed the police violently remove workers from other occupied businesses across the city of Buenos Aires. For instance, one night in 2003, federal police forcibly evicted the workers at Brukman, a recuperated garment factory a short cab ride away from the hotel. Upon hearing the news, Bauen workers rushed to the factory, mobilizing with over three thousand other demonstrators in support until Brukman workers were able to reenter the factory.[2]

Despite their tenuous legal position, the workers occupying the Hotel Bauen launched a public campaign to establish their claim to the hotel and secure popular support. In the weeks and months that followed, state officials, social movement organizations, and politicians supported the workers' efforts to form a cooperative, negotiate with the bankruptcy judge and property owner, and eventually reopen the facility.[3] These initial efforts were fruitful: a commercial judge in the city of Buenos Aires named the newly formed BAUEN Cooperative the temporary custodian of the property. When this temporary authorization expired in October 2003, workers negotiated a subsequent agreement with the property owners and the Buenos Aires City Council to continue operations.

Despite this series of successful but temporary agreements, the cooperative needed to permanently secure its use of the downtown hotel. Recall from chapter 1 that Bauen workers sought help from activists to occupy their former workplace. Tito, a founding member who was one of the group's first presidents, reflected on this process: "The truth is that [at the outset] we didn't have a clear idea of what we were looking to do."[4] Representatives from the National Movement of Recuperated Businesses (MNER), which had helped coordinate the initial occupation, proposed a solution: the state could expropriate the hotel on behalf of the cooperative.

Expropriation, also known as *eminent domain*, involves a state agency taking property from private owners for a purpose deemed to be in the public interest.[5] Practiced around the world, expropriation is often used to acquire the land needed to build a road, a dam, or even a border wall. In the case of the BAUEN Cooperative, advocates proposed that the powerful city of Buenos Aires should expropriate the Hotel Bauen and render it a public resource, thereby resolving the cooperative's legal uncertainty.

Daniel, an MNER activist who eventually joined the BAUEN Cooperative, explained how the group originally came to embrace the goal of expropriation: "What we always thought was that if it was legally possible, politically it would be impossible. To expropriate all the companies that workers control is a prerevolutionary process. And here [in Argentina] we don't have the conditions for that. But for us, it was useful as a polestar, a horizon, a utopia we could strive for. And we went to present our case in Congress, in front of all the legislators, [and they] engaged with us." According to this account, BAUEN members acknowledged that their strategy was ambitious, even utopic. But they had few other options that would resolve their legal status. Another longtime member described the campaign for expropriation as "like a race that has to be won no matter what." Embedded activists like Daniel helped direct the political campaign in crucial ways.[6] As Tito put it, "If they [members of the MNER] had not been with us, if they had not articulated a policy to follow, this [occupation] may have resulted in nothing."[7]

The BAUEN Cooperative's strategy seemed, at first glance, paradoxical. The workers had just illegally occupied the hotel, claiming private property for their collective use. But when they set out to negotiate with judges, state officials, and the police, they asked for permission to *break the law* by remaining in a building they did not legally own. As time passed, though, the strategy shifted and the BAUEN Cooperative's maturing campaign appealed for *enforcement* of the law. Esteban Magnani, an Argentine scholar and expert on worker-recuperated businesses, reflects on this shift:

> It's interesting to note that workers, who are sometimes seen as revolutionaries and sometimes as delinquents, mostly just want the laws to be enforced—the same laws that are so often broken by their bosses. Employers repeatedly failed to pay taxes, or took out loans (usually from the state, and often for amounts larger than the value of the business itself), or didn't pay salaries or benefits, etc. These very same employers now present themselves as defenders of legality, talking about legal uncertainty and violations of the constitutional rights of private property. At the same time, they conveniently forget to mention tax evasion, the emptying of accounts, and other such blatantly illegal acts. (2009, 101)

For members of the BAUEN Cooperative, defending the law became an opportunity to build up their legitimacy in the community. Honor Brabazon (2016, 27) calls this tactic a "law as politics" approach in which social movements choose to defend certain parts of the law in order to "catch the government and the [property] owners—as well as the political and legal system more broadly—in their own contradictions" and ultimately "build support for a more far-reaching change." To do so, supportive lawyers and politicians presented legal challenges and drafted bills while the cooperative mobilized its workers and used direct action to organize the campaign.

The expropriation proposal seemed increasingly feasible in the changing political context of Argentina in 2003. With the election of President Néstor Kirchner that year, the country turned away from the neoliberal policies implemented by the military dictatorship and deepened under the democratic administrations of the 1990s. Kirchner marshaled a social-development and left-wing populist governance model, which boded well for worker-recuperated businesses like the Hotel Bauen. Expropriation was also becoming more common as other recuperated enterprises made similar appeals.[8] On a case-by-case basis, expropriations were taking place at the local and provincial levels, girded by a simple argument: "In a context of scarce employment, closed factories should be preserved for the benefit of the whole of society" (Hirtz and Giacone 2013, 94).

In Argentina arguments for the expropriation of private property relied on the rights enumerated in the National Constitution (Article 17) and the

151

National Law on Expropriation (21.499). Private property could be legally expropriated for reasons of public utility; therefore, lawyers representing worker-recuperated businesses argued for expropriation by framing work as a right and jobs as public goods.[9] This required coordinating political, judicial, and labor interests.[10] First, a bill must be approved by a legislature with power to declare an asset a public utility. Next, the corresponding executive (the mayor, governor, or president) must sign the bill into law and allocate state resources for its implementation. Finally, the case must go before a judge, who determines how the expropriated assets can be used. In practice, the jurisdictions of power are far less tidy than this step-by-step process suggests. In this relatively uncharted legal territory, state actors employed a variety of tactics to facilitate or derail expropriation efforts, and many that succeeded would turn out to be only temporary or subject to future revision.[11] As a member of the MNER stated, "You won't be able to figure out all the legal twists and turns, because here they [state actors] can invent whatever they want" (quoted in Magnani 2009, 106). There may have been only a handful of success stories, but expropriation remained the clearest path to ensuring legal certainty.

Betrayed by the City

Members of the BAUEN Cooperative first directed their campaign toward the Buenos Aires City Council. After reopening the hotel to the public, representatives of the cooperative met with city officials to chart a path to legalize its operations. In early 2005 the workers advocated for a local bill that would permanently expropriate the property and preserve the cooperative's management of the facility as a public utility. In the meantime, operating the hotel without the legal title was becoming increasingly difficult as workers faced a series of administrative and operational hurdles. Without any formal paperwork, the property was unable to pass health and safety inspections, a necessary bureaucratic requirement for any hotel. The private owners seized on this fact, allegedly reporting the hotel for violating city code. In response, city officials conducted inspections and threatened the BAUEN Cooperative with an administrative closure three times in 2005 alone. Amid mounting threats, advocates of the cooperative modified their bill under consideration in the city council to try to legalize the occupation as quickly as possible.

By June 2005 a city council member who also worked as a lawyer for the MNER presented a compromise: a bill proposing the temporary expropriation of the hotel for two years. Members of the BAUEN Cooperative then pressured city council members for support. They issued press releases, organized marches, and built alliances with supporters. The campaign, which

152

started in courtrooms and congressional offices, soon spilled out into the streets. "The BAUEN Worker Cooperative is in a permanent state of alert in defense of its source of work," read one press release. "Join us next Wednesday at noon in the entry of the hotel to march to the City Hall and demand the expropriation of the Bauen for its workers."[12] Subsequent releases informed the public and politicians that nearly two thousand people had marched to support expropriation and outlined the cooperative's demands:

- That the hotel be definitively expropriated
- That the state collect the more than AR$5 million that the business owner owed to the city
- That the expropriation entrust the hotel to the BAUEN Cooperative
- That the cooperative be granted a thirty-year payment plan to make up the difference between the cost of expropriation and the outstanding debt

As the BAUEN Cooperative sharpened its demands, it was increasingly clear it was not the only party invested in the outcome of this fight. The private owners of the Hotel Bauen busily lobbied against any bill that would favor the workers.

My archival research—digging into news reports, press releases, and the cooperative's meeting minutes—provides a window into the cooperative's responses to each political turn of events. As the bill for temporary expropriation progressed in the city council, for instance, the private owners filed code-violation complaints, regarded by the cooperative as a series of politically motivated attacks. The group then denounced the city's attempts to conduct inspections as unjust, reflecting a "policy of persecution." After one inspection the cooperative wrote in a press release, "It is clear that the attempts to close [the hotel] are being used for political ends and not requirements for health and security."

After a series of legislative delays, the city council's budget committee finally considered the BAUEN Cooperative's expropriation bill. During that meeting councilman Mario Morando, a member of the conservative Republican Proposal (PRO) party, surprised the cooperative by presenting an alternative plan. This revised bill proposed the formation of a committee to determine the future of the hotel—with the explicit goal of returning the property to private management. Outraged, members of the BAUEN Cooperative intensified their campaign for a resolution in their favor (see figure 6.1). When the bill for temporary expropriation was amended, the cooperative "repudiated" Morando's counterbill and called on its allies to rally in protest. The resulting march to the legislature successfully delayed the first scheduled vote.

6.1 Sign posted in the lobby soliciting signatures for the cooperative's campaign for expropriation. Photo by BAUEN Cooperative.

Lacunza, who was at City Hall that night, remembered, "We knew that we could stop them from voting . . . so when there was quorum, we made a commotion to the point that the police finally forced us out, threw gas at us, a lot of things." Despite the short-term delay introduced by the workers' civil disobedience, the modified bill passed into law with the minimum votes necessary in the early hours of December 7, 2005. Like other social movements, the cooperative may have succeeded in setting the legislative agenda, but it was ultimately unable to secure passage of a law in its favor.[13]

The bill that eventually passed became infamous as the Morando Law. The revised language explicitly favored the private owners and amplified the workers' uncertainty. The BAUEN Cooperative responded by publicly accusing city council members of complicity with the private owners, writing in a press release, "We denounce the bias of legislators [that led them] to pass a law that would restore the hotel to businesspeople who emptied it and left hundreds of workers in the street. We reaffirm our position to defend our 146 jobs . . . and appeal to Jorge Telerman [the mayor of Buenos Aires] to act in favor of our management." Rejecting defeat, BAUEN workers interpreted their legal setback as a call to action, mobilizing their supporters and promising to appeal the law.

Telerman eventually met with members of the cooperative and agreed to support the amendment of the sections of the Morando Law that specifically mandated the hotel's return to private ownership. Other political actors also came to the cooperative's defense. Between 2005 and 2006, national legislators affiliated with leftist political parties and the Front for Victory, a coalition of parties supporting the Kirchner administration, proposed two bills for expropriation and issued three declarations of support for the BAUEN Cooperative.[14] Despite these encouraging signs, the mayor of Buenos Aires ultimately failed to garner the political support needed to modify the Morando Law as promised. Now, the workers asserted in a press release, it was clear: "The [mayor's] response, far from offering a solution, was only a delay that kept workers in a *legal gray zone* with serious economic consequences: we estimate that obtaining definitive expropriation would double the activities of the hotel and, with that, sources of jobs" (my emphasis). In short, the Morando Law stayed on the books but was never enforced by city officials.

Threats of Eviction

Early support from a commercial judge had hinted that the judiciary could chart a course to legalize the cooperative's use of the hotel. But in 2005 the workers learned that a third firm—Mercoteles—had purchased the property during bankruptcy negotiations. The private owners' apparent openness to collaboration officially ended when Mercoteles denounced the workers as "illegitimate occupants" and called for their removal (O'Donnell 2007). The BAUEN Cooperative and its advocates fought back. Recall in chapter 1 how they investigated the sale of the hotel, uncovering irregularities, unpaid debt, and nepotistic ties among the companies involved.[15] The cooperative presented these claims in commercial courts and won a series of rulings in its favor even as Mercoteles submitted certificates of the sale, registered titles, and other state documents to substantiate its ownership claims. Romina, a veteran member of the cooperative, recalled this as "the only time that they wanted to evict us." Then she clarified, "But afterward they couldn't. Whenever there was an attempt to evict us, the cooperative always found out, and before they could do it, there was a march, an event, a mobilization; something was planned." As Romina noted, while members were busy practicing workplace democracy and cooperative hospitality, they were also increasingly active politically.

After years of back and forth, in 2007 a commercial judge ruled that, based on documents presented to the court, the sale of the hotel to Mercoteles was, in fact, legal. On July 20 the judge declared Mercoteles the titleholder of the hotel and issued the first formal eviction notice to the BAUEN Cooperative. In the decision the judge cited the Morando Law, concluding that although it had never been implemented, it "sufficiently protect[ed] the rights of the workers" while affirming the intention to return the property to private ownership. The eviction notice was published in national newspapers, setting a thirty-day term for the cooperative to vacate the hotel.

Defiant, the BAUEN Cooperative pledged resistance: "We [the workers] won't leave the hotel again," they declared to journalists, calling the ruling a "legal abuse" that created "yet another obstacle that we have to overcome" (Lavaca Collective 2007a). Another press release stated, "Our struggle to recuperate our source of work is yet again under threat by those who abandoned the company, this time protected by the accomplice judge and the advance of the political right." Similar to its response to the Morando Law, the cooperative denounced the court's decision and alleged that the private owners held an unfair advantage in the legal process.

Within days of the scheduled eviction, the cooperative filed an appeal for legal protection in a higher court. The president of the cooperative told a reporter, "We are confident that the appeal will be accepted, but we have to be prepared. The first thing is to resist eviction [and then] . . . achieve a definitive solution, which is expropriation" (*Página/12* 2007). In a hopeful turn of events, the judge accepted the request and forwarded the case to the appeals court.

The eviction order was never enforced *or* obviated. Instead, the persistent threat weighed on the members of the cooperative. Lucinda, a founding member, remembered "thousands" of threats that had never come to pass. "Thanks to God and the Virgin, it never happened. And the next day we continued working like nothing had happened.... How did we survive? We had to work.... I don't know how to explain it." Alan also grappled with describing the cumulative effect of working under the specter of eviction:

> The truth is that we work in a cooperative with an eviction order, where there aren't any political resolutions, where one administration leaves and another comes ... and it creates a little bit of discomfort, fear. It's a sensation, you see? Or it's a mix of sensations.... you don't know if you are going to have a job tomorrow, or if tomorrow they are coming to evict you, or ... in that sense, it's ugly. But ... when those types of problems arise, it's like we all unite, and it makes us strong. So, in that sense, I am not scared because I know that we will unite and we will fight for the common good of the cooperative.

By 2014 the cooperative had been fighting for legal protection for nearly a decade. The workers had exhausted a number of different channels for a legal resolution in their favor: the bankruptcy judge continued to renew the eviction order; criminal charges brought against the private owners had been dismissed by a judge who refused to consider the case; and the Supreme Court upheld the decision of the commercial court in favor of the private owners.

Amid the failure of its judicial appeals, the BAUEN Cooperative turned again to brokering a political solution. In 2014, on the brink of yet another threatened eviction, the cooperative pledged to continue: "We are going to keep working like always" (*La Nación* 2014). But advocates also acknowledged that political opportunities were closing; although their situation "must be resolved politically ... we don't see that there is political will in Congress" (Zucchelli 2014). Indeed, in 2014 alone, five more bills for expropriation were introduced in the national House of Representatives, but none made it out of committee.

Executive Rejection
The political landscape shifted abruptly in 2015 with national elections in Argentina. The PRO party and its conservative coalition faced off against the incumbent party—the Kirchner-sponsored Front for Victory—and scored some major victories. The PRO's candidates were elected to serve as the

mayor of the city of Buenos Aires, the governor of the province of Buenos Aires, and the president. Facing this loss of political power with the election of Mauricio Macri, outgoing president Cristina Fernández de Kirchner called an emergency session of Congress. During the final days of her administration, national legislators would consider nearly a hundred bills, including the expropriation of the Hotel Bauen. In a flurry of excitement at the end of the year, BAUEN Cooperative members lobbied legislators, attended committee meetings, and maintained close contact with congressional aides in an all-out effort to mobilize votes in their favor.

On a sunny day in November 2015, I joined a small group of workers advocating for the expropriation bill. We sat in the back of a crowded meeting room in a government building and watched as members of the BAUEN Cooperative's administrative council testified before a congressional committee in the waning days of the Kirchner presidency. The outcome was promising: the bill was approved by the fourth and final congressional committee and would be sent for a final vote.

After the meeting concluded, our delegation returned directly to the Hotel Bauen, where the council members called an assembly to share the news. Daniel, the former MNER activist turned BAUEN member, shared the updates from the day: "For the newer compañeros, the famous expropriation bill that we have presented a thousand times in Congress . . . has advanced through all the levels but never come to a vote. Today what we received was all the committees approved the bill, and so it will go to the floor for a vote by all the representatives. . . . [W]e are almost certain that they will let us know tomorrow that they will vote. It's what we have been working toward for thirteen years, and hopefully we are close to passing it tomorrow." Daniel tempered his tone of certainty by reminding everyone that the cooperative still faced an uphill battle: bringing any bill to a vote required immense coordination.

Excitedly, the group began planning their turnout for the next day. Pilar, who was part of the delegation, channeled our collective energy: "As we have done so many times . . . [tomorrow] a minimal guard will stay behind [at the hotel]. . . . We will send text messages . . . and come tomorrow in your [BAUEN] T-shirts."

Another council member chimed in, "What we plan to do is not only organize as many of us as we can but also call all the cooperatives that we can, all the workers, unions, parties, and people who have accompanied us during this time. . . . We have to [have] a little patience. Those of you who are religious, pray, light a candle to the saints." We then took pictures and filmed a

6.2 Members march from Congress after the approval of their bill in the House of Representatives in 2015. Photo by the author.

video appealing for social media followers to join the cause. As the meeting broke up, I overheard one worker assure another, "We need to have faith."

Tensions were high the next day as BAUEN workers and their supporters marched to Congress, blocking traffic and chanting, "Here comes expropriation" to a chorus of car horns and drums (see figure 6.2). After hours of waiting, first in the streets outside Congress and then inside the chamber, the session made quorum. And in a swift move, legislators voted on and passed over ninety bills that the outgoing administration had promised to consider as a single packet. On November 26, 2015, after almost thirteen years of occupation, operation, and struggle, the BAUEN Cooperative achieved a major legislative coup: their bill for expropriation passed in the House of Representatives.

This vote provided a much-needed victory to members of the BAUEN Cooperative and their supporters, yet it was only a partial success. Not until the following year did both houses of Congress approve the expropriation. But by that time conservative politician Mauricio Macri had taken office as the country's president. In the dawning days of 2017, Macri vetoed the bill, asserting that the expropriation would "exclusively favor a small group without translating into benefits for the community in general."[16] Advocates called the decision "cruel," since the positive votes of both houses of Congress had

159

"generated for the workers the expectation of a favorable resolution until the last minute" (Heller 2016).[17] With renewed resolve, the cooperative and its allies in Congress pledged to keep fighting, this time to overturn Macri's veto.

Alternative Organizational Survival

The BAUEN Cooperative kept the hotel open for business throughout these years of temporary successes, empty threats, and judicial and legislative failures. Economic and organizational factors were both critical to its continuity, but neither is sufficient to fully explain why the cooperative survived without the legal right to the property.[18] There are a series of possible explanations.

Within the cooperative the members commonly attributed the longevity of their organization to its ongoing mobilization and broad social and political networks of support. One evening in his office, Daniel assured me, "No one will come after us." He continued:

> After we showed all the power of this cooperative, the social power— because the judges and the old owners of the Bauen saw it clearly—we organized events in the entryway . . . huge demonstrations with four thousand, five thousand people, so they could see that the cooperative had support. I always thought this: if the judge or the police advance on the cooperative . . . How many people are working today? Forty? Fifty? They would take us by the hair and throw us out. But I promise you that in two hours there will be three thousand people at the door ready to stay here until they let us back in.

Daniel was right that the BAUEN Cooperative's social legitimacy, activist networks, and ability to turn out a crowd played a critical role in its survival. The geographic location of the hotel also mattered, as its site—near a major intersection in downtown Buenos Aires—meant that any eviction attempt would be widely visible and well documented by the media.

Another possible explanation for the cooperative's continued operation was that the Argentine state simply didn't have the capacity to actually enforce its laws and eviction orders. This is often the case in what are called "weak" or "failed" states. There are rich and ongoing debates about the extent and impact of institutional weakness in Latin American democracies.[19] But Argentina is *not* a failed state. In response to worker-recuperated businesses alone, legislatures have passed and implemented expropriation bills, police and local leaders have enforced eviction notices, and government ministries have funded loans to support capital investments and business development. All this signals an involvement that cannot be overlooked.

160

We commonly refer to *the state* in the singular, but states are not mono-lithic entities that operate in coordination and with consistency. A better way to think about the state is as a collection of actors that can behave in conflicting and sometimes contradictory ways.[20] The BAUEN Cooperative's interaction with the Argentine state offers a case in point: workers received conflicting signals from a host of state actors, from judges, politicians, and political parties to government bureaucrats in both municipal and national agencies. In short, the BAUEN Cooperative remained in operation not because state actors were unable to enforce the law but because they were unwilling to do so.

Political scientists call this *forbearance*, meaning the intentional tolerance of legal violations for political gain.[21] In her study of informal politics in Latin America, Alisha Holland (2017) argues that forbearance is actually a form of informal welfare provision. Politicians can practice forbearance to signal their commitment to certain groups and thus maximize their electoral power. Given the centrality of private property to capitalist economies, politicians across parties hesitated to expropriate Argentine businesses. Rather than formally le-gitimizing such appeals, state actors—especially those from leftist parties that rely on working-class votes—publicly stated their support for the workers and then used forbearance to allow the BAUEN Cooperative to continue operating. In most cases, they did not make meaningful changes to the law, nor did they set a formal precedent that could be leveraged by others in the future. This deli-cate balance not only sustained a powerful symbol of working-class power but also signaled a commitment to workers' rights and avoided the negative public-ity of a highly visible eviction. Ultimately, the story of the BAUEN Cooperative's efforts to legalize its operations provides up-close insights into the operation not of a weak state but of an *ambivalent* state that simultaneously enforces and violates its own law in the same time and place.[22]

On the Offensive: The Activist Workplace

When unemployed workers in Argentina occupied their former workplaces, they rallied around a slogan adapted from the landless workers' movement: "Occupy, resist, produce." This simple credo outlined the ideal way to recu-perate a business: take over the property, successfully resist eviction, and restart production. In the Hotel Bauen, however, this process was far from linear. Rather, periods of occupation and resistance became a permanent feature of the workplace while the cooperative improvised the provision of hospitality in a legal gray zone.

161

Daniel bluntly described how theories of social change failed to provide practical guidance for the workers. "There aren't 150 Marxist compañeros gathered here to reclaim the means of production," he asserted. "It's almost like we've reformulated what happens when you reach the stage where you have the means of production. What do you become? An activist for the socialist cause? No . . . I don't know about tomorrow, but [it's not like that] today." Rather than following a Marxist prescription for social change, Daniel explained, the cooperative just tried to move forward—and help move the movement forward: "You help other compañeros who are going through the same situation in their cooperative. . . . You want there to be more worker cooperatives."

As Daniel pointed out, the political challenges confronting the hotel had meaningful effects on the inner workings of the business.[23] Workers reached out to others and cultivated networks of support, guidance, and collaboration. Under deep uncertainty, the BAUEN Cooperative's long-term campaign for expropriation prompted workers to transform the hotel into what I call an *activist workplace*, an organization that has integrated social movement practices into its everyday routines. In the recuperated Hotel Bauen, three practices inscribed the operation with this imprimatur: recognizing and compensating activist labor to build networks, merging solidarity practices into work practices, and using the cooperative's broader purpose to maintain member commitment.

Coordinating the Campaign

Upon its formation, the cooperative immediately began the process of legalizing its use of the downtown hotel. It was clear early on that coordinating the campaign for expropriation would be a full-time job, from collaborating with lawyers, politicians, and advocates to writing press releases and organizing marches, rallies, and music festivals. The cooperative thus formalized activist labor into its growing list of paid positions. Early on, three members left other jobs to form a press sector that was housed in a small office on the third floor of the hotel and charged with spearheading political negotiations and public relations (see figure 6.3).[24] Until that point, when the cooperative confronted threats, Daniel told me, "We asked some of the [supportive] organizations if they could send some activists who would sometimes be on guard and keep an eye on the cooperative." But after forming the press sector, the cooperative was able to develop its own strategies to respond.

Creating and maintaining social and political networks was key to these efforts. As one member who worked in the sector explained, "We put in

6.3 Press office in the Hotel Bauen. Photo by the author.

place mechanisms to maintain political relations. During times that were more relaxed . . . you would call a leader or official that you knew like a friend to chat, to see them, for something else [but] not because there was a threat. So we had all the mechanisms to maintain these relationships." The impact of these phone calls was evident in the press releases written and disseminated by the cooperative, many of which directly acknowledged organizations that had shown up in support of the hotel.[25]

Inaugurating the press sector also concentrated the cooperative's political networks and social capital among a smaller cadre of workers who quickly gained experience as public-facing representatives. Many members and even elected council members felt as though they didn't have the "words" to go in front of politicians and reporters on behalf of the group, and so this centralization helped the cooperative to clearly articulate its identity to the public. Often that meant drawing a stark comparison between worker control and private management. Illustrating a recurring theme of the public-facing messaging, one press release stated, "In contrast to [the former owners], we have

163

opened the hotel without any loans and created more than 140 jobs. At the same time, we have transformed [the hotel] into a public space open to society." Constructing what social movement scholars would call a "diagnostic frame" (Benford and Snow 2000), the BAUEN Cooperative explained its problem and apportioned blame not to state actors but to corrupt businesspeople using their power and resources to undermine working-class jobs.

Responding to each threatened closure, legislative delay, and political setback, members in the press sector distributed press releases and held rallies. At every turn, they amplified their cause and defined the organization as a *worker-managed hotel with a social purpose*. Lacunza made this clear: "We had to go out in the street, organize marches, and try to constantly put the Bauen in the public opinion, [to] show that there was a conflict . . . [to show] why we were doing this, how we were establishing our conduct, why we said that 'the Bauen belongs to the people' [*el Bauen es de todos*]."

In communicating the cooperative's identity, workers also made the case that the expropriation of the hotel was, in fact, a public issue. Tomás explained, "The internal message is that this is everyone's struggle. The BAUEN is not just the Bauen, but it's also the Bauen of the people." Lacunza echoed many of the cooperative's press releases when he justified why the public should support the BAUEN in practical terms: "[It's] because this hotel was built with state-financed loans. That is, most of us who pay taxes are involved in this. So more than just the internal fight here, we also have to keep in mind that the struggle is continued by many compañeros and others who are building pressure. Because here there are debts that are still visible to the government . . . and there is a pressure to make them pay." By positioning the cooperative as ensuring that the law would be upheld on behalf of the people, the workers clearly identified the protagonists and antagonists in their fight. The common phrase Lacunza used—"the Bauen belongs to the people"—intentionally asserted the cooperative's active role in building a broader movement for justice.

Members working in the press sector strategically leveraged the hotel's resources to support their campaign. Daniel, who worked in the press sector at one point, explained, "Here we have a hotel, so it's a lot easier to organize an activity than it would be in a factory." By way of example, he said, "Tomorrow . . . we are organizing an event in the auditorium that's really important because there are four speakers: one is the general secretary of the CTA [Central Workers Union], another is a city representative, [and] the other two are economists." Using the space to benefit activists and social movement organizations was just one way they blended hospitality and activist work and shored up the cooperative's image as a public good.

164

At a practical level, hosting such events was made possible by the hotel's amenities, from its auditorium and ballrooms to its guest rooms and supporting facilities. But unless they worked overtime shifts (described in chapter 5), only a handful of members stayed after their long days to participate in these events. Referring again to that evening's panel, Daniel said, "As we say here, it's really tough on us [*nos cuesta un huevo*] to attend a panel like this. So many times people have criticized me: 'You have the Bauen, you have the auditorium, and the workers don't participate [in the events].' And I always tell them, 'The workers are waiting to finish their shifts to go home, to see their family, play sports, watch television. This is their job. . . . [T]hey don't want to stay three more hours at work to go to a talk or a workshop.'" Unless they were on the clock, it was primarily council members or press sector workers who stayed to attend these events. I understood the time pressures all too well: my careful field notes brimmed with records of my long hours balancing shift work with attending events and following the political campaign. On the day of the panel that Daniel described, for instance, I worked in the hotel from 11 a.m. to 6 p.m., ate dinner in the staff kitchen, and then attended the panel discussion, which lasted until nearly 10 p.m. By the time I arrived home and wrote my field note, I had only a couple of hours left before I was scheduled to be back at the hotel.

The Service of Solidarity

Members of the BAUEN Cooperative knew that they were uniquely positioned to support social movements and other cooperatives—and they soon became known for their commitment to hospitality *and* solidarity.[26] In a congressional hearing, a politician emphasized this on the cooperative's behalf: "The Bauen [is] a place where popular organizations of all types [gather] without discrimination of any kind. Sometimes they need a space to host their activities, to stay when people come from the interior or other places. With all the effort that it represents, the Bauen is always open and available."

The cooperative's first commitment was to support its community, including members and their families, other cooperatives and community organizations, and the movement of worker-recuperated businesses. This frequently meant sharing collective assets so that, for example, BAUEN workers covering late shifts could stay for free in a hotel room rather than commute home. Members' family and friends could also stay at the hotel for a discounted rate (see chapter 5 for more on the practice of extending various forms of credit). In its early days, a group of young people, many the sons and daughters of longtime Hotel Bauen employees, even moved into the

165

tower to form a twenty-four-hour guard in case of eviction. Over time, and as this threat became less imminent, other members moved in with the approval of the administrative council in exchange for a small monthly rent.[27] For nearly a decade, the cooperative allowed members to actually live on certain floors of the hotel that had not yet been renovated for guests.

The BAUEN Cooperative further built community by offering discounted solidarity rates to nonprofits, community organizations, and other cooperatives. This practice started early on. In a news report recognizing the second anniversary of the occupation, a member of the FaSinPat, the cooperative that had recuperated the Zanon tile factory in the south of Argentina, recalled, "When we came from Neuquén for our [political] struggle, and we didn't have a place to spend the night, they [the members of the BAUEN Cooperative] offered the hotel. Although there was no light or hot water, we stayed there anyway."[28]

Over a decade later, this practice had been formalized in the hotel's official room rates. A member who worked in sales explained, "We have a special rate as part of the policy so that cooperatives can come and get to know us." During times of need, the BAUEN Cooperative would often arrange last-minute lodging for other cooperatives' workers, even absorbing the cost of their rooms from time to time. One day, a member of a different cooperative arrived for a last-minute stay in the hotel. Council members introduced me to the guest, who then nervously asked about payment. A council member assured him that he didn't need to pay for their room: "When you're in a time of need, you need to focus on what is important instead of worrying about money."

Solidarity also pushed the cooperative to specifically tailor its lodging for a working-class clientele. Through their collaboration with government agencies, many guests in the hotel were people who traveled to the capital city for medical procedures and stayed at a discounted rate. This service of solidarity, proudly documented in the cooperative's annual reports, extended beyond the hotel's facilities. Members of the BAUEN Cooperative also created organizations to provide resources for worker-recuperated businesses and cooperatives across the country. At the end of 2006, for example, BAUEN workers formed the Argentine Federation of Cooperatives of Self-Managed Workers (FACTA) to support democratic, participative, and self-managed organizations through training, technical guidance, and funding.[29] In the years since, the cooperative maintained close ties to FACTA. Not only did its workers serve on the leadership council, but FACTA's national headquarters and small staff were housed in the Hotel Bauen. Among a handful of secondary and tertiary organizations formed to support worker self-management,

6.4 Members of the Hotel Bauen at a 2014 rally for expropriation.
Photo by Martin Barzilai/Sub Cooperative.

FACTA and its peers set their sights on promoting cooperative businesses and changing the laws under which they operated (proposing, for instance, legislation to modify national laws regulating bankruptcy, communications, and cooperatives).[30]

Commitment and Community

The third way that the BAUEN Cooperative merged activist practices and everyday business was by using its broader purpose to sustain member commitment. In this activist organization, members learned about and embraced the political dimension of their work through active participation not only in everyday tasks, as I described in chapter 3, but also in its expropriation campaign (see figure 6.4). Recall the work of Rosabeth Moss Kanter, who emphasizes the critical role of commitment in community-building efforts.[31] In the Hotel Bauen, members gained clear "purpose, direction, and meaning" through their involvement in the political dealings of the cooperative and the broader social movement of worker-recuperated businesses (Kanter 1972, 70).[32] Among longtime members, the ties between commitment and contentious politics were obvious. One memorably called protest a "tool of inclusion" with "an energy . . . [that] carries you forward."

The Activist Workplace

After the flurry of activity in 2015 with the passage of the expropriation bill, longtime members reflected on their political cause. During a lull in the lobby, Matías told me, "It's like I said the other day, when we went to Congress with all the new guys. It's likely that it was the first time in their lives that they had entered the national Congress, you know?" He paused before asking hypothetically, "What worker goes to Congress? Very few. So these things have an enormous value for us. You can only live in a cooperative and in self-management, there isn't another way for everything that we've gone through. . . . That's why I always encourage the new guys to join in. They have to go so they can feel what we feel." Matías wanted new members in particular to develop an affective commitment to the collective by "feeling what we feel." That way, they could develop a sense of belonging by forming emotional ties to their coworkers and the cooperative as a whole.[33]

Víctor also underlined the importance of the political campaign in forming emotional bonds: "When there was an eviction order, there wasn't a structure or hierarchy. . . . It was like . . . we were all equal. There we were brothers, friends; friendship prevailed; we were all like one, like a mass." The moments of group cohesion formed a pleasant memory for Víctor, who mused, "You know when you are part of a group and you all feel seen? Everyone moves in the same way, and it's really nice . . . all for a moment . . . it's all love and peace. But then it's like, it goes back to how it was, that's it."

A newer member of the cooperative, Alan, captured what many others described during the course of my fieldwork: "What impacts me the most as a member of the cooperative is how we have gone to marches and all those types of things. It's like throughout the year, you have differences, you get in fights, you have all kinds of situations here inside [the cooperative]. But when we have a problem [threat], it's like we all come together. . . . It unites you, and it's nice to live that because differences are left aside and we can all go in the same direction." Under threat, members of the cooperative came together in defense of their work. And in times of relative calm, the cooperative's support for and hosting of community events and social groups were constant reminders that even the normal operation of the hotel was, in its way, political participation.

Lacunza, whom you first met in chapter 1, was a founding member with a long history in the hotel. He explained, "My really active participation began when we started working with other cooperatives and, well, we had to go out and make our appeal and show a lot of things. . . . You had to talk with politicians . . . social organizations . . . sociologists." We smiled at each other as he referred to my academic discipline. He continued, "It's a job [that requires] a lot of activism. . . . You had to be polished and do it well for the other recuperated businesses and cooperatives that were going through this situation too."

As you might have also noticed in these quotes, working in the Hotel Bauen was a source of deep pride for many of its members. While some publicly professed this pride in interviews and at events, many others shared these feelings with me unprompted. Romina, for example, told me about a day that her daughter had come to work with her. As they passed through the lobby, a customer asked Romina about the cooperative and told her that he thought it was an example to the world. Her daughter had heard the whole thing. "Who can say that to their kids?" she mused with a smile.

Sitting in the administrative council's office, Pilar, the president of the cooperative, used similar terms and marveled from behind her dark mahogany desk: "I never thought that I would be here . . . sitting in the same chair as such a powerful businessman and that a worker like myself would be leading a genuine cooperative from the same desk where he sat." She added, "It's really powerful, and sometimes it's like . . . I can't believe it . . . because I'm just a simple worker."

This chapter chronicled the BAUEN Cooperative's long-term campaign to legalize its occupation and operation of the iconic downtown hotel. Through this effort, "simple workers" have meaningfully impacted other recuperated and cooperative businesses as well as state policy, public perception, and visions of how work can be reorganized to promote the public good. Despite operating in a legal gray zone until its closure in 2020 during the global pandemic, the BAUEN Cooperative experienced remarkable success. It stayed open for eighteen years because the cooperative was able to form an *activist workplace* where productive and activist labor combined to help transform the meanings and practices of paid work.

The cooperative's political trials and tribulations are critical because, in addition to addressing the legal right to use the hotel, they have iteratively shaped the internal dynamics of its equality project. Taking a job at the Hotel Bauen provided both a source of work and inside access to a social movement that actively questioned the legitimacy of private property and challenged the role of the state. As the cooperative navigated its way through a legal gray zone, it integrated social movement practices into everyday work routines. After occupying the hotel in 2003, the BAUEN Cooperative pursued its own fight while also establishing the Hotel Bauen as a hub for

169

social movements and other cooperatives. Its unique amenities and strong ties to the activist community ultimately made this illegally occupied tower a place where social movement organizations, cooperatives, and community groups gathered to coordinate their own efforts. Ultimately, the equality project that workers developed within the towering walls of the hotel extended outward, politicizing their labor and extending their fight for justice beyond the workplace.

Chapter Six

The type of dreaming that appeals to me has nothing to do with reverie, an idle daydream. It isn't wishful thinking. Nor is it the type of revelation reserved for the great ones and rightly called vision. What I speak of is a brand of imaginative thinking backed by enthusiasm, vitality, expectation, to which all [people] may aspire.

—CONRAD HILTON, *Be My Guest*

Conclusions

At the beginning of this book, I argued that both scholars and workers must think about *work* in political terms. It's worth repeating here: our labor is political. There are serious inconsistencies between our rights as citizens and our rights as workers. In democratic political systems like those in Argentina and the United States, opportunities to participate abound across public life.[1] But even in democracies, most of us work under authoritarian regimes. Our bosses have unaccountable power over our lives and livelihoods. We have little stake in the organizations for which we labor. And we rarely have a meaningful say in the decisions that shape our working lives. So what does it look like when businesses seek to democratize work?

This book delved into one such case: a worker-run, worker-recuperated business that occupied and restarted an iconic Argentine hotel. I detailed the ways that members of the BAUEN Cooperative transformed their workplace over nearly two decades of operation and focused on their emergent *equality project*—tracing efforts to promote more egalitarian interactions by revaluing authority, skill, and value at work. In this worker-run hotel, members made decisions democratically, participated extensively in hospitality, rotated jobs requiring widely varying skills, and even maintained a policy of equal pay.

For countless reasons, experiences like those I documented in the Hotel Bauen may seem impossible. As workers converted the hotel into a cooperative, they transformed nearly every aspect of work, from the way they cleaned guest rooms to how they made the most important business decisions. This is certainly an extreme case. But when we stop to think about what could be possible in other businesses, I wonder if the hang-up is not the practicalities of it all but our imagination. Even Conrad Hilton himself, the founder of the multinational chain of Hilton hotels, whom we met in the introduction, made a similar point. In his memoir he acknowledges that prayer and hard work—the pillars of his life—are not enough to explain his success. The missing piece, he reveals, is "*You had to dream!*" (Hilton 1994, 21).

Hilton might have been appalled that workers occupied and restarted a downtown hotel without a boss. But he did not discount the importance of the type of dreaming described in the epigraph: "a brand of imaginative thinking backed by enthusiasm, vitality, expectation" (23).[2] The framework of equality projects will help us take dreams seriously to understand such efforts to reimagine work.

Work, Reimagined

Understanding the causes and consequences of inequality is a defining task of social science research. We often focus on diagnosing and critiquing inequalities in access to respect, resources, and rewards.[3] But this doesn't necessarily shed light on how to reduce inequality, let alone *promote equality* in society. Equality may seem like a simple idea, yet the concept is ripe for rethinking.[4] Rather than understanding equality as the absence of individual difference, a sociological approach takes equality as a relational concept enacted in interactions between people. Equality is not the simple absence of inequality. Rather, the unequal social conditions we deem unjust deeply inform our visions of—and actions toward—more equitable social arrangements.

172

Too often we as workers are used to a status quo in which we opt for different types of jobs (and are excluded from others), have unequal access to power and authority, and expect wide wage disparities. These differences in access, opportunity, and reward are not random. Where a person comes from, how much their parents earned, and myriad other factors influence career opportunities and life chances. Decades of social science research have also established that race and gender are enormously consequential in our working lives (with a cascade of attendant consequences for social mobility): women and racial-minority men—even those with similar experience and education—have fewer opportunities to advance than white men.

Ultimately, we make countless justifications for these arrangements, some of which are widely accepted, and others, more suspect. Our collective values are wrapped up in these understandings of the social order. For example, we might reject outright discrimination and try to root out persistent biases while also accepting that workers have little say in their organizations and that people are paid vastly different salaries for the same hours of labor. By studying equality projects, we are better equipped to make sense of the ways that cultural ideals shape efforts to promote justice at work.

Lessons Learned

My extensive research in the BAUEN Cooperative offers three main lessons. First and most fundamentally, organizations can and do change. In ownership, authority, and the division of labor, the BAUEN Cooperative completely transformed the governance and management of a downtown hotel. According to workers' firsthand accounts, the paternalistic boss who oversaw the strict managerial regime that characterized the Hotel Bauen in the late twentieth century would have found the operation unrecognizable by the 2010s. This speaks to a broader point regarding organizations: when we study them as stable and unchanging entities, we risk missing both the enormous potential for and the actual implementation of change. Serious engagement with these ideas requires reimagining organizations as dynamic configurations of resources, people, and positions—a reconceiving that is not so different from how the cooperative I studied reorganized the workplace.

Worker-recuperated businesses in Argentina are certainly an extreme case of organizational change. But as Katherine Chen (2016) points out, extreme cases can help build social theory by rendering the invisible visible. Unlike conventional organizations, worker-recuperated businesses have not one but *two* founding moments: the creation of the original privately owned

173

firm and the subsequent formation of a worker cooperative. As I described in chapter 1, the BAUEN Cooperative's founders drew on the technical, political, and cultural resources available to them to reorganize the hotel under worker control. But rather than being confined to the previous order, they leveraged their experiences laboring under a boss and being fired amid economic upheaval to inspire, justify, and *reimprint* a new way of doing business. This is a radical yet attainable shift.

Over time, workers founded the BAUEN Cooperative and created a hybrid organization, adopting the regularity and predictability of bureaucracy to create jobs and stay open for business while also implementing collectivist practices to realize their shared commitment to democracy, solidarity, and self-management. This points to a second important takeaway from this book: both formal *and* informal dynamics matter.

At the Hotel Bauen, I documented how the cooperative broadly distributed power, opportunities, and resources to facilitate relations of equality among its members. The formalization of political equality was critical to organizing and sustaining workplace democracy. In some ways, the hierarchy of elected officers, managers, and coordinators in the BAUEN Cooperative looked much like the structure of work in a conventional hotel. But rather than vest absolute authority in positions, the cooperative asserted that the Workers Assembly held collective power over all major decisions. And this was not just symbolic: in chapter 2 I described how the membership actively exercised its ability to appeal any and all decisions made by elected officers or appointed managers.

The cooperative's equality project was inscribed in its formal workplace policies, such as democratic voting and an equal base pay rate. But in other respects, the workers very much *resisted* the creation of prescriptive standards and inflexible rules to govern their distributive efforts. As I traced how and why the cooperative codified some aspects of its operations and finances and not others, for instance, I was able to see firsthand how this selective formalization of workplace democracy enabled a functioning organizational culture and such regular exceptions to the rules.

This selective formalization had different consequences for the cooperative's efforts to reorganize hospitality work. The practice of job rotation provided a case in point. In chapter 4 I described how members rotated jobs, which offered them unprecedented opportunities to learn new skills and develop a more holistic understanding of the organization as a whole. Through job rotation, members could re-sort themselves in the workplace and even disrupt gendered patterns of occupational segregation. The deci-

sion to rotate jobs was often motivated by very practical personal and organizational needs. But the practice was also a way for members to reduce
the isolation, exhaustion, and alienation that come with different forms of
physical, intellectual, and emotional labor. Nearly all members rotated jobs
at some point in their careers in the Hotel Bauen. But no formal policy codified how these opportunities were made available. As a result, some members felt disregarded, penalized, or punished if their requests to rotate were
denied or when they were sent to a different sector without having a say in
that change. Ultimately, the lack of formalization around who could rotate
and when made room for inequalities to persist despite this practice's simul-
taneous leveling effect.

This brings me to my third and final point. Many of the practices documented in this book addressed the material foundations of inequality in the
BAUEN Cooperative. Members had identical equity stakes, an equal vote,
and the same base wage. But this equality project also reverberated through
an organizational culture marked by an egalitarian ethos that shaped interpersonal dynamics. In chapter 3 I examined how members integrated as
compañeros into the culture of the cooperative. This process involved not
just joining but being recognized and respected within the group. To convey
these cultural expectations, members of the BAUEN Cooperative envisioned
an ideal worker: someone who was self-motivated, deeply committed, and
had developed a consciousness of work as a political act. While the assumptions around this cultural imaginary looked very different from the starkly
gendered and racialized expectations of many conventional workplaces,
being the ideal self-managed worker continued to demand long hours, personal sacrifice, and political commitment, which was much less possible for
members with outside responsibilities or differing worldviews.

Research on worker cooperatives has long found that members of collectivist organizations tend to be likeminded and demographically similar.
To explain this in-group preference, scholars have focused on the need for
consensus, which often demands that members share underlying moral commitments. As Joyce Rothschild observed in her classic article on collectivist-
democratic organizations, "Unified action is possible only if individuals
substantially agree with the goals and processes of the collective" (Rothschild-
Whitt 1979, 520). Bureaucratic organizations can accommodate greater diversity, owing to the command of authority and the incentives of remuneration,
while collectivist organizations require a degree of homogeneity. My research   175
in Argentina offers an additional explanation for the tendency toward homogeneity, demonstrating that the BAUEN Cooperative constructed and

relied on an image of an ideal worker to direct the process of workplace integration—to help turn workers into compañeros.

Equality projects require ongoing relational work to revalue the categories that orient social practice. As I described in chapter 2, members of the BAUEN Cooperative not only practiced workplace democracy but also collectively negotiated the meanings of fairness bound up in those practices. Take the cooperative's elections. Beyond the policies for meeting and voting to elect the next administrative council, I witnessed weeks of deliberation over what constituted a fair election and how members should think about their democratic participation. These debates were prompted not by policy implementation but by something that many have argued is detrimental to work culture: *rumors*.

Research on informal communication often attributes the existence of workplace rumors to a lack of transparency—higher-level employees closely guard bureaucratic secrets, leaving room for lower-level employees to speculate about processes they are not allowed to shape. But in the BAUEN Cooperative, where members had extensive access to official information and decisions, rumors flourished. As I traced fleeting rumors throughout my time in the field, I found that rumors constituted both a form of collective surveillance and an informal accountability mechanism for elected officers.

Informal dynamics and communication channels were critical to ensuring and upholding the core practices of workplace democracy at the Hotel Bauen. In conversations that unfolded throughout the workday, members deliberated on the purposes and consequences of their organizational practices, shared information relevant to collective decision-making, and ultimately kept their leaders accountable to the group as a whole. Rather than simply undermining formal practices or reproducing inequalities, informal workplace dynamics were key to understanding the interactive labor behind the cooperative's equality project.

This was particularly clear in debates about wages and value that spilled out of formal assemblies and into the halls of the hotel. As I explained in chapter 5, from its inception the BAUEN Cooperative paid all its members the same base rate. I traced how, over time, the group created and justified small differences in pay that introduced a degree of discrepancy in wages. While these changes introduced differences, they were bounded and transparent: all members knew the values of different types of work and the reasoning behind them.

176   The organization's commitment to equal pay had both material impacts and symbolic repercussions. The cooperative valued its members equally not just in discourse but also in material rewards. Women and men, older and

younger people, and founders and new members were compensated as equals. By equalizing purchasing power (which, importantly, is different from equalizing pay), the cooperative took meaningful steps to level symbolic power, a key equality-producing process. Of course, dissent and concern about the policy of equal pay remained as members worried about differences in commitment, hours, and effort. These daily debates arguably served to motivate members to contribute their fair share and discourage free riding, again using informal communication as a source of social control.

The ongoing conversations about equal pay also spurred a unique organizational effort to reimagine wages. The cooperative constantly tried to increase pay, just as it implemented compensatory innovations to address the common pressures of low-wage service work. As I described in chapter 5, the cooperative's system of *survival finance* was based on a broad view of the resources with which it could compensate its members. Money wages were important, but for the BAUEN Cooperative, so too was the ability to provide access to zero-interest loans, bulk-buying benefits, and a system for banking future paid time off. In combination, these forms of compensation meaningfully changed the experience of work. Whereas extensive research on work in the twenty-first century has documented trends that have made service work even more precarious (tendencies toward ever-longer hours, lower pay, and irregular hours and schedules), the notion of survival finance provides a way to discuss organizations' creative nonwage attempts to fairly compensate low-wage laborers. This, of course, is no substitute for living wages, benefits, and a robust social safety net. But given the structural constraints on the BAUEN Cooperative, the organization prioritized helping its members make ends meet and ultimately making work *work* for them.

Equality Projects

Equality is often thought of as an ideal or value in the domain of philosophers and activists. In this book I argued that equality is also a meaningful sociological concept that begs empirical study. Equality is not a preexisting, objective "thing" to uncover but rather a context-specific and ultimately plastic social construction. We thus need to document and analyze *equality projects*, efforts to promote more egalitarian relations between people by reorganizing and revaluing the categories that orient social action.

Sociologists are well equipped to examine how people interpret and act in situations they define as just or unjust. But we need to broaden our conversation from an almost exclusive focus on inequality to include the study of equality projects. This is not a singular task but part of a broader trend toward the development of problem-solving sociology and emancipatory social science. Erik Olin Wright (2006, 94) describes this as a mandate "to generate knowledge relevant to the collective project of challenging human oppression and creating the conditions in which people can live flourishing lives."[5]

The case of the Hotel Bauen highlights a series of equality-producing processes that help explain how organizations promote justice at work. The first involves shifting power. Organizations that are collectively owned fundamentally reshape the classic capitalist arrangement of work based on domination. Rather than extracting value from another person's labor, the process of *inclusion* distributes power by integrating people into the value they add to a group. A second key process relates to how we share opportunities and resources. Scholars have identified opportunity hoarding as a key mechanism of social closure that explains how and why inequality persists. My research signaled that this process is not unidirectional. People can also share resources with those outside their network by engaging in *opportunity distribution*. Finally, equality projects involve addressing the cultural meanings that justify what we do. A third equality-producing process, *symbolic leveling*, refers to the discursive emphasis on peoples' equivalent ability to participate in decision-making, learn new skills, and contribute value to a group. Taken together, these concepts hold theoretical and practical value, sensitizing us to generic processes that explain the production of relational equality and also signaling ways to reconfigure power, distribute opportunity across difference, and change cultural meanings.

Efforts to produce equality populate many realms of society, from intimate relationships and families to schools, organizations, and governments. In worker cooperatives, equality projects tend to be readily evident, developed, negotiated, and codified in organizational practice over time. Yet equality projects are not limited to instances of worker ownership. Traditional businesses can also more broadly distribute access to power, opportunities, and resources. Many companies, for example, have replaced the command-and-control mentality of bureaucratic management with a greater emphasis on participatory and team-based work arrangements.[6] Others have adopted employee ownership, profit sharing, and other forms of shared capitalism.[7] Some of these are certainly veiled efforts to increase productivity without extending rewards.[8] Yet other undertakings not only improve work conditions but allow for important and possibly transformative deliberation over the legitimacy of differences in pay, authority, and recognition.[9] Divergent types of organizations can teach each other a great deal about promoting equality in practice, no matter how fundamentally different they may appear.

Asking and answering normative questions about what is *good* and *just* is hugely important to understanding social change and advancing movements for justice.[10] As I finish writing in late 2021, democracy is under threat. Corporations and the billionaires who make up the "1 percent" hold a disproportionate amount of resources and power to influence our democratic institutions. Around the globe, populist movements (on both the right and the left) are undermining the validity and viability of representative democracy by drumming up support for ideologues whose leadership degrades the value of civil deliberation and prevents the construction of coalitions across difference. Simultaneously, social movements are passionately advocating for social change, broader distributions of power, and equality along multiple axes. As protesters decrying police violence and racial injustice marched in cities across the United States, organizers in Argentina mobilized to demand women's rights and an end to gender-based violence through the Ni Una Menos (Not One More) campaign. Structural forces and institutions may seem intractable, but there are countless examples of peoples' remarkable efforts to imagine a more just and equal world. This is ongoing work, and it is largely coordinated through unpaid labor atop subsistence employment.

The problem is that we don't usually think about our workplaces as sites of social struggle. For most, activism is separate from employment. But we are also witnessing major changes in employment relations. Entrepreneurship is a rising cultural ideal, and workers are encouraged to follow their passion and "reinvent themselves" as the once expected relationship of employer responsibility erodes amid the disappearance of retirement, seniority, and retention efforts. Lifetime careers are a thing of the past. "Bullshit jobs" proliferate.[11] And novel employment models like gig work are changing familiar ways of working and frequently amplifying the precarity of the 99 percent.

What if we directed this momentum not exclusively to making a profit for a few but to improving work for many? Worker cooperatives offer one way to harness collective power to change our everyday working conditions. Most businesses today are drivers of inequality. Research on alternative work organizations teaches us that businesses can also be *radical levelers* that adopt equality projects to broadly distribute power and opportunity, redirect resources to promote relational equality, and ultimately change the rules of the game.[12] Rather than limit ourselves to "narrowly pragmatic reforms," we should make what Kathi Weeks (2011, 176) calls "utopian demands" to transform

179

the present configuration of employment relations.[13] This must happen at multiple levels, from individual homes and workplaces to collective appeals to state actors that play such an important role in the fate of cooperative businesses.

All of this requires zooming out, yet again, to think about social change. I often return to Karl Marx's famous quote: "People make their own history, but under circumstances existing already, given and transmitted from the past."[14] Who we are, where we come from, and what happens in the world all shape our opportunities to make our own history. As we saw in the Hotel Bauen, the spirits of the past manifested in old ways of doing and thinking about work, while hope for the future drove the vision and practice of the cooperative's equality project. Economists and social scientists may often assume otherwise, but people don't make economic and organizational decisions as rational actors with full information. Rather, we are motivated to act based on an imagined future state informed by incomplete information, cultural scripts, and our sense of the possible. Jens Beckert (2016) argues that these fictional expectations appear as stories, theories, and discourses that can constrain us *and* provide a source of creativity.[15] In thinking about equality, the word *project* captures this future-casting—we project into the future and we undertake projects to get there. Like real utopias guided by "dreams and practice," equality projects are shaped by our ability to imagine—despite the cliché—that another world is possible (Wright 2010, 4).

The BAUEN Cooperative was never isolated from the world around it. Its members weathered political blows, economic turmoil, and a global pandemic. And its equality project was never finalized, even if I hoped to write a tidy concluding chapter. The Uruguayan writer Eduardo Galeano's (2020) poem "Window on Utopia" offers an alternative perspective on such equality projects:

> She lies on the horizon . . .
> I walk two steps, she moves two steps away.
> I walk ten steps and the horizon runs ten steps ahead.
> No matter how much I walk, I'll never reach her.
> What good is utopia? That's what: it's good for walking.

Equality is not an end state. It is a guide for directing action. It is my hope that the possibilities and pitfalls of working for justice revealed in my account of the Hotel Bauen become landmarks along the way.

Epilogue: Surviving (Another) Crisis

In March 2020 the BAUEN Cooperative celebrated its seventeenth year operating without a boss. But the anniversary of this iconic Buenos Aires hotel was muted by news that would reshape people's lives around the world: we were entering a global pandemic as COVID-19 rapidly spread.

From my home in Texas, I exchanged messages with longtime friends and respondents in Buenos Aires. "How are you? Is everyone safe?" My US state's response to the pandemic was lax in comparison to that of the Argentine capital, which had entered a full lockdown. Residents observed mandatory isolation in their homes and ventured out only in their neighborhoods and to shop for basic supplies like food and medications. Movement

Epi.1. The shuttered entrance in November 2020 after workers vacated the downtown hotel. Photo by BAUEN Cooperative.

was restricted, and businesses shut down. Hotels were also ordered to close. During the first weeks of the pandemic, the Hotel Bauen remained open with a skeleton staff, accommodating the handful of travelers in the city for medical procedures or other approved exceptions. Eventually, following state orders, the cooperative closed the facility (*Clarín* 2020).

In 2020 the Argentine government passed a series of measures to support struggling businesses and people out of work owing to the pandemic. But cooperative organizations did not receive adequate lifelines.[1] As the months passed, the BAUEN Cooperative's situation became increasingly untenable. With the hotel still closed for business, debts piled up as revenues tanked. By August the situation was desperate, so the cooperative organized an online fundraiser streamed live through Facebook. Three days of musical and artistic performances were punctuated by appeals to donate directly to the cooperative using the hashtag #TodxsConElBAUEN. I tuned in from Texas. But the fundraiser wasn't enough.

Weeks later, the members decided, mournfully, to close the Hotel Bauen's doors and sell off some of the hard-earned assets they had invested in over the years (see figure Epi.1). The cooperative's current president told a local news outlet, "We always said that this building was the state's, but because we didn't have a resolution, we need to support our source of work. . . . It's a really distressing situation because the debt to our suppliers is large. We can't run this place."[2] She shared the interview with me over WhatsApp, part of a longrunning conversation that would continue through the tough decisions ahead.

Many of the challenges I outlined in chapter 6 are unique to worker-recuperated businesses and the Hotel Bauen in particular. The global pandemic, however, is all-inclusive. The hotel industry has been one of the hardest hit by the travel restrictions, prohibitions on group gatherings, and local public health efforts to stop the spread of COVID-19. By the end of 2020, 40 percent of hotel workers in the United States were out of a job, and hotel occupancy rates were well below 50 percent (Uhler 2020). In Buenos Aires just 1 percent of the thousand-plus hotels in the city were open for business in September 2020, and many shuttered hotels have now been listed for sale (*El Observador del Sur* 2020).

The years since I completed fieldwork for this book have also been marked by a series of additional challenges. In 2019, I returned to Buenos Aires to revisit the hotel and share my work with my respondents. As I checked in for my first stay as a guest in the Hotel Bauen, I discovered that the majority of the people I had worked with in 2015 were still active members of the cooperative. I was generously received by the cooperative, taking up residence in a small room with two single beds on an upper floor of the tower. I slept and ate in the hotel for three weeks, reconnecting with workers, sharing my research findings, and keeping my promise to remain in touch. Occupancy and events continued in much the same way as I had observed during my previous periods of fieldwork. But life inside and outside the hotel felt dramatically changed.

Even before the pandemic brought the country to a screeching halt, the cooperative's hard-fought effort to expropriate the hotel had been vetoed at the highest level of power (see chapter 6). Under the leadership of then-president Mauricio Macri, cooperatives and alternative organizations lacked political support amid the economic policies of *macrismo*, grappling with everything from changes to tax policies and utility regulation to increased scrutiny over businesses' daily operations.[3]

What's more, this political drama unfolded amid broader economic troubles and rising inflation. In 2015 when I exited the field, the official exchange rate was approximately AR$5 to US$1. In 2018 the Argentine peso lost about half its value on the dollar, and by my visit in 2019, the exchange rate was shockingly close to AR$20 to US$1. Because of currency issues, prices for everyday goods crept up while wages stayed more or less the same.

The social impacts of this economic reality were visible on the streets. One evening in 2019, when I stepped out of the hotel to take a walk in the Congreso neighborhood, I passed by three young children curled up under blankets. There, in the shadow of the Hotel Bauen, they huddled as their mother kept a watchful eye on a stroller overflowing with their belongings. I would see them there nearly every night for the duration of my stay, a living, breathing reminder of the impact of official statistics: about a third of Argentines lived in poverty, and the number of people living in "extreme poverty" in Buenos Aires doubled between 2015 and 2018, to reach 6.5 percent.[4]

In the BAUEN Cooperative, workers had expanded their practices of survival finance (see chapter 5). They converted an unfinished basement room into a fully stocked general store specifically for co-op members, which they jokingly called the *almacén* (food pantry). Other unused spaces in the hotel had also been converted to support community members and generate additional income streams. Alongside the cooperative federations that had operated out of offices in the hotel for some time, the building was now home to a host of newer worker cooperatives, including an alternative newspaper (*La Garganta Poderosa*), a fair-trade store, and a theater collective (El Descubridor).[5] Members now described the hotel as a "cooperative complex" that sustained not only the livelihoods of the hotel workers but also a whole network of organizations of self-managed workers.

The future of the BAUEN Cooperative remains uncertain at the time of writing. Before the cooperative's public announcement that they would vacate the property, members told me privately that they intended to continue working together. It would just be in another location. Once they announced the news, the cooperative's president told a reporter, "We know the world is reinventing itself, and that's why we are looking for other spaces, but we will continue with the cooperative to maintain our sources of work. So much struggle and so many sacrifices, so many times that we invested in this building instead of buying bread. It's really sad, but we will continue in another place. There were many years of struggle, of joy, and of marches under the workers' flag. My pride is that we are going to continue working and that the compañeros are not going to be left without food in their house."[6] By 2021 there was no sign that this vision might become a reality, especially as subsequent waves of COVID-19 prompted new restrictions on movement in Buenos Aires.

Does this mean that the BAUEN Cooperative's equality project was a failure? My answer to this question is an emphatic *no*. We tend to judge a business's success by its profitability and longevity. Indeed, the vast majority of research on recuperated businesses (and organizations in general) focuses on "successful" cases that were able to stay open for business. But as María Inés Fernández Álvarez (2012, 3) reminds us, focusing exclusively on the ability to compete in a capitalist market glosses over "the potential of these experiences as spaces of political construction." Those who study alternative organizations often highlight different metrics of "success," emphasizing an organization's role in developing nonmarket logics like cooperation, reciprocity, and redistribution.[7] Beyond questions about productivity and profit, has an organization promoted cooperation? Supported and motivated its members? Cultivated networks within the community? The BAUEN Cooperative may be closed for business, but the impact of its equality project fundamentally changed the way that workers in the hotel related to each other and themselves. Moreover, the BAUEN Cooperative's equality project had reverberating effects, extending outward to tackle inequalities beyond the workplace. In its last years, this became even clearer as other cooperatives moved into the space and joined the effort to create a cooperative hub in the center of the city. This, in my mind, does not constitute a failure. It's an impetus to reconsider what we mean by success.

In 2020, when they vacated the hotel, members of the BAUEN Cooperative published an open letter to the public. Rather than using poetry, as I did in my original conclusion to this book, the workers included the lyrics of a ballad by Attaque 77, an Argentine rock band that had vocally supported the cooperative and even performed at some of its most memorable events. After promising "This is only a short pause," the cooperative quoted:

> A thousand years may pass,
> You will see many fall,
> But if we come together
> They will not stop us.[8]

According to the letter, this "working-class symphony"—so "embedded in the walls of the hotel and in the folds of our memories"—had guided the cooperative over its seventeen years as a worker-recuperated business.[9] Whether and how the BAUEN Cooperative will reinvent itself remains to be seen. But if their history is any guide, these skillful and innovative people will continue to respond to crisis with creativity and ingenuity, advancing the BAUEN Cooperative's equality project in an effort to provide good jobs and community support.

Epilogue

Methodological Appendix

I never considered becoming a sociologist until I walked into the Hotel Bauen one balmy spring day in 2008. The jacaranda trees were starting to bloom in Buenos Aires, flowering with soft purple blossoms that littered the city's plazas. I had spent the semester studying social movements and human rights in Argentina, traveling from the bustling capital city, where I learned about urban activism, to the interior of the country, where I studied indigenous organizing and peasant farming in the plains of the Pampas, the seven-colored sands of the northern provinces, and eventually the altiplano sweeping across the Southern Cone toward the Andes.

A couple of years before, I sat at a long dining room table in a white stucco house in Austin, just a stone's throw from the campus of the University of Texas. I was there for the monthly meeting of the Inter-Cooperative Council, a group that provided affordable student housing. As the organization's recently elected president, I was charged with overseeing nine properties that had been creatively converted into student-run, democratically managed homes. My affordable monthly rent ($550 in 2006), along with my contribution of a set number of weekly work hours, covered the cost of a slightly drafty room over a garage and five meals per week.

In the two-story blue house I called home, I joined fourteen other students to take turns cooking, cleaning, and administering the house in the roles of kitchen manager, labor czar, and board representative. We held regular meetings, set our own rules, and voted on decisions democratically. Unbeknownst to me at the time, I had begun a crash course in participatory democracy. To my surprise—and despite moments of conflict and turmoil—our housing cooperative *worked*. We self-managed, held each other accountable, fed each other, and had a lot of fun.

My housing co-op felt like a world unto itself. Still, I became curious about other types of cooperation. Young and energetic, I launched a personal study of the history of the cooperative movement.[1] As I explored its mainstream roots in England, I was also exposed to critiques of cooperatives as White utopian projects and began to reorient my understanding of collectivist practices within a broader history of indigenous practices and communities of color around the globe.[2]

I was most intrigued by how and why people formed cooperatives. Cooperatives seemed like an obvious tool to confront the growing student loan crisis, the lack of jobs and affordable housing, and the repercussions of neoliberal globalization. But I had never actually encountered one until I found myself enmeshed in the student housing cooperative movement. From there, a series of trips to Ann Arbor, Michigan, to attend institutes organized by the North American Students of Cooperation exposed me to another world of cooperatives—worker-recuperated businesses—formed during and after Argentina's 2001 crisis. I wanted to learn more, so when I had the incredible opportunity to study abroad, I set my sights on South America.

Back in Buenos Aires, an adviser put me in contact with members working in the press sector at the Hotel Bauen. When I arrived for an afternoon meeting, I nervously presented myself to a group of workers I would come to know well over the next decade. For reasons I may never know, they invited me to stop by daily to learn more about the hotel. At the time, the

188

cooperative was busy preparing to protest an eviction order. As the small group planned a demonstration and music festival to take place in the street outside the hotel, I listened, asked questions, and offered to help by translating announcements and press releases into English. When I returned to the University of Texas to finish my undergraduate degree, my curiosity had blossomed like the jacaranda trees that spring day.

Organizational Ethnography

This book is based on the long-term relationship I have cultivated with members of the BAUEN Cooperative since 2008. After starting my training in ethnographic and qualitative methods as a graduate student in sociology, I returned to Buenos Aires in the summers of 2011, 2013, and 2014, each time considering different research questions and study designs, which included my original case study of the Hotel Bauen. In 2015 I received a Fulbright award to support my longest period of fieldwork conducting an organizational ethnography of the worker-run hotel.[3] I started by meeting with the BAUEN administrative council, which approved the project and helped me coordinate the logistics of my stay, from documentation and insurance to scheduling and compensation.

I explained to the council members that I did not need to be paid since I received a stipend from my grant, but they insisted that anyone who worked in the cooperative needed to be compensated for their time: "We don't think anyone should work for free." We negotiated the specifics and the cooperative ended up paying me a monthly *viático*, or transportation stipend. We agreed that I would rotate among all the sectors of the hotel and I would ask for permission to shadow or interview workers individually. My fieldwork was called an internship (*pasantía*), but although I worked in the hotel, I would not become a full member of the cooperative, replace the position of a full-time worker, vote, or seek to influence democratic processes.

After working out these details one night in the council's office, I filled out a simple form with my name and address and made copies of my insurance cards, passport, and visa in order to be covered by the cooperative's insurance. The next day—excited and nervous—I arrived at the hotel ready to begin this new phase of fieldwork.

Observant Participation

The bulk of this project draws on data collected over ten months in 2015 when I worked part-time in the BAUEN Cooperative. I set out to immerse myself in the cadence of everyday work practices. I spent long days in the

189

Hotel Bauen, often arriving early and staying late for meetings and events in addition to working my shift. As a foreigner and nonnative Spanish speaker, I soon became known as someone who asked a lot of questions. When the hotel was busy, I stayed late with my informants, feeling the sting of long hours and exhaustion the next day. And on the many days that business was slow, I endured the quiet spells alongside my coworkers—relishing the time to ask deeper questions. I remember, in the administrative office, when Romina told me I could leave if I wanted because "nothing was happening," I was very happy to stay.

During this period I transitioned from a participant observer to the role of "observant participant," "a subtle shift" that allowed me to "see beyond the social front that informants present to strangers in their everyday lives" (Moeran 2009, 148).[4] My early access to the organization via the press sector offered an ideal position from which to observe and ask questions about its history, organizing, and activism. I then set out to learn more about how work was done in other sectors, eventually rotating through purchasing, reception, reservations, sales and events, administration, the member office, the administrative council, maintenance, the staff kitchen, the lobby bar, housekeeping, and the laundry.[5] At this point, in 2015, I was invited to attend internal meetings to which I had not had access in previous years. In total, I attended two orientations for new members, five sector meetings, seventeen weekly council meetings, and eighteen formal assemblies and informative meetings that gathered all members of the cooperative.

I was also interested in the stories of the members themselves. I conducted forty-five interviews with members, asking about their personal histories before joining the cooperative, their work experiences in the hotel, and their hopes and plans for the future. Most of these interviews took place after a member's shift in the hotel's break rooms or offices, though some were held in coffee shops and bars, at people's homes, and even in transit. I decided early on not to rush into these but to wait until I had worked with members for weeks or months before asking for and conducting interviews.[6] I did this to establish our relationship before initiating the intrusion of an interview, which Pierre Bourdieu (1996, 18) describes as an "attempt to bring out the representation the respondent has of the situation." Every interview began with a discussion about informed consent and the promise that I would not share the information we discussed with others in the cooperative; for most of my participants, this was satisfactory.[7] Because I had gotten to know most of them well before these interviews, I utilized this one-on-one time to learn more about people's beliefs, motivations, meanings, and feelings about their work and to document their work histories in their own words instead of just relying on my own reconstructions.

Over time, and as participants watched me rotate through different sectors, many expressed an investment in this project. When I explained my research plan, Romina thought it was good that I would see all the different parts of the hotel. "Actually, we are supposed to do that in the cooperative, too," she observed, relating my fieldwork to the opportunities available to others to change positions through job rotation.

Pilar also appreciated that I was taking the time to learn about the cooperative by actually working—she commented that this would ensure my project was "not just [based in] theory" but in practice, "the day-to-day. I can tell you how it is, [but] there is nothing that could possibly obscure what you are seeing because the doors are open . . . not to just anyone who wants to come." She went on, "But you are different. The truth is that we have sincerely opened ourselves and the compañeros to you, and you have been in all the places. There is nothing else that can better tell the truth." To me as an ethnographer, her words were reassuring.

Over the years, the members of the BAUEN cooperative had become accustomed to hosting journalists, students, and researchers to share their story and make the case for expropriation, as I describe in chapter 6. At the outset of this project, my field notes were filled with similar narratives that focused on the hotel's history and the cooperative's goals. It took time for me to move beyond these shared stories to learn more about the complexities of individuals' experiences in the worker-run hotel. I regularly explained that the intent of my project was to learn about how people worked in the cooperative, setting it apart from accounts of the group's history or opinion pieces arguing for the legitimacy of the organization. As my participants became familiar with my intent, they began to open up and joke around more. After one of the more contentious sector meetings I observed, Lacunza assured me jokingly that no one was going to believe my book. Over time, I realized that perhaps the most effective way to move beyond well-worn narratives was simply to show up daily, arriving early and staying late, and, as Pilar mentioned, "be[ing] in all the places." Pilar and others recognized this ethnographic approach as a method that would allow me to go beyond my theories about the cooperative or about work and politics in general. She also rightly identified it as a way to better understand the individual interpretations that I collected in my interviews.

I originally planned on rotating jobs by working in one sector and then moving on to the next. But as my fieldwork progressed, the lines between the sectors became increasingly blurry. I would move out of a certain sector, only to have a manager request that I return to help or fill in for someone who was absent. One member laughed that she was willing to "loan me to [another sector] . . . but just for one day!" When this happened, I did my best to make sure these stints did not take time away from my current work sector. The result was often that I worked longer hours to make up for the moves. Even after I changed sectors, I also continued to attend as many meetings as possible, including the administrative council's weekly meetings. Soon my presence was unremarkable. In fact, when I later studied the meeting minutes, I noticed that after the initial sessions, my name was omitted from the listed attendees, as if the participants no longer registered my presence.[8]

In sectors made up of fewer than three people (stock and accounts receivable), I spent just a single shift working with them and conducting interviews. I did not work in three sectors (the breakfast room, kitchens, and security) because they had sufficient overlap with other groups. For example, while working the morning shift in the Utopia Café, I interacted with the two members who oversaw the breakfast operations for overnight guests. When I joined the staff kitchen, I worked alongside members who oversaw the commercial kitchen, which shared the same spaces. I never actually cooked for events but usually was stationed behind the bar serving drinks or restocking buffet tables. This, too, brought me into the orbit of the kitchen. And when I worked in reception, I regularly interacted with members in security, whose proximity to the reception desk allowed me to observe their routines and interventions.

My attempt to work in every sector of the hotel left only one real gap: custodial services. Though I interviewed many members who had worked as janitors, I was never put in contact with the manager of the custodial sector. In retrospect, I could have been clearer in communicating my interest in working all of the jobs, even those that involved cleaning or more intense physical labor. I noticed that I was not usually asked to do physical work—I had to request such tasks explicitly. For example, in housekeeping, after repeated requests, members taught me how to properly tuck the sheet corners so they stayed put, how to clean a bathroom efficiently, and how to wash the windows without leaving streaks. But I was never left to perform those tasks on my own.

Anonymity and Transparency

192 Many organizational ethnographies use pseudonyms to mask certain identifying features of a business and its employees. As should now be clear, the Hotel Bauen would be very difficult to anonymize. Not only was the BAUEN

Cooperative a leader in the movement of worker-recuperated businesses, it was also one of the few recuperated hotels in Argentina and the only one that enjoyed such extensive visibility. I realized early on that even if I promised to guarantee anonymity, it would be all but impossible to make good on that assurance. In the digital age, interested parties need only seconds to search "recuperated hotels in Argentina" online. The Hotel Bauen is the first hit.

This forced me to delve further into debates about ethics and transparency in ethnographic research.[9] As part of a growing movement toward data transparency in the social sciences, ethnographers are questioning the long-established convention of *masking*: "the practice of concealing or distorting identifying information about people, places, and organizations" (Jerolmack and Murphy 2019, 802). What are the justifications for changing certain pieces of identifying information? Of course, there are serious reasons to protect the people and places we study through masking. As Randol Contreras (2019) points out in his reflection on crime research in the United States, *unmasking* can put both the ethnographer and the participants in harm's way. These risks, however, are not exclusive to research on seemingly dangerous topics like crime, violence, deviance, and war. As Rebecca Hanson and Patricia Richards (2017, 588) expertly show, the emphasis on solitude, danger, and intimacy as standards of ethnographic research has been "used to explain, if not justify, the harassment and assault faced by women ethnographers."

At the same time, there are benefits to ethnographic transparency. First, seemingly small modifications can potentially obscure information that may be important to evaluating conclusions and considering alternative explanations.[10] Second, masking the actual location of fieldwork can not only overstate the generalizability of a particular case but also make it difficult to compare cases across time and revisit past studies. Finally, the ethical implications of naming people and places are not universal, especially with technologies that facilitate identification. As anthropologist Nancy Scheper-Hughes (2012, 226) described after a reporter unmasked the location of her study in Ireland (well before the advent of social media), "I have come to see that the time-honored practice of bestowing anonymity on 'our' communities and informants fools few and protects no one—save, perhaps, the anthropologists' own skin." And, we could add, a university's legal liability.[11]

Questions about what to mask and what to name have been constant considerations throughout this research. I've opted for partial disclosure. With the consent of the BAUEN Cooperative, I have used its real name in my publications.[12] But I have also gone to great lengths to protect the confidentiality of

193

the people I worked with in the cooperative. I include real personal biographies and work histories throughout this text, but I change the participants' names, work roles, and other small personal details to prevent individual identification.

Discrepant Roles

In his classic book *The Presentation of Self in Everyday Life*, Erving Goffman developed a dramaturgical theory of social interaction that has also been useful in understanding my fieldwork experiences. Like performances in a theater, social interactions take place on both a frontstage and a backstage, where people can "step out of character" (1959, 112). Access to these different regions of social life directly affects our access to information. For example, Goffman (144) explains, "those who perform; those performed to; and outsiders who neither perform in the show nor observe it" are distinguished based on what they know about the interactive performance.[13]

On occasion, however, "discrepant roles" trouble the neat divisions between performers and their audience. According to Goffman (151), discrepant roles include "the *informer*, the *shill* . . . and the *go-between*. In each case we find an unexpected, unapparent relation among feigned role, information possessed, and regions of access." Ethnographers frequently occupy discrepant roles, navigating the misalignment of our function, information, and access to different social spaces. Sometimes we risk becoming *informers*— people who pretend to be a performer and can access the backstage but then openly reveal secrets of the show to the audience. At other times, we are *shills*, acting like audience members when we are actually performers. Perhaps most commonly we are *go-betweens*, learning the secrets of each side and giving the impression of loyalty to each.

Members of the BAUEN Cooperative were closely attuned to my discrepant role in the hotel as I gained access to the organization's backstage. When I met one of my new coworkers and told him about my family in Texas, he playfully asked whether I was a "spy for George Bush." As people around us laughed, others chimed in, asserting that if not working for Bush, then I must be a "spy for Obama." Though I brushed off the jokes, the concern that I was a spy or had some ulterior purpose persisted. Months later, a coworker revealed that a group in another sector had been speculating about my research and lightheartedly shared that they thought I was a spy. While she laughed at the suggestion, I was disturbed. "Who would I be spying for?" I asked. This only made her laugh more.

194

As time passed, my loyalties continued to be questioned. Some asked me who was I working *for*, while others pushed me to identify my "favorite" sector in the hotel. After rotating from one sector to another on schedule, a member teased that I had "abandoned her." On another occasion when I stopped by an office I had worked in months before, one member joked that she was "mad" at me because I "didn't hang out" with her anymore.

Later in the year, during an informal gathering in the hotel, yet another member called me "la stiuso." I had no idea what it meant, but everyone else seemed to understand perfectly. Normally I felt free to ask directly about the definitions of words and phrases outside my vocabulary. But on this day I felt inexplicably ashamed. After reflecting on what happened, I tried and failed to clarify the meaning of the nickname on my own. So weeks later, I gathered the gumption to ask. Eyes twinkling, a member finally explained, "It's not a word! It's a last name!" Everything became clear. Members had been calling me "la stiuso" as a dark reference to an ex-intelligence officer (Antonio "Jaime" Stiuso) who was involved in the mysterious death of a high-profile lawyer the year before.[14] Again, the joke was that I was some sort of spy.

Despite the trust I gained from my participants—resulting in access to every part of the building, entrée to meetings and events, and invitations to work and be present in the hotel—I was never able to move past my discrepant role. Michel Anteby (2015, 198) argues that paying attention to such instances of *field resistance* is analytically important: "Their reactions say as much about them as they say about you." Given the constant threat of eviction and discredit, my participants were rightly skeptical of any intrusion into their social world. Would I expose the "dark side" of the cooperative? Would I pass information to their opponents? It turns out that I was not the only target of suspicion. Members of the BAUEN Cooperative also discouraged each other from maintaining contact with workers in the adjoining (and still privately owned) Bauen Suites, and stories of moles and shills cropped up throughout my research. All of this meaningfully shaped the data I collected in the hotel and the ways that my mobility (through job rotation), my access to information (from having studied the history of the hotel and from working with and talking to many different members), and my unclear role (as a customer buying a cup of coffee in the café, a worker doing shift work, a researcher from a different country) were interpreted by the people around me. Ultimately, these ongoing japes and nicknames not only sensitized me to the mismatch between my position as a researcher and my role as a worker in the cooperative but also helped me to analyze the deep uncertainty of an organization operating in a legal gray zone.

195

Immersion and Distance

This project is an ethnographic study of relational equality, democratic participation, and organizational change in a worker cooperative. To do this research, I used my own participation in the hotel to study participation itself. This web of participation—as a researcher and as a worker (but never a full member) in the cooperative—posed special challenges.

Feminist ethnographers have long called on scholars to engage in reflexivity to account for their unique standpoints (Collins 2000).[15] Rather than consider one or two aspects of my social position, I have sought to dissect throughout this project my use of social capital and personal characteristics as part of what Victoria Reyes (2020) calls an "ethnographic toolkit." My embodiment and positionality meaningfully shaped my research as I navigated this social world without the linguistic dexterity, national familiarity, or work experience of an insider.

Over the years, I followed the advice given to many an ethnographer to immerse myself in life within the hotel, adopting new routines in an effort to reduce the social distance I had as an outsider to the organization. As a student from the United States living and working in Argentina, I tried my best to settle in, however difficult this might be.[16] I had previous work experience in childcare and administration, but I had never had a job in a service workplace like a restaurant or hotel. Moreover, growing up in Texas, I had learned Spanish in school and continued my language training into adulthood. But even after months of living in Argentina, speaking the language rarely felt like second nature.

All of this guided what I paid attention to and prompted me to ask questions about words, practices, and meanings that I didn't understand. Often I felt I had to observe social and interactional patterns many times before I could identify them as such. Still, while I was an outsider in many respects, I came to study worker-recuperated businesses as an insider to the cooperative movement and as a person deeply interested in the possibilities of participatory democracy and self-management. Having served as president of a student housing cooperative, I brought my own opinions about what I thought could elicit broad-based participation and how to balance efficiency with equality in decision-making. Ultimately, my curiosity about the possibilities of democratic participation afforded me the patience to sustain this long-term project. Along the way, I have also gone to great lengths to interrogate my own assumptions and the ways in which they impact my analysis of workplace democracy.

196

It's common for advocates and allies to conduct research projects on movements in which they participate. I am no exception. This practice demands that scholars adopt a critical lens to make sense of their work. For example, as part of their study of the paradoxes of participation, Gianpaolo Baiocchi and Ernesto Ganuza (2016, 15) call for researchers to adopt "a critical distance and a sense of estrangement from these [participatory] processes." They continue, "We have come to believe that greater agnosticism would benefit critical scholars evaluating participatory processes, rather than relying on what anthropologists call 'ontological complicity.'" The way out of this conundrum, according to Pierre Bourdieu, Jean-Claude Chamboredon, and Jean-Claude Passeron (1991), is not to deny our participation but to interrogate our place in the field by breaking from scientific, commonsensical, and ethnocentric pressures. Throughout this research I have sought to reflect on the impacts of my individual embodiment, moral orientations, and epistemic commitments. Rather than romanticizing the efforts of members of the BAUEN Cooperative by placing my analytic focus solely on their successes and innovations, I have tried to examine the many challenges and contradictions members confronted in order to present a vivid portrait of efforts to address inequality and reorganize work in a capitalist economy.

At the end of 2015, I said goodbye to my coworkers, participants, and now friends in the BAUEN Cooperative. Their response to my exit caught me off guard: they organized goodbye meals, threw a going-away party, and even gave me a plaque recognizing my time in the cooperative. Their kindness and generosity were touching, and I have had the good fortune to stay in contact with many of them to this day.

It is worth noting that I didn't start this project with a grand plan to study the Hotel Bauen for an extended period of time. Make no mistake, long-term ethnographic research is logistically complicated and emotionally trying. But there are also analytic and methodological benefits to collecting multiple sources of data over the years. First off, it changed how I conceptualized the object of my study: the organization itself. Unable to freeze the workplace in time, I was forced to consider the BAUEN Cooperative not as a static entity but as a dynamic and changing web of relations. This had meaningful impacts on the theoretical framing of this book and the development of the concept of equality projects. Second, forming relationships with people and a place over time not only helped me with access but also reinforced my commitment to the cooperative ethos of accountability. In addition to staying in touch virtually, I returned to the Hotel Bauen in 2019

197

with a draft manuscript in hand to share my arguments and publishing plans with members of the cooperative.

Building the Case

Over nearly a decade, I collected different types of qualitative and historical data on worker-recuperated businesses in Argentina. The primary data for this project were my own written ethnographic field notes. I carried a small notebook with me in the field, where I would take short notes and jot down direct quotes throughout the day. At the end of each period of fieldwork, I would find a quiet place to type up my notes. I spent many hours carefully reconstructing the events, conversations, and insights of each day.[17] Since both service work and cooperative participation require feeling management, I recorded affective dynamics that I observed and experienced in the workplace, noting when people explicitly stated their feelings, how they displayed emotions through their bodies, and what my own emotional reactions were to workplace dynamics.[18]

In addition to these hundreds of pages of field notes, my extensive data also include in-depth interviews that I conducted in Spanish and audio-recorded with the consent of my participants.[19] I wrote field notes immediately after each interview to capture the setting, context, and emotional tenor of the conversation. A paid assistant in Argentina transcribed most of the interviews, and I reviewed all the text files while listening to the original audio to make any corrections needed.

Finally, I collected historical documents about the movement of worker-recuperated businesses and the Hotel Bauen specifically. My data from the BAUEN Cooperative included all meeting minutes for the Workers Assembly and the administrative council from 2003 through the end of 2015 as well as founding documents and internal memos. I scanned and digitized all these documents for later analysis. I also collected press releases published online, newspaper and scholarly articles in both English and Spanish about worker-recuperated businesses, and legal files and state documents related to the property (including all the bills for expropriation and the proceedings of the commercial courts hearing the case). Throughout my fieldwork I also took photos and collected many other visual records. Some are reproduced in this book.

I organized my data collection by uploading all these documents and images to the qualitative data-analysis software ATLAS.ti. I then used open and focus coding to guide my analysis (Emerson, Fretz, and Shaw 1995). I proceeded abductively, applying codes to capture themes that emerged from the data as well as general theoretical codes related to external factors, such as state intervention and legal issues, as well as internal factors, such as decision-making, participation, job rotation, and pay. I refined these broad codes by adding relevant subthemes. I then reexamined codes and code groups individually, considering patterns and divergences when data excerpts were delinked from their source. Throughout this process I wrote memos related to analytic and methodological themes I was noticing, which I also stored in ATLAS.ti. Because my relationships with my participants evolved over time, I also maintained memos on individuals that allowed me to link interactions and conversations that took place across different periods of fieldwork.

For some data, such as meeting minutes, I supplemented this coding with a different approach. For example, I cataloged meetings in an Excel spreadsheet to analyze how they were called, what topics they dealt with, and what decisions (if any) were made. This allowed me to quantify meetings by type and outcome and to create the figures that appear in this text. As it came time to combine these diverse sources of data, I applied the evidentiary criteria normally used for ethnographic research, assigning higher value to patterns of conduct reported by multiple observers (Becker 1970; Katz 2001). Unless otherwise noted, direct quotes and ethnographic vignettes that appear in this text are meant not as exceptional or discrete comments but as encapsulations of broad patterns that I observed repeatedly and in multiple data sources.

Of course, transforming a wealth of data into a sociological object involves more than just careful coding or smart software. Andrew Deener (2018, 296) describes this as a process of *narrowing down*: "No researcher can include every empirical instance from their field sites into their sociological cases. They produce rich and varied data sets over lengthy periods of time, but just as importantly, they learn how to narrow down what they focus on . . . to make their research relevant to other sociologists." As I set out to study workplace democracy, I sought to complicate common assumptions about work and organizations, which usually focus on the production of inequality at the microlevel, the arrangements of hierarchy at the mesolevel, and the ways these processes reflect and reinforce broader political-economic pressures. I paid careful attention to how these taken-for-granted approaches to seeing inequality and hierarchy shaped not only my data collection but also my analysis and writing. My long-term fieldwork allowed me to explore these processes over time, from the official narratives and problems so clearly defined by the group to the spaces of deliberation that emerged through mundane practices.

The winnowing process of data analysis necessarily involves establishing boundaries to define the ethnographic case. While this is an ethnography of a place with clear spatial boundaries (a recuperated hotel), my guiding question about *how organizations construct equality* took me beyond the twenty-story tower and into congressional hearings, street protests, and other cooperative workplaces across the city of Buenos Aires. Similarly, I ended up putting my observational data in conversation with a historical event: the occupation of the hotel. Time, for this project, extended back into the not-too-distant past, and I used historical records to trace how workers changed organizational processes over time.

The future also weighed heavy on my mind. Just as the threat of eviction nagged at my participants, I, too, was concerned about when the hotel might close. Although I wrote the bulk of this manuscript while the BAUEN Cooperative was still open for business, I revised the final draft to account for the hotel's closure. This involved practical updates as well as more substantive reflections on the implications of my findings in the conclusion and epilogue. In the writing process, I have endeavored to include the stories of members from different positions in the organization, re-creating dialogues and debates that took place rather than presenting a settled picture of social reality. When discussing the cooperative itself, I included voices of council members who had been elected by their compañeros to speak on their behalf. Throughout this book, rather than construct an "ethnographic present," I have chosen to write in the past tense to reinforce the particular time and place in which these data were collected. This underscores that the BAUEN Cooperative constantly changed and evolved as members shaped an organization to meet their needs. While this appendix is not an exhaustive reflection of the many decisions about what I included and omitted and what relations and boundaries I tried to study systematically, I hope it offers a window into the research process that is useful for others who undertake ethnographic work.

Notes

Introduction

1. Scholars of inequality rarely address the normative assumptions and implications of these theories. A recent exception is Dustin Avent-Holt (2020). Applying egalitarian frameworks to rent theory, he argues that it fundamentally fails to capture why distributional inequalities are normatively problematic. See also Wright (2006, 2010).

2. Gisela was a vocal advocate for the cooperative and regularly spoke in public forums about her experience in the hotel. I conducted three interviews with Gisela over the course of my fieldwork. To recount her story in her own words, I also draw on excerpts from an interview that Gisela had with a journalist I met and hosted for an afternoon while I was working in the Hotel Bauen in 2015. I use

excerpts from this transcript with permission. All translations are my own unless otherwise noted.

3. Between 1976 and 1983, a military junta held power in Argentina, part of a cycle of civilian and military governments that had begun in the 1950s with the ousting of Juan Domingo Perón. This period of military rule also coincided with violent state-sponsored terrorism supported by Operation Condor, a US-led intelligence operation to fight communism in South America (Brennan 2018; McSherry 2005).

4. For more information on how social activism flourished during and after the 2001 crisis, see Svampa, Bombal, and Bergel (2003). On the lasting impacts of the crisis twenty years later, see Pérez and Sobering (2022).

5. On the organization and emergence of *piqueteros* in Argentina, see Svampa and Pereyra (2003). For a fascinating update that examines what has happened to *piqueteros* since the movement surged, see Pérez (2018).

6. On the MNER, see Magnani (2009). On bankruptcy in Argentina and the effects of the 2011 reforms to the Bankruptcy Law on worker-recuperated businesses, see Ruggeri (2014a, 21–24).

7. *Compañero* translates to "comrade," "compatriot," or "colleague" and is generally used to refer to someone of equal status. Unlike other synonyms for "coworker" (i.e., *colega*), *compañero* has political connotations. It is not only used by activists to refer to one another but also commonly used to refer to members of the Peronist party.

8. When referring to the physical location, many people still call the tower the Hotel Bauen, so I have followed that usage. When I refer explicitly to the cooperative, I use the organization's name, BAUEN.

9. Scott Harris (2006a) breaks down uses of equality into four approaches: (1) operationalizing equality in a rational manner; (2) identifying factors that promote or reduce equality in a given situation; (3) determining the beneficial and negative effects of the presence of inequality; and (4) recommending social reforms to address inequalities and their consequences. See also White (2007).

10. As Thomas DiPrete and Brittany Fox-Williams (2021, 3) state, sociological research "makes a strong case for the desirability of inequality reduction, and it points to large-scale social transformations that might accomplish this objective, but it often neglects or insufficiently engages in the task of elucidating how this social transformation might occur." See also Cancian (1995).

11. By centering this project on equality rather than inequality, I do not intend to reify equality. When applied without differentiation or attention to the complexities of a given context, equality is a dangerous idea that can deny differences and "bleach away the variation of human experience" (Rae 1981, 18). I neither seek to promote a single idea of equality nor argue that equality stands for nothing (Westen 1982) but rather to advocate for the study of equality in practice. Terms like *egalitarian*, *equity*, and *equality* are sometimes distinguished but often used interchangeably. In this book I use the term *equality* to bridge interdisciplinary debates on equality and inequality in the humanities and social sciences.

12. A long line of egalitarian thinkers have debated equality in principle. A simple understanding of equality refers to a static state in which all people are

treated as if they are interchangeable. Scholars who meaningfully consider these questions usually adopt a complex definition of equality, acknowledging that people can be equally valued even though they have different skills, interests, and talents (Walzer 1984).

13. To Dietrich Rueschemeyer (2005), political equality is deeply shaped by social inequalities in power, status, and resources. Thus, unless societies limit the effects of these inequalities, the possibility for meaningful political equality will be constrained.

14. Most basically, justice means fairness, or the application of impartiality free from personal biases and vested interests. John Rawls (2005) promoted this "justice as fairness" approach. For a more detailed discussion of a Rawlsian conception of justice, see Sen (2009, chap. 2). A long line of social theorists— from Thomas Hobbes, Jean-Jacques Rousseau, and Immanuel Kant to Ronald Dworkin—have sought to identify the rules and arrangements of "just institutions." Amartya Sen (2009, 6–8) calls these "contractarian" modes of thinking because they identify a social contract that specifies the terms of justice.

15. There are a host of proposed approaches to distributive equality. One approach focuses on material resources, or what Rawls (2005) calls "basic goods," while others focus on equality of opportunities to access advantages, may it be through a fair lottery system (where everyone has the same chances of winning) or through the creation of "starting-gate equality" (where young people are ensured equal opportunities). A second approach considers the notion of equal access as a criterion for equality. Similar to the idea of equal opportunity, equal access does not mean that all people should make the same hourly wages or that everyone must flourish equally. Rather, a just society is one in which the failures to do so are not the result of inequalities in basic access to social and material resources (Wright 2010). A third approach contends that social arenas or "spheres" should follow different criteria for the distribution of social goods. According to Michael Walzer (1984, 19), "complex equality means that no citizen's standing in one sphere or with regard to one social good can be undercut by his standing in some other sphere, with regard to some other good."

16. I understand recognition as the social practices through which people communicate mutual respect and validate their standing as moral equals within a society (Anderson 1999; Fraser 2000; Lamont 2018).

17. Douglas Rae (1981, 4) describes this as the process through which "equality" in the abstract fissions into "equalities" in practice.

18. This approach to studying inequality reflects a substantialist ontology that characterizes various kinds of things, beings, and essences as the fundamental units of inquiry (Emirbayer 1997). As Donald Tomaskovic-Devey and Dustin Avent-Holt (2019, 14) argue, "The assumption that social causes inhere in individuals, rather than social relationships, is simply wrong."

19. Joan Acker (2006) differentiates between people's awareness of inequalities and the legitimacy of inequalities, both of which vary by organization, by the position of an individual within that organization, and by political and economic context. As Acker explains, "Class is highly legitimate in US organizations, as

class practices, such as paying wages and maintaining supervisory oversight, are basic to organizing work in capitalist economies [. . . whereas] gender and race inequality are less legitimate than class" (453), given civil rights and labor laws.

20. See Mishel and Wolfe (2019). In comparison to the United States, corporate executives in Argentina make far less (US$77,000 per year on average in 2019) but still more than the average annual salary across all workers (US$41,000). See Rebón (2019).

21. On the Occupy movement, see Graeber (2014).

22. Definitions of equality and inequality are the product of interpretation and are socially constructed in practice (Harris 2003, 2006a, 2006b). How people collectively make sense of equality and inequality is deeply contextual, takes constant work, and can also break down (Waldron 2017).

23. I define organizations as "socially constructed spaces in which individuals' efforts are coordinated to jointly accomplish a set of tasks to fulfill some goal or set of linked goals" (Tomaskovic-Devey and Avent-Holt 2019, 2; see also Kellogg 2009; Roscigno 2011; Weick 2000). Throughout this book I use the terms *organization* and *workplace* interchangeably. On the importance of organizations for understanding inequality, see Baron and Bielby (1980); Reskin (1993); Tilly (1998); and Tomaskovic-Devey (1993).

24. The idea of equality as an ongoing project is also consistent with the work of relational egalitarian theorists (Wallimann-Helmer, Schuppert, and Fourie 2015). If a just society is one in which members can relate to each other on an equal footing, the task is then to determine what institutional arrangements and social practices enable such interactions. As Samuel Scheffler (2015, 30–31) explains, "Sustaining an egalitarian relationship requires creativity, the exercise of judgement, and ongoing mutual commitment, and even the sincere efforts of the parties are no guarantee of success, although success is a matter of degree."

25. Building on the work of Charles Tilly (1998), relational inequality theory outlines a series of processes that explain how and why inequalities are produced and persist over time (see also Avent-Holt and Tomaskovic-Devey 2010; Tomaskovic-Devey et al. 2009; Tomaskovic-Devey 2014; Weeden 2002; Wilson and Roscigno 2014). Feminist scholars have long modeled a fundamentally relational approach, understanding gender not simply as the study of women's issues but as an interactional accomplishment that uses gender to legitimize male domination (Acker 2006; Chodorow 1978, 2000; Rich 1980). On relational sociology, see also Emirbayer (1997).

26. Acker's (2006) notion of "inequality regimes" has been widely used to understand the organizational production of inequality (Tomaskovic-Devey and Avent-Holt 2019, chap. 4; see also Meyers and Vallas 2016). Inequality regimes vary by organization and over time. Given this variation, Tomaskovic-Devey and Avent-Holt (2019, 81) call for more attention to the variation between organizations to recognize more (or less) egalitarian contexts.

27. Inclusion is key to organizational change processes. As Katherine Kellogg (2009) argues in her study of operating rooms in the United States, the success

relies on the creation of *relational spaces*, a type of free space that includes people from different positions to support and sustain reforms against defenders of the status quo.

28. Equality is not a preexisting "thing" to discover but rather a social construction with multiple meanings that are context specific (Rae 1981). As Harris (2006a, 9) points out, "This does not mean that 'it is forbidden' for sociologists to construct their own 'objective' definitions for equality—'objective,' that is, from the perspective of a particular community of researchers."

29. Here, I build on Michael Omi and Howard Winant's (2014, 13) conceptualization of projects as social processes that link social structures and representations.

30. My use of the word *project* draws on the notion of "projectivity" developed by Alfred Schutz (1967) to capture the future-oriented dimension of social action (see Beckert 2016; Mische 2009).

31. The Real Utopias Project has been far-reaching, analyzing issues from market socialism and participatory governance to universal basic income and gender equality (Wright 2010).

32. G. A. Cohen (2008) developed the concept of an "egalitarian ethos" to critique Rawls's theory of justice. While Cohen focuses on individual-level action, I use the term to think about organizational culture. Following Tim Hallett (2003), I understand organizational culture as a negotiated order that emerges through interactions and is influenced by those with the symbolic power to define the situation. Culture is a system of widely shared values and beliefs that are used to organize social processes. In organizations, as William Foote Whyte and Kathleen King Whyte (1991, 270–71) explain, culture emerges out of efforts to solve social, economic, and political problems.

33. On the participatory theory of democracy and arguments for democratizing the workplace, see Carole Pateman (1970, 2012).

34. Workplaces, Elizabeth Anderson (2017) argues, should be understood as a form of *private government* that is unaccountable to the people it governs. The legal authority of private employers to regulate employees extends beyond the workday, from control over their politics and speech to their choice of sexual partners, recreational drug use, and physical activities. Other scholars have documented workers draw this analogy unprompted. For example, an IT professional in Erin Kelly and Phyllis Moen's (2020, 13) study of organizational change called the management style at his firm "more of a dictatorship than anything."

35. Worker-owned businesses are just one type of cooperative association. According to the International Cooperative Alliance (n.d.), a cooperative can be defined as "an autonomous association of persons united voluntarily to meet their common economic, social, and cultural needs and aspirations through a jointly-owned and democratically-controlled enterprise." Cooperatives are generally classified into three types: (1) producer cooperatives that pool resources to purchase shared supplies and equipment (i.e., agriculture and craft co-ops); (2) consumer cooperatives that coordinate the provision of affordable goods and services to their members (i.e., food and retail co-ops, childcare collectives, credit

unions); and (3) worker cooperatives that provide job security and democratic economic participation to workers.

36. While the international cooperative movement traces its historical roots to white cooperators like the Rochdale Pioneers, movements for Black civil rights and economic equality are a critical part of the contemporary cooperative movement. In her important book, Jessica Gordon Nembhard (2014) expertly shows how democratic economic participation has been practiced in low-income communities and by Black communities and people of color in the United States.

37. These principles were codified by the International Cooperative Alliance, which was formed in 1895 to support cooperatives around the globe. On cooperative legal structures in different countries, see Cracogna, Fici, and Henrÿ (2013).

38. For a collection of recent work on cooperatives, see Chen and Chen (2021). On worker cooperatives in the United States, see Gunn (1984); Mansbridge (1980); Mellor, Hannah, and Stirling (1988); Rothschild and Whitt (1986); and Viggiani (1997). On retail worker cooperatives in California, see Meyers (2022). On Cooperative Home Care Associates, the largest worker cooperative in the United States, see Berry (2013) and Berry and Bell (2018). On Mondragón, see Cheney (1999); Hacker (1989); and Kasmir (1996). On small health care cooperatives, see Kleinman (1996).

39. For a review of gender inequality in worker cooperatives, see Sobering, Thomas, and Williams (2014). See also Meyers and Vallas (2016).

40. On the theory of gendered organizations, see Acker (1990, 2006). On understanding organizations as racialized structures, see Ray (2019) and Wooten and Couloute (2017).

41. According to Patricia Yancey Martin (1990, 189), the focus on failures is connected to the problem of assessing organizational purity such that any inconsistencies or conflicts among goals, practices, and outcomes "are depicted as fatal or disqualifying flaws." On the interesting debates over whether feminist organizations can be effective, see Staggenborg (1995).

42. This perspective has been advanced by theories of organizational ecology (Hannan and Freeman 1977) and institutional isomorphism (DiMaggio and Powell 1983). Although organizations often imitate each other, workers still resist (Burawoy 1979; Roscigno and Hodson 2004; Vallas 2006) and demand dignity at work (Hodson 1995, 2001).

43. Responding to the critiques of neoinstitutionalism, Tim Hallett and Marc Ventresca (2006, 226) develop an "inhabited" approach to institutions that focuses on the "people whose social interactions infuse those institutions with force and meaning."

44. On initiatives to "redesign and redefine work," see Correll et al. (2014); Correll (2017); and Kelly and Moen (2020).

45. J. K. Gibson-Graham (2003) calls these "capitalocentric" logics. For research on the motivations to form alternative organizations, see the edited volumes by Maurizio Atzeni (2012) and Martin Parker and colleagues (2014).

46. Surveys of worker-recuperated businesses have been conducted by the Open Faculty Program (Programa Facultad Abierta) at the University of Buenos

Aires since 2003 (Programa Facultad Abierta 2003; Ruggeri 2011, 2014a, 2016; Ruggeri, Trinchero, and Martinez 2005; Ruggeri and Vieta 2015; Vieta 2019).

47. Private firms have been recuperated in other national contexts. For an insightful analysis of case studies in the United States and Latin America, see Ranis (2016). On Brazil, see Henriques et al. (2013). On Uruguay, see Rieiro (2009). On Greece, see Kokkinidis (2015). On Italy, see Vieta, Depedri, and Carrano (2017).

48. Directed by Avi Lewis and written by Naomi Klein, *The Take* (2004) documents workplace occupations in the early twenty-first century, focusing on the story of workers in a metallurgical factory called FORJA San Martín. For an update on the case of FORJA and an exploration of why some alternative organizations survive and others cease to operate, see Sobering and Lapegna (2021).

49. The North American Students of Cooperation continues to meet annually in Ann Arbor, Michigan.

50. For just one of many examples, see Kennard and Caistor-Arendar (2016).

51. The multiple periods of fieldwork I conducted are similar to what Michael Burawoy (2003) calls *focused revisits*. A focused revisit "occurs when an ethnographer undertakes participant observation, that is, studying others in their space and time, with a view to comparing his or her site with the same one studied at an earlier point in time, whether by him or herself or by someone else" (646). I used each period of fieldwork to continue data collection and also to compare data over time. This required an attention to not only changes in the cooperative and its environment but also my shifting involvement as an observer as well as the theories I brought with me. See the appendix for more on this reflection.

Chapter One: Recuperating the Hotel Bauen

1. Following Christopher Marquis and András Tilcsik (2013, 199), I understand imprinting as "a process whereby during a brief period of susceptibility, a focal entity develops characteristics that reflect prominent features of the environment, and these characteristics continue to persist despite significant environmental changes in subsequent periods." For a review of the concept of imprinting, which began with the work of Arthur Stinchcombe (1965), see Marquis and Tilcsik (2013).

2. Victoria Johnson (2007) argues that organizational imprinting happens through a process of cultural entrepreneurship, which involves both the creativity of the founders and the constraints and opportunities of their particular historical context. Imprinting is an agency-driven process, whereby "key stakeholders . . . may reinforce or thwart entrepreneurs' plans, whether these be isomorphic or innovative in nature" (117).

3. Despite trends toward flexible organizational forms, much organizational theory focuses on change-inhibiting forces, explaining organizations' structural rigidities, inertial tendencies, institutionalization, and path dependencies (DiMaggio and Powell 1983; Hannan and Freeman 1977; Sydow, Schreyögg, and Koch 2009).

4. Christopher Marquis and András Tilcsik (2013, 221) argue that imprinting is not limited to an organization's founding moment but can also take place during

what they call "sensitive periods"—times of upheaval, transition, and instability. Organizations are thus "layers of imprints" that build up over time.

5. Debates about the lasting effects of imprints highlight the ongoing tension in organizational research between their inertial and adaptive tendencies. But imprinted characteristics are not unchangeable. While they may persist or decay over time, some research shows that firms explicitly try to modify or revise these features (Kriauciunas and Kale 2006; Marquis and Huang 2010).

6. This was not the first time the military had taken political power. Argentina experienced six coups d'état in the twentieth century. For a more complete history, see Jozami, Paz, and Villareal (1985).

7. When Argentina returned to democracy, the new government set out to investigate the human rights violations that took place during the military dictatorship. The results of the National Commission on Disappeared Persons were published in a report entitled "Nunca Más: Informe de la Comisión Nacional sobre la Desaparición de Personas" (Never Again: Report from the National Commission on Disappeared Persons) that confirmed that the disappearances and assassinations were organized by the military (Comisión Nacional sobre la Despaparición de Personas 2011).

8. Members of the BAUEN Cooperative collaborated with the Open Faculty at the University of Buenos Aires to publish an in-depth examination of the illicit ties of the former owners (Ruggeri, Alfonso, and Balaguer 2017).

9. Political scientists have described the entrenchment of economic power in Argentina as the result of elite cartels. As Michael Johnston (2014, 151) explains, "To a remarkable extent Elite Cartels have withstood, even capitalized upon, democratization and other systemic reforms, such as transparency measures, regional and international agreements, and above all market-oriented neoliberal reforms." For more detailed analysis of the role of corruption and the impunity enjoyed by the economic elite, see Guillan-Montero (2011) and Manzetti (2009).

10. *Precarious work* refers to "employment that is uncertain, unpredictable, and risky from the point of view of the worker" (Kalleberg 2009, 2), largely brought about by the decline of unions and the weakening of labor protections.

11. On the changing regulatory context related to worker-recuperated businesses in Argentina, see Echaide (2007, 84) and Magnani (2009, 110–11).

12. The National Development Bank had issued the original loan to the Bauen Corporation. The national bank operated from 1944 until 1993, when it was liquidated amid various scandals. From 1970 to 1993, the bank financed companies with "softer" loans than conventional banks offered. In other words, it provided loans at no interest or at below-market interest rates with extended grace periods and longer amortization schedules. For more on these irregularities, see *La Nación* (2007).

13. The *corralito* refers to economic measures implemented by Domingo Cavallo, then minister of the economy, to freeze all bank accounts in Argentina in 2001. *Cacerolazos* are a form of popular protest consisting of people making noise by banging pots and pans.

14. For more details on these transactions and the arguments against them, see Pierucci and Tonarelli (2014) and Ruggeri, Alfonso, and Balaguer (2017).

15. On the lasting effects of the 2001–2002 crisis, see Pérez and Sobering (2022).

16. Data can be found in Economic Commission for Latin America and the Caribbean (n.d.).

17. On the history of Chilavert, the recuperated graphics factory, see Vieta (2019, 40–61).

18. Trade unions have taken different positions on worker-recuperated businesses. While some have provided support, others have fully opposed their tactics and collaborated with management to undermine workers' organizing efforts. For example, in a 2013 survey, approximately half of recuperated businesses maintained connections with unions (Ruggeri 2014a). While workers in the BAUEN Cooperative did not receive active support, the Union of Tourism, Hospitality, and Gastronomy Workers later supported the recuperation of six restaurants in the city of Buenos Aires. On the role of unions, see Vieta (2019, 126–29); and Clark and Antivero (2009).

19. Interview conducted by the Lavaca Collective in 2005.

20. In Argentina there were procedures for workers to receive money owed to them when businesses closed, but these were lengthy and sometimes unreliable. For a detailed analysis of the emergence of worker-recuperated businesses in Argentina, see Magnani (2009).

21. Research has found that social movements can promote diverse organizational forms like cooperatives (Schneiberg, King, and Smith 2008). In Argentina the decision to form a cooperative was practical. Worker cooperatives offered a legitimate and accessible way to reorganize work and benefit from preexisting exemptions from the tax on revenues. Unlike in the United States, worker cooperatives in Argentina are incorporated at the national level. On the benefits of the cooperative organizational form, see Cheney et al. (2014); for Argentina, see Fajn (2003).

22. For a discussion of worker-recuperated businesses in relation to the broader cooperative movement in Latin America, see Larrabure, Vieta, and Schugurensky (2011) and Vieta (2010).

23. Honor Brabazon (2016, 23) outlines two tendencies of worker occupations outside a revolutionary context. In the first, most of which are "short lived and brutally repressed," workers occupy businesses independent from state actors in efforts to create spaces independent from capitalist constraints. The second general pattern includes cases of worker control supported by the state, which free workers from certain demands of capitalist production without ceding control. See Ness and Azzellini (2011) for more on these cases.

24. In her analysis of the landless peasants' movement in Bolivia and worker-recuperated businesses in Argentina, Brabazon (2016) argues that both adopt a "radical legal praxis" that informs their engagement with the law. For more on their creative use of the law, see Magnani (2009, 101–2).

25. Workplace recuperations have taken place in various Latin American and European countries, including Brazil, Colombia, Italy, Greece, and Uruguay (Ruggeri and Vieta 2015).

26. Collective authority is a distinguishing feature of all worker cooperatives.

27. On the evolution of labor processes in other worker-recuperated businesses, see Pizzi and Icart (2014) and Rebón and Salgado (2007).

28. For internal meetings, the secretary was required to document what was said and done, along with vote tallies. This involved taking detailed notes, typing them up, and then presenting them for approval at the next meeting.

29. In their study of worker-recuperated businesses in Buenos Aires, Julián Rebón and his coauthors (2006) detail how the economic crisis impacted social change and workplace innovation.

30. Position by position, the members created a hierarchy of authority. In bureaucratic organizations this arrangement can create an "isomorphic" distribution of power and privilege whereby hierarchy is used to institutionalize and justify inequality (Rothschild-Whitt 1979). Chapter 2 examines how the BAUEN Cooperative blended bureaucratic and collectivist practices to distribute power in the workplace.

31. For a detailed report on the cooperative's growth and challenges, see Pierucci and Tonarelli (2014).

32. The administrative council initially consisted of the three members required by law. In 2006 the cooperative increased the size of the council to add two at-large members to fill in for the three primary council members as needed. In 2009 the workers voted to increase the size of the council again, this time to nine.

33. Research on cooperatives has documented that family ties ease hiring but have other trade-offs. This is similar to the creation of "fiefdoms" that Robert Jackall (1988) describes in corporations, which are based on loyalty. Research shows that while sometimes discounted as a remnant of the past, patrimonialism—"an organization of authority in which a leader assumes power through networks based on trust, loyalty and tradition" (Neely 2018, 366)—continues to be an organizing logic in contemporary firms like hedge funds (Neely 2022).

34. The minutes from this first recorded assembly in 2005 (Acta No. 1)—which none of my respondents clearly remembered in interviews—recounted the debate over whether members had spent enough time reviewing the document. But in the end, the council vote approving the document was recorded as unanimous.

35. Some of these threats were coordinated into smear campaigns. For example, there was a website titled The True History of the Bauen, which sought to debunk many of the cooperative's claims. The website (www.laverdaddelbauen .com.ar, accessed April 25, 2018) no longer exists.

36. This is the case for many worker-recuperated businesses. See Vieta (2010) for similar cases.

37. Recent research examines transparency in new organizational forms. For example, Catherine Turco (2016) studies how an entrepreneurial technology firm practices "radical transparency"—sharing extensive information and encouraging open communication and greater voice among employees. Yet studies of information sharing often underplay the democratic possibilities of these initiatives.

38. Archon Fung (2013) developed the concept of democratic transparency as defined here. In its original conception, "infotopia" results from democratic

transparency at a societal level, where (1) information that affects citizen interests is widely available; (2) the amount of information is proportional to the extent to which organizations jeopardize social life; (3) information is organized and accessible; and (4) individuals can take action based on these public disclosures (Fung, Graham, and Weil 2008).

39. In Sobering (2019b), I use the case of the Hotel Bauen to develop a framework for studying democratic transparency in organizations.

Chapter Two: Democracy at Work

1. Organizational scholars have argued that decision-making is part of broader sensemaking processes in organizations, whereby members read into their situations to both rationalize past actions and identify patterns of meaning (Weick 2000). Deliberation is a way that organizational sensemaking takes place. As Francesca Polletta (2002) points out, this deliberative approach is different from an adversarial one, in which people (supposedly) know their preferences and opinions before the deliberation.

2. For a review, see Dahl (2007) and Verba (2001). Scholars often discuss political equality on a spectrum of participation, where a strong ideal of equality is a situation in which each person has equal voice and an equal vote, which are ensured by fundamental rights.

3. For a conceptual justification of applying the term *government* to work organizations, see Anderson (2017, 41–48).

4. Workplace democracy is a system of organizational governance that varies according to the degree of control that workers enjoy over decisions, the ways in which that control is exercised, and the organizational level at which participation takes place (Bernstein 1983). On participatory theories of democracy and their application in the workplace, see Pateman (1970).

5. Joyce Rothschild (Rothschild-Whitt 1979) builds on the work of Max Weber (1946), who emphasized the tensions between bureaucracy and democracy and went so far as to say that democracy must actively oppose bureaucracies to prevent them from becoming completely isolated from the people they serve. Collectivist-democratic organizations, in theory, reject instrumentally rational behavior and instead are guided by what Weber called "value rationality" (Rothschild-Whitt 1979, 24).

6. Max Weber's (1946) theory of bureaucracy is part of his broader typology of social action that corresponds to different forms of authority. In contrast to traditional and charismatic authority rooted in time-tested institutions and emotional appeals, legal-rational authority is founded on formalized rules and actualized in bureaucratic organizations.

7. For example, in her study of two worker cooperatives in northern California, Joan Meyers (2022) shows how the arrangements of authority, formal rules, and job specialization can support more egalitarian levels of earnings, authority, and autonomy on the job. Research on feminist organizations has also documented hybrid organizational practices (Ferree and Martin 1995; Iannello 1992; Martin 1990).

8. For research on efforts to create self-managed teams in corporate work-places, see Lee and Edmondson (2017) and Bernstein et al. (2016). See also Smith (1997) and Rothschild (2000).

9. During the 1980s, companies removed layers of managerial hierarchy and created teams to be more flexible and responsive to the market (Appelbaum et al. 2000; Hodson 2002; Kalleberg et al. 2006; Kunda 2006; Smith 1997; Turco 2016; Vallas 2003). On participation as a management strategy, see Hodson (1995, 2002) and Heller et al. (1998).

10. In her study of a privately owned start-up tech firm, Catherine Turco (2016) shows how the company encouraged participation not only by soliciting opinions from employees but also by sharing information that was previously off-limits, redesigning office spaces to facilitate open communication, and leveraging online forums and new technology to make all this possible. On the impact of flat organizations on gender inequality, see Neely (2022).

11. *Participatory democracy* refers to systems in which decisions are made by the people who are affected by them. On efforts to create equity in bureaucratic organizations, see Dobbin, Schrage, and Kalev (2014).

12. See Vincent Roscigno's (2011) dynamic theory of power, which emphasizes the role of legitimation and discursive processes.

13. Karl Weick (1993, 635) defines sensemaking as an "ongoing accomplish-ment that emerges from efforts to create order and make retrospective sense of what occurs."

14. Katherine Chen (2009, 3) argues that there are unintended consequences to both formalization and ad hoc approaches: "If members underorganize, their organization does not have enough structures, such as designated rules, positions, or procedures, or enough coordination to support members' efforts. If members overorganize, structures and coercive control constrain rather than enable organ-izing efforts." On the importance of informal dynamics at work, see also Freeman (1972); Lopez (2007); and Roy (1959).

15. On the problems of underorganizing in alternative organizations, see Chen (2009); Freeman (1972); Hernandez (2006); and Kleinman (1996).

16. On issues related to overorganizing, see Chen (2009, 13–18); see also Hod-son (2001); Ogasawara (1998); and Sewell (1998).

17. Drawing on research in a high-tech firm and service workplace, Van Maanen and Kunda (1989) examine what they call the "dark side of culture," demonstrating how corporate organizations use rituals to manipulate emotions in order to elicit compliance and solidify managerial control.

18. In contrast to what political theorists call *substantive democracy*, in which all groups participate equally, *procedural democracy* centers on an electoral process that delegates certain responsibilities of participation. On the shifting meanings of democracy in community organizations, see Rothschild and Stephenson (2009).

19. This was most evident along gender and class lines and was heavily influ-enced by the social, economic, and sexual inequalities that exist in the private sphere (Hacker 1989; Kleinman 1996; Pateman 1970, 1989). On gender dynamics in the BAUEN Cooperative, see Sobering (2016).

212

20. I regularly observed members of the cooperative bring their children to work, where they often sat quietly in back offices or behind desks. On a handful of occasions, I encountered children playing in the hallways of certain floors. Until 2015 some members of the cooperative also lived in the hotel. While most were young, unmarried members who could guard the property, others stayed there with their families for a variety of personal reasons.

21. On effectiveness and efficiency in consensus-based decision-making, see Leach (2016).

22. This is similar to the businesslike approach that cooperatives can develop to address market pressure. In his analysis of restructuring processes at Mondragón, Peter Leigh Taylor (1994) argues that concepts like efficiency are socially constructed by organizations and can displace collective goals and values of equality, job security, and working conditions.

23. Elections were held every two years, and nearly all members participated.

24. The administrative council was elected as a unit, not by individual positions. This was debated by the members before the internal election in 2015. Some members speculated that it would be better if they could choose the candidate who was most experienced for each position. Others thought that since the council members had to work so closely together, it was better to elect them as a group to ensure interpersonal dynamics would not be a problem. Despite these debates, no changes were made to the electoral format that year.

25. According to the council members, all members of the cooperative voted in the election with the exception of a handful of members who were on medical leave and unable to vote in person.

26. On clientelism in Argentina, see Auyero (2007); Brusco, Nazareno, and Stokes (2004); and Grindle (2016). Clientelism is neither dead nor unique to countries in the Global South. In her study of contemporary community-based organizations in New York, Nicole Marwell (2004) shows how elected officials may not directly control these organizations but still serve as the conduit of resources.

27. Rumors are just one type of hearsay (DiFonzo and Bordia 2007). They are analytically distinguished from gossip (talking about absent third parties) and urban legends (rumors that take a narrative form), although these forms of informal communication often co-occur in everyday life (Rosnow and Fine 1976). See also Kapferer (1990).

28. I use the term *favoritism* (*amiguismo*) to refer broadly to practices of favoring one person over another for reasons other than merit. A series of overlapping terms can be used to describe favoritism, including *patronage*, *nepotism*, and *cronyism* (Nadler and Schulman 2015). *Merriam-Webster* defines *nepotism* as "favoritism (as in appointment to a job) based on kinship," whereas *cronyism* refers to partiality toward friends ("cronies"), which takes place among insider networks. *Merriam-Webster*, s.v. "nepotism," accessed October 15, 2021, https://www.merriam-webster.com/dictionary/nepotism.

29. Longtime members of the cooperative adopted nicknames for each other based on their resemblance to certain animals, for example, "porcupine," "tadpole," and "crow."

30. On the theoretical foundations of the civic spillover hypothesis, see Pateman (1970). For a contemporary examination of this hypothesis using data on democratic firms in the United States, see Schlachter and Már (2020).

Chapter Three: Hospitality in Cooperation

1. The documentary, "B.A.U.E.N.: Lucha, Cultura, Trabajo," was produced by Grupo Alavío, a media collective that once held office space in the Hotel Bauen (see Grupo Alavío 2015).

2. Compañero is normally translated as "companion" or "comrade." In Argentina the word is also associated with people who identify as Peronist. Juan and Eva Perón regularly used the word to address the nation. For an analysis of Peronism in contemporary Argentina, see Levitsky (2003).

3. In her landmark study of flight attendants, Hochschild (2012) argues that emotions are not simply the reflections of authentic feelings but the managed expression of those feelings based on the social context. Emotional labor thus requires "the coordination of mind and feeling" as an individual works "to induce or suppress feeling in order to sustain the outward countenance that produces the proper state of mind in others" (7).

4. This has a long history in labor process theory. On the extension of labor process theory into the realm of service work, see Leidner (1993) and Hochschild (2012).

5. For an analysis of self-management from a business perspective, see Chung-Herrera, Enz, and Lankau (2003); see also Crawford-Welch (1989).

6. I understand neoliberalism as "a theory of political economic practices that proposes that human well-being can best be advanced by liberating individual entrepreneurial freedoms and skills within an institutional framework characterized by strong private property rights, free markets, and free trade" (Harvey 2005, 2; see also Crowley and Hodson 2014; and Gershon 2011). On an understanding of neoliberalism rooted in the Global South, see Connell and Dados (2014). On discourses of personal branding, see Vallas and Christin (2018).

7. For examples, see Ness and Azzellini (2011).

8. Marcelo Vieta (2019) theorizes autogestión through the lived experiences of workers, providing a detailed analysis of the possibilities and challenges of alternative work organizations (see also Calloway, Colombari, and Iorio 2013). He warns against using the translation—*self-management*—without including the context and history of worker self-management in Argentina. I thus follow his lead to use autogestión in this text.

9. Feminist scholars have argued that changing interactional norms requires a politics of transformation aimed at reconfiguring gendered power relations (Chafetz 1990). To Judith Lorber (1999), subverting the gendered, heterosexist, racist social order must take place at three levels: value and meaning, individual agency and collective action, and institutional practices.

10. In her study of worker cooperatives in the United Kingdom, Elizabeth Hoffmann (2016) also finds that in organizations with shared governance, members must engage in intraorganizational emotional labor that goes well beyond simply doing their jobs.

11. Following the 2001 crisis, the federal government created a series of welfare programs that provided cash payments (called *planes*) for eligible individuals. *Piquetero* organizations like the one Rafi describes were just one type of entity that distributed welfare plans to recipients (Pérez 2018; Svampa and Pereyra 2003).

12. All members of worker cooperatives in Argentina are classified as "self-employed workers" (*monotributos*). Individuals must complete official paperwork (*trámites*) to ensure they receive health insurance and retirement benefits. On the problems of this employment designation in worker cooperatives, see Fernández Vilchez et al. (2011).

13. In 2015, I joined the cooperative as an intern, which allowed me to rotate jobs to gain broad work experience in the hotel. Although I attended orientations and meetings, I never formally joined the cooperative as a voting member. I detail the reasons for this in the appendix.

14. On the importance of emotional dynamics of workplace democracy in the BAUEN Cooperative, see Sobering (2021a).

15. For studies that build on Acker's (1990) concept of an ideal worker to examine how women navigate conflicting cultural schemas of work and family, see Collins (2019); Blair-Loy (2003); and Williams (2001).

16. For women and people of color in conventional organizations, the cultural ideology that supports this definition of an ideal worker creates norms that are often impossible to achieve, thus setting people up for failure. Changing the "ideal worker" norm is possible but difficult. In their study of an organization implementing an innovative workplace initiative to transform the company culture, Erin Kelly and her coauthors (2010) find that even when formal policies change, a masculinized ideal persists.

17. *Porteño* refers to anything that comes from a port city; the term is commonly used to describe people and things from Buenos Aires.

18. Opportunities for participation in the workplace have been associated with overwork. In her study of investment banks in the United States, Alexandra Michel (2014) finds that participatory practices intensified the pace of work and spurred overwork that was self-chosen. As I describe in chapter 5, overwork was also a problem in the BAUEN Cooperative. Members were attentive to this problem, referring to it as a pernicious form of self-exploitation (*autoexploitación*).

19. For a review of the concept of psychological ownership, see Dawkins et al. (2017).

20. On the role of affective commitment in cooperatives, see Jussila, Byrne, and Tuominen (2012).

21. Interview conducted by the Lavaca Collective in 2005.

22. For a review of passion as a cultural schema, see Rao and Neely (2019).

Chapter Four: Rotating Opportunity

1. On the impact of institutional closure devices like licensing, credentialing, certification, and unionization, see Weeden (2002).

2. Both supply factors like workers' occupational choices and demand factors like employer practices are important to understanding occupational segregation (Kanter 1977; Reskin 1993; Reskin, McBrier, and Kmec 1999). See also Bielby and Baron (1987); Glass (1990); Tomaskovic-Devey (1993); and Williams (1995).

3. In his study of hotel housekeepers in the United States, David Brody (2016) details both the intentional design and extensive ongoing labor involved in keeping certain maintenance hidden from customers. He traces much of this to historical hospitality labor processes. Codified in the Statler Service Code (named after the early twentieth-century hotelier E. M. Statler, whose company was later purchased by Hilton), hotels around the globe adopted internal rules for managing the service encounter along with the design of standardized rooms to hide workers from the customer experience. On the dynamic of architecture and labor process in Hilton hotels, see Wharton (2001).

4. An internal labor market distributes workers in an organization through "a set of rules defined independently of the external labor market" (Burawoy 1983, 593; see also Burawoy 1979).

5. Rachel Sherman (2007), however, finds that one hotel she studied had an active internal labor market, providing promotion opportunities and career ladders to its employees.

6. For a critique of post-Fordism, see Vallas (1999).

7. On flexible workplace practices, see Kalleberg (2003); Kelly and Kalev (2006); and Smith (1994, 1997).

8. For examples, see Appelbaum et al. (2000) and Kanter (1989).

9. On the organization of work in hotels, see Otis (2008); and Sherman (2007). Some luxury hotels have avoided such low-road practices, taking an interest in internal labor markets, career development, and functional flexibility (Knox and Walsh 2005).

10. Scholars have documented practices of job rotation in worker cooperatives since the 1970s (Jackall and Levin 1984; Rothschild and Whitt 1986). On job rotation in recuperated businesses in Argentina, see Atzeni and Ghigliani (2007).

11. More specifically, Tomaskovic-Devey et al. (2006) find that between 1966 and 1980, occupational segregation by sex and race and ethnicity declined, but after 1980, only sex segregation continued this downward trend. On the history of equal opportunity legislation, see Dobbin (2009).

12. Using EEO-1 reports from the US Equal Employment Opportunity Commission, Tomaskovic-Devey et al. (2006) analyze patterns of occupational segregation in workplaces, disaggregating findings at the national level to understand industry, regional, and between-group differences. On the gendered outcomes of occupational desegregation, see Roos and Reskin (1992).

13. See also Bielby and Baron (1987) and Tomaskovic-Devey et al. (2006).

14. On the process of opportunity hoarding, see Tilly (1998); Tomaskovic-Devey (1993); and Weeden (2002).

15. *Quinceañeras* are parties that families organize for their daughters when they turn fifteen years old.

16. *Tereré* is a tasty infusion of yerba maté that is prepared with cold water and poured over ice.

17. Men in housekeeping worked as valets, a gendered division of labor characteristic of hotel work (see Reskin and Roos 1998). Whereas housekeepers cleaned guest rooms, valets operated cleaning machinery (i.e., industrial carpet cleaners) in the hallways and hauled the linens to and from the laundry room, located at the very top of the hotel.

18. While some studies measure skill based on the degree of complexity and autonomy in a job (Vallas 1990), constructivist approaches contend that skill is an ideological category that can be used as a mechanism of social closure (Attewell 1990; see also Korczynski 2005; Lafer 2004; Steinberg 1990; and Warhurst, Tilly, and Gatta 2017).

19. On racialized and gender-typed jobs, see Glenn (1992). On the devaluation of care work, see England, Budig, and Folbre (2002).

20. On the nature of work and requisite skills in interactive service jobs, see Gatta, Boushey, and Appelbaum (2009).

21. Sherman (2007, 69–70) also finds that some managers characterize hospitality work as something "you can't teach," instead focusing on hiring and retaining the right "type" of worker. Other studies have also found that managers focus on hiring rather than training (Hochschild 2012; Leidner 1993).

22. As Chris Warhurst, Chris Tilly, and Mary Gatta (2017, 74) make clear, "excluders now need to justify their actions with a discourse of merit—which in the case of jobs translates into skills and who is and isn't deemed to be skilled." On skill recognition in the service sector, see Hampson and Junor (2010, 2015).

23. According to Cynthia Cockburn (1983), skill has three dimensions: (1) it resides in the worker as human capital (Becker 1964); (2) it is part of the job requirement (Braverman 1975); and (3) it involves society's valuation of the first two dimensions. In the BAUEN Cooperative, skill was redefined along all three dimensions.

24. See Belt, Richardson, and Webster (2002) and Moore (2009).

25. A survey conducted by the National Institute to Combat Discrimination, Xenophobia, and Racism found that 71 percent of respondents perceived discrimination toward migrants from neighboring countries like Paraguay. For more information, see Mapa Nacional de la Discriminación (2013).

26. Research has found that antidiscrimination efforts are most effective when job assignment and mobility paths are formalized (Baron, Mittman, and Newman 1991), although even merit-based practices do not completely eliminate bias (Castilla 2008).

27. In their study of women utility workers in the United States, Reskin and Padavic (1988) find a similar process at play. After participating in a strike,

supervisors relied on gender stereotypes to reassign women who had been working in male-typed jobs to more traditionally female jobs. In other words, they used their individual discretion to reinforce gender inequality by re-creating occupational segregation in the workplace.

Chapter Five: The Politics of Equal Pay

1. On ways that different movements have reconfigured the social basis of value, see Collins (2017).

2. On the concept of survival finance, see Sobering (2021b). On survival strategies, see Edin and Lein (1997); Stack (1975); and, more recently, Desmond (2012).

3. In 2020 this fund was managed by the Associates in Critical Need Trust, a nonprofit organization. Many thanks to Adam Reich for pointing out the similarities with corporate practices at Walmart.

4. Considerable research explores the causes and consequences of differences in pay (Cohen and Huffman 2007; Tomaskovic-Devey and Skaggs 2002; Western and Rosenfeld 2011), but very few question the basic presumption that workers are paid differently in the first place.

5. Joan Acker (1989, 6) defines comparable worth as "a strategy for raising the wages of jobs in which the pay is low, due, in part, to the predominance of workers who are members of low status groups, women, or discriminated-against minorities."

6. For a review of research on techniques of job evaluation in comparative worth schemes, see England and Dunn (1988). On how advocates proposed implementing pay adjustments, see Steinberg (1984).

7. On the impacts of the comparable-worth movement, see Blum (1991). Outside the United States, many countries have passed equal-pay legislation. In countries that have more centralized wage-setting practices, government wage boards and unions collaborate to establish minimum pay rates for public- and private-sector employment and are thus able to make modifications to address explicit discrimination.

8. After the passage of the US Equal Pay Act (1963), for example, twenty states implemented comparable-worth policies to address the gender wage gap among public employees. In the private sector, some companies self-report their progress toward pay equity (Michael, Hartmann, and O'Farrell 1989). For a recent example, see Wiener-Bronner (2018).

9. This is what scholars call *vertical pay dispersion*. This contrasts with within-job discrimination and extreme differences in pay, as in the case of some corporate executives who have benefited from the surge in executive compensation (DiPrete, Eirich, and Pittinsky 2010).

10. In fact, as David Graeber (2012) shows, people actually developed credit systems well before the development of currencies. In the nineteenth century, proponents of labor money included John Ruskin and Pierre-Joseph Proudhon, among others. For a review, see Dodd (2016, 342–46).

11. These include Robert Owen's short-lived utopian experiment, the kibbutz movement (Simons and Ingram 2000), and the contemporary intentional community of Twin Oaks, which has been operating since the 1960s in Virginia (Rothschild and Tomchin 2006). One of the businesses associated with the community, Twin Oaks Indexing, created the index for this book.

12. On the connection between this aphorism and contemporary understandings of work, see Chayka (2017).

13. In this noncash exchange, there is no distinction between producer and consumer, prompting theorists to study time banking as a form of coproduction (Cahn 2000). For research on time banks, see Collom, Lasker, and Kyriacou (2016) and Cooper (2013).

14. On alternative currency movements, see North (2007). On alternative currencies in Argentina, see DeMeulenaere (2000) and Pearson (2003).

15. As Gómez (2010) argues, *clubes de trueque* do not offer a meaningful solution to reduce poverty. In Argentina, they were gendered spaces where mostly unemployed middle-class women were able to access goods and services but did not address structural inequalities.

16. At the turn of the twentieth century, Georg Simmel ([1907] 2004) warned against taking money and wages for granted as if they stayed the same across time and space. For more on the context of post-Fordist capitalism, see Krippner (2005).

17. In Argentina, for example, the average family has just over AR$35,000 in debt, which is lower than in countries like the United States.

18. On the growth of the financial sector and its connections with rising inequality, see Lin and Neely (2020). On the ways that financialization has transformed the gendered labor of social reproduction, see Adkins and Dever (2014).

19. Credit markets operate differently than labor markets (Lapavitsas 2014). Both depend on the formal equality of the parties involved. But the extension of credit creates a relationship between debtor and creditor that is fundamentally unequal. This is an interesting consideration for studies of democratic lending. Yet as Greta Krippner (2017, 3) argues in her study of credit in the United States, certain dimensions of credit can mediate status inequality, in particular, "the capacity of borrowers to anchor their demands in the most foundational of rights claims—claims of ownership."

20. All numbers are reported in Argentine pesos. In 2015 the exchange rate was approximated AR$3 to US$1, but this varied substantially over the period of fieldwork.

21. In her study of gendered pay inequalities in five cooperatives in Buenos Aires, Collette Oseen (2016) finds that cooperatives that allowed pay inequalities were not only male-dominated, but also had fewer opportunities for members to participate in democratic decision-making. On the perennial issue of gender inequality in worker-owned businesses, see Sobering, Thomas, and Williams (2014).

22. Although workplace protections have eroded over time, Argentine workers in the formal economy benefit from a national minimum wage, a required annual

bonus, annual vacation time, and required contributions to pensions and health care plans.

23. For a discussion of the free-rider problem in cooperatives, see Lichbach (1996).

24. Pay secrecy is common in the United States. For a review of policies that forbid discussing wages and salaries in US workplaces, see Rosenfeld (2017).

25. There is very little research on the impacts of pay transparency on inequality owing to the very limited data available for private-sector firms. However, using data from Britain, Jake Rosenfeld and Patrick Denice (2015) find that financial disclosure results in higher wages for workers after adjusting for profit, productivity, and other workplace characteristics.

26. In Argentina the *canasta básica* is a combination of forty-five products that are considered the minimum amount required to get necessary calories per person, and the costs of these goods are used to track inflation.

27. Viviana Zelizer's (1994) now-classic work shows how people attribute social meanings to money. As she argues, "Even estimating the quantity of money requires a social accounting involving more than purely rational market calculation" (19).

28. In his study of the social use of money in an Argentine slum, Ariel Wilkis (2015) makes a compelling case that no study of low-wage work in Argentina should neglect the important role of credit and debt.

29. Accounting practices can challenge capitalist logics of profitability. Alice Bryer (2010) shows that while some worker-recuperated businesses retained bureaucratic financial controls, others (like the BAUEN Cooperative) democratized their accounting practices to promote self-management and social responsibility.

30. In case of the BAUEN Cooperative, workers access credit through their ownership stake in the cooperative itself.

31. This peer-to-peer donation is similar to other practices used in firms to acknowledge or compensate work. For example, at Google, employees can nominate coworkers for a cash bonus through an online tool.

32. While this benefit relieves the pressure of relying on loans from family members or loans with high interest rates, it might also (ironically) deepen workers' exposure to outside requests for help since they have access to organizational support (Wherry, Seefeldt, and Alvarez 2019).

33. As a symbolic change, the BAUEN Cooperative renamed the ballroom from El Embajador (the Ambassador) to Simón Bolívar, the name of the Venezuelan military and political leader who helped many South American states win independence from Spain in the early nineteenth century.

Chapter Six: The Activist Workplace

1. Alisha Holland (2017, 13) defines forbearance as "the intentional and revocable nonenforcement of law," often done by politicians to withhold sanctions to maximize votes and rents. In contrast to situations of institutional weakness, Holland analyzes cases where politicians are unwilling to enforce the law. Using

the case of street vendors and urban squatters in Latin America, she shows how politicians use forbearance to mobilize voters and signal their commitment to distributive politics.

2. For an account of evictions in Buenos Aires, see Kabat (2011). For a description of the "Brukman Battle," see Fernández Álvarez (2016); and Klein (2009).

3. These various actors in government, politics, civil society, and the private sector provided what scholars call *certification* to the occupation of the Hotel Bauen (McAdam, Tarrow, and Tilly 2001).

4. Interview conducted by the Lavaca Collective in 2005.

5. While the idea of expropriation may seem extreme, this tactic is regularly used in countries around the globe. In the United States, expropriation is more often referred to as *eminent domain*, when state agencies take private land to build public roads and schools. For a comparison of the use of eminent domain to promote cooperatives in the United States and Argentina, see Ranis (2014).

6. Timo Böhm (2015) defines embedded activists as those integrated into both political and social movement networks, which allows them to combine resources and use insider tactics to build trust.

7. Interview conducted by the Lavaca Collective in 2005.

8. Sixty percent of worker cooperatives have been granted legal protection through expropriation (Palomino et al. 2010). Expropriation, however, is just one way for worker-recuperated businesses to legalize their operations. For a discussion of different political and legal solutions, see Fajn (2003) and Magnani (2009, 101–28).

9. On the clash between the labor rights and private property rights, see Ranis (2010).

10. There has been limited coordination across democratic institutions in Argentina. See Llamazares (2005) for an overview and Levitsky and Murillo (2005) for more information on institutional weakness in Argentine democracy.

11. An exception is IMPA. This recuperated metallurgical factory located in Buenos Aires was expropriated at the national level in 2015. For a history of IMPA, see Kasparian (2009).

12. See the methodological appendix for details on this archival data collection and analysis.

13. Movement size and organizational diversity can impact policy outcomes. On the case of the environmental movement in the United States, see Johnson (2008).

14. For a background on the back-to-back Kirchner administrations in Argentina, see Levitsky and Murillo (2008).

15. For an exposé published in a national newspaper, see O'Donnell (2007). See also Ruggeri, Alfonso, and Balaguer (2017).

16. Boletín Oficial, Decreto 1.302 (2017). Macri was certainly familiar with the BAUEN Cooperative's cause. Before his election to the presidency, he was mayor of Buenos Aires from 2007 to 2015.

17. Carlos Heller had authored one of the bills for expropriation.

221

18. Geographic location, labor process, and political networks are important components in explaining the survival of alternative work organizations. Through a comparative analysis of a worker-recuperated business that survived (the BAUEN Cooperative) and one that failed (FORJA San Martín), Pablo Lapegna and I show that the geographic location not only shapes internal workplace dynamics but also impacts the formation of social and political networks that are key to the continuity of these businesses (Sobering and Lapegna 2021).

19. For a contemporary review, see Brinks, Levitsky, and Murillo (2020).

20. On the "many hands of the state," see Morgan and Orloff (2017).

21. To Holland (2016, 233), forbearance, "or intentional and revocable government leniency toward violations of the law," has three components. First, governments must have the capacity to enforce the law. Cases of other worker-recuperated businesses that were evicted testify to the Argentine state's ability to enforce eviction notices. Second, forbearance requires intention on the part of a politician to change enforcement. The story of the BAUEN Cooperative's legal limbo is filled with rumors of backroom negotiations and interventions on the part of politicians, but I don't have definitive evidence that politicians directly intervened on the cooperative's behalf. Holland admits that this is a "high evidentiary bar," but it is necessary to distinguish forbearance from what scholars call "institutional drift," which results from bureaucratic noncompliance (234). Finally, forbearance must be revocable in practice. The constant threat of eviction experienced by the BAUEN Cooperative is a case in point: their informal permission to use the hotel was always subject to reversal.

22. On theorizing the state as ambivalent, see Auyero and Sobering (2019). In his study of three other recuperated businesses in Argentina, Marcelo Vieta (2019, 438–52) also characterizes their relationship with state actors as ambivalent.

23. Research on worker-recuperated businesses has found that the process of struggle (*lucha*) has meaningful impacts on the types of self-management that each organization adopts and the practices developed inside the business (Fajn and Rebón 2005).

24. Two of these members had previous experience participating in social movements. Professional activists tend to institutionalize activist tactics into organizations, which ultimately helps to maintain social movements when environmental conditions change (Staggenborg 1988).

25. In just one example, after a march to the city council in 2005, a press release disseminated the next day said, "Some of the organizations, assemblies, parties, and movements of the unemployed that accompanied us in the march yesterday were: delegates from the Subway, workers from FaSinPat—ex Cerámica Zanón, workers from Brukman, UTP, M26 de Junio, MTR CUBA, MTD Resistir y Vencer, Comedor Infantil 'Los Pibes,' Barrios de Pie, Cooperativa Manos, Asamblea San Telmo, Interbloque de Izquierda, Ex petroleros de YPF Jujuy y Salta, B.O.P, UTDOCH, OLP, Izquierda Unida, PC, MST, PO, PTS y FTC (Solano, Garay, Temperley, Lomas de Zamora), and others."

26. Denise Kasparian (2012) calls these "non-market interactions" that are generally motivated by solidarity instead of economic rationality.

27. For years, approximately twenty members lived on the unused floors of the Hotel Bauen. In 2014 the Workers Assembly decided to end the practice to facilitate political efforts to expropriate the property. They also voted to support members to move out by providing zero-interest loans to help with the costs. Members explained to me that the cooperative would look more official if no one lived there. In early 2015 only three members still resided in the hotel, but they were transitioning to other housing arrangements.

28. FaSinPat stands for *fábrica sin patrón* (factory without a boss).

29. FACTA went on to help form a higher-level organization, the National Confederation of Worker Cooperatives (CNCT). For an analysis of the latter, see Faulk (2016).

30. Karen Ann Faulk (2016, 296) traces the utopian visions that underpin these umbrella organizations, explaining how the National Confederation of Worker Cooperatives, which is made up of thirty federations of worker cooperatives in Argentina, seeks to "(1) advocate for dignified working conditions; (2) extend and deepen the idea and practice of worker self-management; and (3) lay the foundation of an alternative, social economy."

31. This subtitle draws on the title of Kanter's book *Commitment and Community: Communes and Utopias in Sociological Perspective* (1972).

32. For a contemporary analysis of the creation of community in communes in the United States, see Vaisey (2007).

33. On the emotional dynamics of workplace democracy, see Sobering (2021a).

Conclusions

1. On the breadth and challenges of civic engagement, see Lee, McQuarrie, and Walker (2015).

2. Although he certainly didn't mean it as such, Hilton's call to dream is similar to Ernst Bloch's defense of utopian thinking as "a mode of thought in which reason is allied with the imagination" (Weeks 2011, 187).

3. In setting the agenda for an emancipatory social science, Wright (2010) explains that the starting point is to identify the ways that social structures systematically impose harm on people. The second task, he argues, is to develop theories of alternatives to existing institutions that would eliminate or mitigate these injustices.

4. Equality is a central sociological concept but remains "open to extensive reformulation in terms of relational thinking" (Emirbayer 1997, 291).

5. The study of real utopias is part of a broader chorus of scholars calling for the development of what Monica Prasad (2018) calls *problem-solving sociology* (see also Graizbord 2019).

6. More flexible and humane work practices are not only important for reducing inequality, but also can significantly improve workers' physical and mental health (Kelly and Moen 2020). For a review of participatory practices in organizations, see Lee (2015).

223

7. Shared capitalism refers to a system in which workers become partial owners in their firms. On the extent and impact of these organizational arrangements in the US, see Kruse, Freeman, and Blasi (2011).

8. Carole Pateman (1970, 69) calls participation used to increase efficiency without including people in decision-making processes *pseudo-participation*.

9. Decades of research shows that sharing knowledge and power with workers and allowing them greater discretion over their everyday tasks is good for business (Appelbaum et al. 2000; Kelly and Moen 2020). For a review of the business case for workplace democracy, see Johnson (2006).

10. See Wright (2010). I'd like to thank Dustin Avent-Holt for encouraging me to take on this normative question and articulate a "Sobering egalitarianism" to open debates about equality projects.

11. David Graeber (2018) argues that "bullshit jobs" are those that are so completely pointless that even the person performing them doesn't see their value.

12. Cooperative business development requires not only dedicated people, but public policy and state support. On the challenges and opportunities of workplace recuperation, see Ranis (2016).

13. By "utopian demands," Weeks (2011, 176) refers to "a political demand that takes the form not of a narrowly pragmatic reform but of a more substantial transformation of the present configuration of social relations."

14. This is my adaptation. Originally published in 1852 in "The Eighteenth Brumaire of Louis Bonaparte," the original quote exclusively references "men" (Marx 1978, 595).

15. According to Beckert (2016, 2), a theory of fictional expectations is based in "the unique human ability to imagine future states of the world that are different from the present."

Epilogue

1. In March 2020 Argentina modified the Productive Recovery Program, which guaranteed a salary for up to twelve months for workers affected by the pandemic. Self-managed workers also received some support from the Ministry of Labor, but the cooperative didn't receive support from a law passed to support the tourism industry (Sustaining and Reactivating Tourism Law, No. 27.563). The Ministry of Social Development created a program called Recuperar to provide small subsidies to worker-recuperated businesses. See Tonarelli (2020). On the impacts of the pandemic on worker cooperatives and recuperated businesses, see Ruggeri (2020).

2. This interview was originally broadcast on Radio Sur and reported in numerous news articles. See Moreno (2020).

3. On worker resistance to *macrismo*, see Ruggeri and Gigliarelli (2021). On the specific case of the BAUEN Cooperative, see Meyer (2017).

4. By 2020, this number had jumped to over 40 percent (INDEC n.d.).

5. Over the years, multiple federations had been housed in the Hotel Bauen. These include FACTA, Red Gráfica, and the National Confederation of Worker Cooperatives.

6. The interview conducted by *El Grito del Sur* (2020) was reproduced by multiple media outlets.

7. On the idea of survival in alternative organizations, see Sobering and Lapegna (2021).

8. Attaque 77, "Donde las Águilas se Atreven," track 4 on *Obras Cumbres*, BMG Ariola Argentina, 2006.

9. For the open letter in Spanish, see BAUEN Cooperative (2020).

Methodological Appendix

1. For a history of the cooperative movement, see Curl (2009).

2. Andrea Smith's keynote speech on November 3, 2007, at the North American Students of Cooperation Institute about her participation in the radical feminist network INCITE! Women of Color against Violence (now called INCITE! Women, Gender Non-Conforming, and Trans People of Color against Violence) and the work of Jessica Gordon Nembhard (2014) were particularly influential to me.

3. On the merits of ethnography as an approach to studying organizations, see Tope et al. (2005).

4. Observant participation inverts the traditional approach to participant observation by calling for a deeper involvement in the field. For a recent review, see Seim (2021). See also Hoang (2018); Mears (2013); and Wacquant (2015).

5. Organizational ethnographies are shaped by the researcher's position in the workplace. In my case, as I detail in chapter 4, members of the BAUEN Cooperative also had opportunities to rotate jobs, so my experience of different sectors of the hotel—while accelerated—wasn't totally foreign to the people working there.

6. Familiarity and social proximity are two ways that Pierre Bourdieu (1996) suggests can create more "nonviolent" forms of communication.

7. I was particularly careful when confronted with workplace gossip. Different from the rumors that I analyze in chapter 2, *gossip* refers to negative talk about absent third parties. While I did not remove myself from conversations involving gossip, I refrained from sharing personal details about members I had worked with in different sectors. On the problems of gossip in ethnographic access, see Carmel (2011).

8. For meetings I attended, my name was rarely included in the minutes.

9. On three models of transparency in ethnographic research (naming places, naming people, and sharing data), see Reyes (2018).

10. Mitchell Duneier (2011), for example, proposes two types of thought experiments—the ethnographic trial and the inconvenience sample—to help ethnographers produce more reliable data.

11. Many features of human subject research are regulated through institutional review boards. On the politics of this ethics review process in the United States, see Babb (2020).

12. The elected officers during the time of my fieldwork approved my research and granted me access to the organization. The project was approved by the Institutional Review Board at the University of Texas at Austin (Study #2013-10-0081).

225

13. Interestingly, this observation was informed by his own ethnographic research in the Shetland Hotel. See Goffman (1959, 116–18, 121–23).

14. Alberto Nisman was an Argentine lawyer who served as the chief investigator of the 1994 bombing of the Argentine Jewish Mutual Association (AMIA), a Jewish center in Buenos Aires, that killed eighty-five people. In the final days of 2014, Nisman had accused then-president Cristina Fernández de Kirchner of covering up the role of Iran in the country's deadliest terrorist attack. The day before he was scheduled to testify, he was found dead in his home in an apparent suicide. The details of the death, including the role of former intelligence officers like Stiuso, were regularly reported on in newspapers throughout 2015. In 2017 a judge concluded that Nisman had been murdered, and the former president and other high-ranking officials were indicted for treason.

15. On the paradoxes of feminist ethnography, see Stacey (1988) and, more recently, Fields (2013).

16. What Goffman (1989, 125) calls "getting into place" requires "subjecting yourself, your own body and your own personality, and your own social situation to the set of contingencies that play upon a set of individuals so that you can physically and ecologically penetrate their circle of response to their social situation, or their work situation." As part of this immersion, I worked the long hours and late nights in the hotel, experiencing what Kimberly Kay Hoang (2015) calls the "embodied costs" of getting deeply involved in a field site and in research subjects' lives.

17. This totaled over eight hundred and fifteen single-spaced pages of field notes based on over one thousand hours of participant observation in the Hotel Bauen.

18. While qualitative research methods are different from psychoanalytic and therapeutic techniques, ethnographers can experience transference (when the researcher awakens an emotional reaction in the respondent) and countertransference (when the researcher responds to the transference). As Yiannis Gabriel and Eda Ulus (2015, 44) observe, "Reflecting on our own emotion . . . can offer powerful insights into elusive unconscious emotions, and can also help us make sense of the emotional dynamics of the interview situation itself."

19. Only two people asked not to be audio-recorded. For those interviews I took detailed notes to ensure that I captured direct quotes accurately.

References

Acker, Joan. 1989. *Doing Comparable Worth: Gender, Class, and Pay Equity*. Philadelphia: Temple University Press.

Acker, Joan. 1990. "Hierarchies, Jobs, Bodies: A Theory of Gendered Organizations." *Gender and Society* 4 (2): 139–58.

Acker, Joan. 2006. "Inequality Regimes: Gender, Class, and Race in Organizations." *Gender and Society* 20 (4): 441–64.

Adkins, Lisa. 2015. "What Are Post-Fordist Wages? Simmel, Labor Money, and
the Problem of Value." *South Atlantic Quarterly* 114 (2): 331–53.

Adkins, Lisa, and Maryanne Dever. 2014. "Housework, Wages and Money: The
Category of the Female Principal Breadwinner in Financial Capitalism."
Australian Feminist Studies 29 (79): 50–66.

Adler, Patricia A., and Peter H. Adler. 2004. *Paradise Laborers: Hotel Work in the Global Economy*. Ithaca, NY: Cornell University Press.

Anderson, Elizabeth S. 1999. "What Is the Point of Equality?" *Ethics* 109 (2): 287–337.

Anderson, Elizabeth S. 2017. *Private Government: How Employers Rule Our Lives*. Princeton, NJ: Princeton University Press.

Anteby, Michel. 2015. "Denials, Obstructions, and Silences: Lessons from Repertoires of Field Resistance (and Embrace)." In *Handbook of Qualitative Organizational Research: Innovative Pathways and Methods*, edited by Kimberly D. Elsbach and Roderick M. Kramer, 197–205. New York: Routledge.

Appelbaum, Eileen, Thomas Bailey, Peter Berg, and Arne L. Kalleberg. 2000. *Manufacturing Advantage: Why High Performance Work Systems Pay Off*. Ithaca, NY: Cornell University Press.

Attewell, Paul. 1990. "What Is Skill?" *Work and Occupations* 17 (4): 422–48.

Atzeni, Maurizio, ed. 2012. *Alternative Work Organizations*. New York: Palgrave Macmillan.

Atzeni, Maurizio, and Pablo Ghigliani. 2007. "Labour Process and Decision-Making in Factories under Workers' Self-Management: Empirical Evidence from Argentina." *Work, Employment and Society* 21 (4): 653–71.

Auyero, Javier. 2007. *Routine Politics and Violence in Argentina: The Gray Zone of State Power*. Cambridge: Cambridge University Press.

Auyero, Javier, and Katherine Sobering. 2019. *The Ambivalent State: Police-Criminal Collusion at the Urban Margins*. New York: Oxford University Press.

Avent-Holt, Dustin. 2020. "An Egalitarian's Cautionary Note on Rent Theory." Unpublished manuscript, Department of Social Sciences, Augusta University, Augusta, GA.

Avent-Holt, Dustin, and Donald Tomaskovic-Devey. 2010. "The Relational Basis of Inequality: Generic and Contingent Wage Distribution Processes." *Work and Occupations* 37 (2): 162–93.

Babb, Sarah. 2020. *Regulating Human Research: IRBs from Peer Review to Compliance Bureaucracy*. Stanford, CA: Stanford University Press.

Baiocchi, Gianpaolo, and Ernesto Ganuza. 2016. *Popular Democracy: The Paradox of Participation*. Stanford, CA: Stanford University Press.

Baker, John, Kathleen Lynch, Sarah Cantillon, and Judy Walsh. 2004. *Equality: From Theory to Action*. 2nd ed. London: Palgrave Macmillan.

Baron, James N., and William T. Bielby. 1980. "Bringing the Firms Back In: Stratification, Segmentation, and the Organization of Work." *American Sociological Review* 45 (5): 737–65.

Baron, James N., Brian S. Mittman, and Andrew E. Newman. 1991. "Targets of Opportunity: Organizational and Environmental Determinants of Gender Integration within the California Civil Service, 1979–1985." *American Journal of Sociology* 96 (6): 1362–401.

BAUEN Cooperative. 2020. "Carta abierta de los trabajadores del Bauen." *Tiempo Argentino*, October 6, 2020. https://www.tiempoar.com.ar/politica/carta -abierta-de-los-trabajadores-y-trabajadoras-de-la-cooperativa-bauen/.

Becker, Gary S. 1964. *Human Capital: A Theoretical and Empirical Analysis.* Chicago: University of Chicago Press.

Becker, Howard S. 1970. *Sociological Work: Methods and Substance.* Chicago: Aldine.

Beckert, Jens. 2016. *Imagined Futures: Fictional Expectations and Capitalist Dynamics.* Cambridge, MA: Harvard University Press.

Belt, Vicki, Ranald Richardson, and Juliet Webster. 2002. "Women, Social Skill and Interactive Service Work in Telephone Call Centres." *New Technology, Work and Employment* 17 (1): 20–34.

Benford, Robert D., and David A. Snow. 2000. "Framing Processes and Social Movements: An Overview and Assessment." *Annual Review of Sociology* 26:611–39.

Bernstein, Ethan, John Bunch, Niko Canner, and Michael Lee. 2016. "Beyond the Holacracy Hype." *Harvard Business Review,* July–August. https://hbr.org /2016/07/beyond-the-holacracy-hype.

Bernstein, Paul. 1983. *Workplace Democratization: Its Internal Dynamics.* New Brunswick, NJ: Transaction Books.

Berry, Daphne P. 2013. "Effects of Cooperative Membership and Participation in Decision Making on Job Satisfaction of Home Health Aides." In *Sharing Ownership, Profits, and Decision-Making in the 21st Century,* edited by Douglas Kruse, 3–25. Advances in the Economic Analysis of Participatory and Labor-Managed Firms 14. Bingley, UK: Emerald.

Berry, Daphne P., and Myrtle P. Bell. 2018. "Worker Cooperatives: Alternative Governance for Caring and Precarious Work." *Equality, Diversity and Inclusion: An International Journal* 37 (4): 376–91.

Bielby, William T., and James N. Baron. 1987. "Undoing Discrimination: Job Integration and Comparable Worth." In *Ingredients for Women's Employment Policy,* edited by Christin. E. Bose and Glenna D. Spitze, 211–29. Albany: State University of New York Press.

Blair-Loy, Mary. 2003. *Competing Devotions: Career and Family among Women Executives.* Cambridge, MA: Harvard University Press.

Blum, Linda M. 1991. *Between Feminism and Labor: The Significance of the Comparable Worth Movement.* Berkeley: University of California Press.

Böhm, Timo. 2015. "Activists in Politics: The Influence of Embedded Activists on the Success of Social Movements." *Social Problems* 62 (4): 477–98.

Bourdieu, Pierre. 1996. "Understanding." *Theory, Culture and Society* 13 (2): 17–37.

Bourdieu, Pierre, Jean-Claude Chamboredon, and Jean-Claude Passeron. 1991. *The Craft of Sociology: Epistemological Preliminaries.* Edited by Beate Krais. Translated by Richard Nice. New York: Walter de Gruyter.

Brabazon, Honor. 2016. "Occupying Legality: The Subversive Use of Law in Latin American Occupation Movements." *Bulletin of Latin American Research* 36 (1): 21–35.

Braverman, Harry. 1975. *Labor and Monopoly Capital: The Degradation of Work in the Twentieth Century.* New York: Monthly Review Press.

Brennan, James P. 2018. *Argentina's Missing Bones: Revisiting the History of the Dirty War.* Berkeley: University of California Press.

Brinks, Daniel M., Steven Levitsky, and María Victoria Murillo, eds. 2020. *The Politics of Institutional Weakness in Latin America*. Cambridge: Cambridge University Press.

Brody, David. 2016. *Housekeeping by Design: Hotels and Labor*. Chicago: University of Chicago Press.

Brusco, Valeria, Marcelo Nazareno, and Susan Carol Stokes. 2004. "Vote Buying in Argentina." *Latin American Research Review* 39 (2): 66–88.

Bryer, Alice. 2010. "Beyond Bureaucracies? The Struggle for Social Responsibility in the Argentine Workers' Cooperatives." *Critique of Anthropology* 30 (1): 41–61.

Burawoy, Michael. 1979. *Manufacturing Consent: Changes in the Labor Process under Monopoly Capitalism*. Chicago: University of Chicago Press.

Burawoy, Michael. 1983. "Between the Labor Process and the State: The Changing Face of Factory Regimes under Advanced Capitalism." *American Sociological Review* 48 (5): 587–605.

Burawoy, Michael. 2003. "Revisits: An Outline of a Theory of Reflexive Ethnography." *American Sociological Review* 68 (5): 645–79.

Cahn, Edgar S. 2000. *No More Throw-Away People: The Co-production Imperative*. Washington, DC: Essential Books.

Calloway, Cecilia, Bruno Colombari, and Santiago Iorio. 2013. "Invenciones y resistencias: Construyendo autogestión en las fábricas y empresas recuperadas." *Revista del Observatorio Social sobre Empresas Recuperadas y Autogestionadas (OSERA)*, no. 8. http://webiigg.sociales.uba.ar/empresasrecuperadas/PDF/PDF_08/Invenciones_y_resistencias.pdf.

Cancian, Francesca M. 1995. "Truth and Goodness: Does the Sociology of Inequality Promote Social Betterment?" *Sociological Perspectives* 38 (3): 339–56.

Carmel, Simon. 2011. "Social Access in the Workplace: Are Ethnographers Gossips?" *Work, Employment and Society* 25 (3): 551–60.

Castilla, Emilio J. 2008. "Gender, Race, and Meritocracy in Organizational Careers." *American Journal of Sociology* 113 (6): 1479–526.

Chafetz, Janet Saltzman. 1990. *Gender Equity: An Integrated Theory of Stability and Change*. Newbury Park, CA: Sage.

Chayka, Kyle. 2017. "Time Is Money, but You Don't Need to Work Non-Stop." *Pacific Standard*, June 14, 2017. https://psmag.com/economics/time-money-doesnt-mean-need-work-non-stop-81438.

Chen, Katherine K. 2009. *Enabling Creative Chaos: The Organization behind the Burning Man Event*. Chicago: University of Chicago Press.

Chen, Katherine K. 2016. "Using Extreme Cases to Understand Organizations." In *Handbook of Qualitative Organizational Research: Innovative Pathways and Methods*, edited by Kimberly D. Elsbach and Roderick M. Kramer, 33–44. New York: Routledge.

Chen, Katherine K., and Victor T. Chen, eds. 2021. *Organizational Imaginaries: Tempering Capitalism and Tending to Communities through Cooperatives and Collectivist Democracy*. Research in the Sociology of Organizations 72. Bingley, UK: Emerald.

Cheney, George. 1999. *Values at Work: Employee Participation Meets Market Pressure at Mondragón.* Ithaca, NY: Cornell University Press.

Cheney, George, Iñaki Santa Cruz, Ana Maria Peredo, and Elías Nazareno. 2014. "Worker Cooperatives as an Organizational Alternative: Challenges, Achievements and Promise in Business Governance and Ownership." *Organization* 21 (5): 591–603.

Chodorow, Nancy J. 1978. *The Reproduction of Mothering: Psychoanalysis and the Sociology of Gender.* Berkeley: University of California Press.

Chodorow, Nancy J. 2000. "Reflections on *The Reproduction of Mothering*— Twenty Years Later." *Studies in Gender and Sexuality* 1 (4): 337–48.

Chung-Herrera, Beth, Cathy Enz, and Melenie Lankau. 2003. "Grooming Future Hospitality Leaders: A Competencies Model." *Cornell Hotel and Restaurant Administration Quarterly* 44 (3): 17–25.

Clarín. 2020. "Por la cuarentena, cada vez hay más hoteles de 4 y 5 estrellas al borde del cierre, dice la Asociación de Hoteles de Turismo." September 25, 2020. https://www.clarin.com/viajes/cuarentena-vez-hoteles-4-5-estrellas -borde-cierre-dice-asociacion-hoteles-turismo_0_uizrdojzP.html.

Clark, Gabriel, and Javier Antivero. 2009. "La intervención sindical en las empresas recuperadas en Argentina: Hacia la reconstrucción selectiva de un model de justicia social." In *Las empresas recuperadas: Autogestión obrera en Argentina y América Latina,* edited by Andrés Ruggeri, 125–37. Buenos Aires: Facultad de Filosofia y Letras, Universidad de Buenos Aires.

Cockburn, Cynthia. 1983. *Brothers: Male Dominance and Technological Change.* London: Pluto.

Cohen, G. A. 2008. *Rescuing Justice and Equality.* Cambridge, MA: Harvard University Press.

Cohen, Philip N., and Matt L. Huffman. 2007. "Working for the Woman? Female Managers and the Gender Wage Gap." *American Sociological Review* 72 (5): 681–704.

Collins, Caitlyn. 2019. *Making Motherhood Work: How Women Manage Careers and Caregiving.* Princeton, NJ: Princeton University Press.

Collins, Jane L. 2001. "Flexible Specialization and the Garment Industry." *Competition and Change* 5 (2): 165–200.

Collins, Jane L. 2003. *Threads: Gender, Labor, and Power in the Global Apparel Industry.* Chicago: University of Chicago Press.

Collins, Jane L. 2017. *The Politics of Value: Three Movements to Change How We Think about the Economy.* Chicago: University of Chicago Press.

Collins, Patricia Hill. 2000. *Black Feminist Thought: Knowledge, Consciousness, and the Politics of Empowerment.* New York: Routledge.

Collom, Ed, Judith N. Lasker, and Corinne Kyriacou. 2016. *Equal Time, Equal Value: Community Currencies and Time Banking in the US.* New York: Routledge.

Comisión Nacional sobre la Despaparición de Personas (conadep). 2011. *Nunca Más: Informe de la Comisión Nacional sobre la Desaparición de Personas.* Buenos Aires: Eudeba. https://www.digitaliapublishing.com/a/32618.

Connell, Raewyn, and Nour Dados. 2014. "Where in the World Does Neoliberalism Come From?" *Theory and Society* 43 (2): 117–38.

Contreras, Randol. 2019. "Transparency and Unmasking Issues in Ethnographic Crime Research: Methodological Considerations." *Sociological Forum* 34 (2): 293–12.

Cooper, Davina. 2013. *Everyday Utopias: The Conceptual Life of Promising Spaces.* Durham, NC: Duke University Press.

Correll, Shelley J. 2017. "sws 2016 Feminist Lecture: Reducing Gender Biases in Modern Workplaces: A Small Wins Approach to Organizational Change." *Gender and Society* 31 (6): 725–50.

Correll, Shelley J., Erin L. Kelly, Lindsey Trimble O'Connor, and Joan C. Williams. 2014. "Redesigning, Redefining Work." *Work and Occupations* 41 (1): 3–17.

Cracogna, Dante, Antonio Fici, and Hagen Henrÿ, eds. 2013. *International Handbook of Cooperative Law.* Vol. 14. Berlin: Springer.

Crawford-Welch, Simon. 1989. "Self-Management in Hospitality Organizations: A Conceptual Analysis." *Hospitality Education and Research Journal* 13 (3): 435–47.

Crowley, Martha, and Randy Hodson. 2014. "Neoliberalism at Work." *Social Currents* 1 (1): 91–108.

Curl, John. 2009. *For All the People: Uncovering the Hidden History of Cooperation, Cooperative Movements, and Communalism in America.* Oakland, CA: PM Press.

Dahl, Robert A. 2007. *On Political Equality.* New Haven, CT: Yale University Press.

Dawkins, Sarah, Amy Wei Tian, Alexander Newman, and Angela Martin. 2017. "Psychological Ownership: A Review and Research Agenda." *Journal of Organizational Behavior* 38 (2): 163–83.

Deener, Andrew. 2018. "The Architecture of Ethnographic Knowledge: Narrowing Down Data and Contexts in Search of Sociological Cases." *Sociological Perspectives* 61 (2): 295–313.

DeMeulenaere, Stephen. 2000. "Reinventing the Market: Alternative Currencies and Community Development in Argentina." *International Journal of Community Currency Research* 4 (3). https://ijccr.net/2012/05/22/reinventing-the-market-alternative-currencies-and-community-development-in-argentina/.

Desmond, Matthew. 2012. "Disposable Ties and the Urban Poor." *American Journal of Sociology* 117 (5): 1295–1335.

DiFonzo, Nicholas. 2008. *The Watercooler Effect: An Indispensable Guide to Understanding and Harnessing the Power of Rumors.* New York: Avery.

DiFonzo, Nicholas, and Prashant Bordia. 2007. "Rumor, Gossip and Urban Legends." *Diogenes* 54 (1): 19–35.

DiMaggio, Paul J., and Walter W. Powell. 1983. "The Iron Cage Revisited: Institutional Isomorphism and Collective Rationality in Organizational Fields." *American Sociological Review* 48 (2): 147–60.

DiPrete, Thomas, Greg Eirich, and Matthew Pittinsky. 2010. "Compensation Benchmarking, Leapfrogs, and the Surge in Executive Pay." *American Journal of Sociology* 115 (6): 1671–712.

232

DiPrete, Thomas A., and Brittany Fox-Williams. 2021. "The Relevance of In-equality Research in Sociology for Inequality Reduction." *Socius: Sociological Research for a Dynamic World* 7. https://journals.sagepub.com/doi/full/10.1177/23780231211020199.

Dobbin, Frank. 2009. *Inventing Equal Opportunity*. Princeton, NJ: Princeton University Press.

Dobbin, Frank, Daniel Schrage, and Alexandra Kalev. 2014. "Resisting the Iron Cage: The Effects of Bureaucratic Reforms to Promote Equity." Social Science Research Network, September 30, 2014. http://papers.ssrn.com/abstract=2513869.

Dodd, Nigel. 2016. *The Social Life of Money*. Princeton, NJ: Princeton University Press.

Duneier, Mitchell. 2011. "How Not to Lie with Ethnography." *Sociological Methodology* 41 (1): 1–11.

Echaide, Javier. 2007. "Sobre lo político y lo jurídico: La batalla legal de las empresas recuperadas." *Revista Idelcoop* 34 (176): 82–102.

Economic Commission for Latin America and the Caribbean. n.d. "CEPALSTAT: Bases de Datos y Publicaciones Estadísticas." Accessed October 15, 2021. http://estadisticas.cepal.org/cepalstat/WEB_CEPALSTAT/Portada.asp.

Edin, Kathryn, and Laura Lein. 1997. "Work, Welfare, and Single Mothers' Economic Survival Strategies." *American Sociological Review* 62 (2): 253–66.

El Grito del Sur. 2020. "La cooperativa del Hotel Bauen dejará el histórico edificio de Avenida Callao." ANRed: Agencia de Noticias RedAcción. September 24, 2020. https://www.anred.org/2020/09/24/la-cooperativa-del-hotel-bauen-dejara-el-historico-edificio-de-avenida-callao-es-muy-doloroso-pero-seguiremos-en-otro-lado/.

Emerson, Robert M., Rachel I. Fretz, and Linda L. Shaw. 1995. *Writing Ethnographic Fieldnotes*. Chicago: University of Chicago Press.

Emirbayer, Mustafa. 1997. "Manifesto for a Relational Sociology." *American Journal of Sociology* 103 (2): 281–317.

England, Paula, Michelle Budig, and Nancy Folbre. 2002. "Wages of Virtue: The Relative Pay of Care Work." *Social Problems* 49 (4): 455–73.

England, Paula, and Dana Dunn. 1988. "Evaluating Work and Comparable Worth." *Annual Review of Sociology* 14 (1): 227–48.

Fajn, Gabriel. 2003. *Fábricas y empresas recuperadas: Protesta social, autogestión y rupturas en la subjectividad*. Buenos Aires: Centro Cultural de la Cooperación, Instituto Movilizador de Fondos Cooperativos.

Fajn, Gabriel, and Julián Rebón. 2005. "El taller ¿sin cronómetro? Apuntes acerca de las empresas recuperadas." *Revista Herramienta*, no. 28. https://herramienta.com.ar/articulo.php?id=300.

Faulk, Karen Ann. 2016. "'Recuperar el trabajo': Utopia and the Work of Recovery in an Argentine Cooperativist Movement." *Journal of Latin American and Caribbean Anthropology* 21 (2): 294–316.

Fernández, Ana María, Xabier Imaz, and Cecilia Calloway. 2006. "La invención de las fábricas sin patrón." In *Política y subjetividad: Asambleas barriales y*

233

fábricas recuperadas, edited by Ana María Fernández, 201–42. Buenos Aires: Tinta Limón.

Fernández Álvarez, María Inés. 2012. "Ocupar, resistir, producir . . . sostener: El problema de la sustentabilidad en las experiencias de gestión colectiva del trabajo." *Revista del Observatorio Social sobre Empresas Recuperadas y Autogestionadas (OSERA)*, no. 7. http://webiigg.sociales.uba.ar /empresasrecuperadas/PDF/PDF_07/F_ALVAREZ.pdf.

Fernández Álvarez, María Inés. 2016. "Productive Work as Political Action: Daily Practices of Struggle and Work in a Recovered Factory." *Journal of Latin American and Caribbean Anthropology* 21 (2): 254–75.

Fernández Álvarez, María Inés, and Florencia Partenio. 2010. "Empresas recuperadas en Argentina: Producciones, espacios y tiempos de género." *Tabula Rasa: Revista de Humanidades*, no. 12, 119–35.

Fernández Vilchez, Iliana Irupé, María Eleonora Feser, Valeria Mutuberría Lazarini, and Facundo Ureta. 2011. "Seguridad social y empresas recuperadas por sus trabajadores: Problemáticas en Argentina." *Revista del Observatorio Social de Empresas Recuperadas y Autogestionadas (OSERA)*, no. 5. http:// webiigg.sociales.uba.ar/empresasrecuperadas/PDF/PDF_05/Mutuberria5.pdf.

Ferree, Myra Marx, and Patricia Yancey Martin, eds. 1995. *Feminist Organizations: Harvest of the New Women's Movement*. Philadelphia: Temple University Press.

Fields, Jessica. 2013. "Feminist Ethnography: Critique, Conflict, and Ambivalent Observance." *Journal of Contemporary Ethnography* 42 (4): 492–500.

Franklin, Benjamin. 1748. "Advice to a Young Tradesman." Founders Online, National Archive. July 21. https://founders.archives.gov/documents/Franklin /01-03-02-0130.

Fraser, Nancy. 2000. "Rethinking Recognition." *New Left Review*, no. 3, 107–20.

Freeman, Jo. 1972. "The Tyranny of Structurelessness." *Second Wave* 2 (1): 1–6.

Fung, Archon. 2013. "Infotopia: Unleashing the Democratic Power of Transparency." *Politics and Society* 41 (2): 183–212.

Fung, Archon, Mary Graham, and David Weil. 2008. *Full Disclosure: The Perils and Promise of Transparency*. Cambridge: Cambridge University Press.

Gabriel, Yiannis, and Eda Ulus. 2015. "'It's All in the Plot': Narrative Explorations of Work-Related Emotions." In *Methods of Exploring Emotions*, edited by Helena Flam and Jochen Kleres, 36–45. London: Routledge.

Galeano, Eduardo. 2020. "'Ventana sobre la Utopía,' Texto de *Las Palabras Andantes*." In *Homenaje a Eduardo Galeano*, 18. Madrid: Siglo XXI de España Editores. http://sigloxxieditores.com/media/imagenes/Homenaje_a _Galeano.pdf.

Gasalla, Juan. 2017. "La brecha salarial entre hombres y mujeres crece en empleos menos calificados." *Infobae*, March 7, 2017. https://www.infobae.com /economia/2017/03/07/la-brecha-salarial-entre-hombres-y-mujeres-crece -en-empleos-menos-calificados/.

Gatta, Mary, Heather Boushey, and Eileen Appelbaum. 2009. "High-Touch and Here-to-Stay: Future Skills Demands in US Low Wage Service Occupations." *Sociology* 43 (5): 968–89.

Gershon, Ilana. 2011. "'Neoliberal Agency.'" *Current Anthropology* 52 (4): 537–55.

Gibson-Graham, J. K. 2003. "Enabling Ethical Economies: Cooperativism and Class." *Critical Sociology* 29 (2): 123–61.

Glass, Jennifer. 1990. "The Impact of Occupational Segregation on Working Conditions." *Social Forces* 68 (3): 779–96.

Glenn, Evelyn Nakano. 1992. "From Servitude to Service Work: Historical Continuities in the Racial Division of Paid Reproductive Labor." *Signs* 18 (1): 1–43.

Goffman, Erving. 1959. *The Presentation of Self in Everyday Life*. Garden City, NY: Anchor Books.

Goffman, Erving. 1989. "On Fieldwork." *Journal of Contemporary Ethnography* 18 (2): 123–32.

Gómez, Georgina M. 2010. "What Was the Deal for the Participants of the Argentine Local Currency Systems, the Redes de Trueque?" *Environment and Planning A* 42 (7): 1669–85.

Graeber, David. 2012. *Debt: The First 5,000 Years*. Brooklyn Melville House.

Graeber, David. 2014. *The Democracy Project: A History, a Crisis, a Movement*. New York: Penguin.

Graeber, David. 2018. *Bullshit Jobs: A Theory*. New York: Simon and Schuster.

Graizbord, Diana. 2019. "Toward an Organic Policy Sociology." *Sociology Compass* 13 (11): 1–14.

Grindle, Merilee. 2016. "Democracy and Clientelism: How Uneasy a Relationship?" *Latin American Research Review* 51 (3): 241–49.

Grupo Alavío. 2015. "B.A.U.E.N.: Lucha, Cultura, Trabajo." YouTube video, 1:14:27, posted June 5, 2015. https://www.youtube.com/watch?v=oq5-lRAgjk4.

Guillan-Montero, Aranzazu. 2011. "As If: The Fiction of Executive Accountability and the Persistence of Corruption Networks in Weakly Institutionalized Presidential Systems; Argentina (1989–2007)." PhD diss., Georgetown University, Washington, DC.

Gunn, Christopher E. 1984. *Workers' Self-Management in the United States*. Ithaca, NY: Cornell University Press.

Hacker, Sally. 1989. *Pleasure, Power, and Technology: Some Tales of Gender, Engineering, and the Cooperative Workplace*. Boston: Unwin Hyman.

Hallett, Tim. 2003. "Symbolic Power and Organizational Culture." *Sociological Theory* 21 (2): 128–49.

Hallett, Tim, and Marc J. Ventresca. 2006. "Inhabited Institutions: Social Interactions and Organizational Forms in Gouldner's 'Patterns of Industrial Bureaucracy.'" *Theory and Society* 35 (2): 213–36.

Hampson, Ian, and Anne Junor. 2010. "Putting the Process Back In: Rethinking Service Sector Skill." *Work, Employment and Society* 24 (3): 526–45.

Hampson, Ian, and Anne Junor. 2015. "Stages of the Social Construction of Skill: Revisiting Debates over Service Skill Recognition." *Sociology Compass* 9 (6): 450–63.

Hannan, Michael T., and John Freeman. 1977. "The Population Ecology of Organizations." *American Journal of Sociology* 82 (5): 929–64.

Hanser, Amy. 2008. *Service Encounters: Class, Gender, and the Market for Social Distinction in Urban China*. Stanford, CA: Stanford University Press.

Hanson, Rebecca, and Patricia Richards. 2017. "Sexual Harassment and the Construction of Ethnographic Knowledge." *Sociological Forum* 32 (3): 587–609.

Harris, Scott R. 2003. "Studying Equality/Inequality: Naturalist and Constructionist Approaches to Equality in Marriage." *Journal of Contemporary Ethnography* 32 (2): 200–232.

Harris, Scott R. 2006a. *The Meanings of Marital Equality*. Albany: State University of New York Press.

Harris, Scott R. 2006b. "Social Constructionism and Social Inequality: An Introduction to a Special Issue of *JCE*." *Journal of Contemporary Ethnography* 35 (3): 223–35.

Harvey, David. 2005. *A Brief History of Neoliberalism*. New York: Oxford University Press.

Heller, Carlos. 2016. "BAUEN: Frente al veto de Macri, en 2017 vamos por una nueva sanción de 2/3 de los votos en ambas cámaras." Distribuir major para seguir creciendo, December 27, 2016. http://www.carlosheller.com.ar /2016/12/27/bauen-frente-al-veto-de-macri-en-2017-vamos-por-una-nueva -sancion-con-23-de-los-votos-en-ambas-camaras/.

Heller, Frank, Eugen Pusic, George Strauss, and Bernhard Wilpert. 1998. *Organizational Participation: Myth and Reality*. Oxford: Oxford University Press.

Henriques, Flávio Chedid, Vanessa Moreira Sígolo, Sandra Rufino, Fernanda Santos Araújo, Vicente Nepomuceno, Mariana Baptista Giroto, Maria Alejandra Paulucci, Thiago Nogueira Rodrigues, Maíra Rocha Cavalcanti, and Maurício Sardá de Faria. 2013. *Empresas recuperadas por trabalhadores no Brasil*. Rio de Janeiro: Editora Multifoco.

Hernandez, Sarah. 2006. "Striving for Control: Democracy and Oligarchy at a Mexican Cooperative." *Economic and Industrial Democracy* 27 (1): 105–35.

Hilton, Conrad N. 1994. *Be My Guest*. New York: Simon and Schuster.

Hirtz, Natalia Vanesa, and Marta Susana Giacone. 2013. "The Recovered Companies Workers' Struggle in Argentina: Between Autonomy and New Forms of Control." *Latin American Perspectives* 40 (4): 88–100.

Hoang, Kimberly Kay. 2015. *Dealing in Desire: Asian Ascendancy, Western Decline, and the Hidden Currencies of Global Sex Work*. Oakland: University of California Press.

Hoang, Kimberly Kay. 2018. "Gendering Carnal Ethnography: A Queer Reception." In *Other, Please Specify: Queer Methods in Sociology*, 230–46. Berkeley: University of California Press.

Hochschild, Arlie Russell. 2012. *The Managed Heart: Commercialization of Human Feeling*. Berkeley: University of California Press.

Hodson, Randy. 1995. "Resistance and Power in Organizations: Agency, Subjectivity, and the Labour Process." *Work and Occupations* 22 (3): 364–66.

Hodson, Randy. 2001. *Dignity at Work*. New York: Cambridge University Press.

Hodson, Randy. 2002. "Worker Participation and Teams: New Evidence from Analyzing Organizational Ethnographies." *Economic and Industrial Democracy* 23 (4): 491–528.

Hoffmann, Elizabeth A. 2016. "Emotions and Emotional Labor at Worker-Owned Businesses: Deep Acting, Surface Acting, and Genuine Emotions." *Sociological Quarterly* 57 (1): 152–73.

Holland, Alisha C. 2016. "Forbearance." *American Political Science Review* 110 (2): 232–46.

Holland, Alisha C. 2017. *Forbearance as Redistribution: The Politics of Informal Welfare in Latin America.* Cambridge: Cambridge University Press.

Iannello, Kathleen P. 1992. *Decisions without Hierarchy: Feminist Interventions in Organization Theory and Practice.* New York: Routledge.

International Cooperative Alliance. n.d. "Cooperative Identity, Values and Principles." Accessed October 15, 2021. https://www.ica.coop/en/cooperatives/cooperative-identity.

Instituto Nacional de Estadística y Censos de La República Argentina (INDEC). n.d. "Línea de Pobreza." Accessed October 15, 2021. https://www.indec.gob.ar/indec/web/Nivel4-Tema-4-46-152.

Itzigsohn, José, and Julián Rebón. 2015. "The Recuperation of Enterprises: Defending Workers' Lifeworld, Creating New Tools of Contention." *Latin American Research Review* 50 (4): 178–96.

Jackall, Robert. 1988. *Moral Mazes: The World of Corporate Managers.* Oxford: Oxford University Press.

Jackall, Robert, and Henry M. Levin, eds. 1984. *Worker Cooperatives in America.* Berkeley: University of California Press.

Jerolmack, Colin, and Alexandra K. Murphy. 2019. "The Ethical Dilemmas and Social Scientific Trade-Offs of Masking in Ethnography." *Sociological Methods and Research* 48 (4): 801–27.

Johnson, Erik W. 2008. "Social Movement Size, Organizational Diversity and the Making of Federal Law." *Social Forces* 86 (3): 967–93.

Johnson, Phil. 2006. "Whence Democracy? A Review and Critique of the Conceptual Dimensions and Implications of the Business Case for Organizational Democracy." *Organization* 13 (2): 245–74.

Johnson, Victoria. 2007. "What Is Organizational Imprinting? Cultural Entrepreneurship in the Founding of the Paris Opera." *American Journal of Sociology* 113 (1): 97–127.

Johnston, Michael. 2014. *Corruption, Contention and Reform: The Power of Deep Democratization.* Cambridge: Cambridge University Press.

Jozami, Eduardo, Pedro Paz, and Juan Villarreal. 1985. *Crisis de la dictadura argentina: Política económica y cambio social, 1976–1983.* Buenos Aires: Siglo Veintiuno.

Jussila, Iiro, Noreen Byrne, and Heidi Tuominen. 2012. "Affective Commitment in Co-operative Organizations: What Makes Members Want to Stay?" *International Business Research* 5 (10): 1–10.

237

Kabat, Marina. 2011. "Argentinean Worker-Taken Factories: Trajectories of Workers' Control under the Economic Crisis." In *Ours to Master and to Own: Workers' Councils from the Commune to the Present*, edited by Immanuel Ness and Dario Azzellini, 365–81. Chicago: Haymarket Books.

Kalev, Alexandra. 2009. "Cracking the Glass Cages? Restructuring and Ascriptive Inequality at Work." *American Journal of Sociology* 114 (6): 1591–643.

Kalleberg, Arne L. 2003. "Flexible Firms and Labor Market Segmentation: Effects of Workplace Restructuring on Jobs and Workers." *Work and Occupations* 30 (2): 154–75.

Kalleberg, Arne L. 2009. "Precarious Work, Insecure Workers: Employment Relations in Transition." *American Sociological Review* 74 (1): 1–22.

Kalleberg, Arne L., Peter V. Marsden, Jeremy Reynolds, and David Knoke. 2006. "Beyond Profit? Sectoral Differences in High-Performance Work Practices." *Work and Occupations* 33 (3): 271–302.

Kanter, Rosabeth Moss. 1968. "Commitment and Social Organization: A Study of Commitment Mechanisms in Utopian Communities." *American Sociological Review* 33 (4): 499–517.

Kanter, Rosabeth Moss. 1972. *Commitment and Community: Communes and Utopias in Sociological Perspective.* Cambridge, MA: Harvard University Press.

Kanter, Rosabeth Moss. 1977. *Men and Women of the Corporation.* New York: Basic Books.

Kanter, Rosabeth Moss. 1989. "The New Managerial Work." *Harvard Business Review*, November–December. https://hbr.org/1989/11/the-new-managerial-work.

Kapferer, Jean-Noel. 1990. *Rumors: Uses, Interpretation and Necessity.* New Brunswick, NJ: Routledge.

Kasmir, Sharryn. 1996. *The Myth of Mondragón: Cooperatives, Politics, and Working-Class Life in a Basque Town.* Albany: State University of New York Press.

Kasparian, Denise. 2009. "Situación de IMPA." *Revista del Observatorio Social sobre Empresas Recuperadas y Autogestionadas (OSERA)*, no. 2. http://webiigg.sociales.uba.ar/empresasrecuperadas/PDF/coyuntura/IMPA1.pdf.

Kasparian, Denise. 2012. "De alianzas y solidaridades: Las articulaciones no mercantiles en las empresas recuperadas de la ciudad de Buenos Aires." *Revista del Observatorio Social sobre Empresas Recuperadas y Autogestionadas (OSERA)*, no. 8. http://webiigg.sociales.uba.ar/empresasrecuperadas/PDF/PDF_08/De_alianzas_y_solidaridades.pdf.

Katz, Jack. 2001. "From How to Why: On Luminous Description and Causal Inference in Ethnography (Part I)." *Ethnography* 2 (4): 443–73.

Kellogg, Katherine C. 2009. "Operating Room: Relational Spaces and Micro-institutional Change in Surgery." *American Journal of Sociology* 115 (3): 657–711.

Kelly, Erin L., Samantha K. Ammons, Kelly Chermack, and Phyllis Moen. 2010. "Gendered Challenge, Gendered Response Confronting the Ideal Worker Norm in a White-Collar Organization." *Gender and Society* 24 (3): 281–303.

Kelly, Erin L., and Alexandra Kalev. 2006. "Managing Flexible Work Arrangements in US Organizations: Formalized Discretion or 'a Right to Ask.'" *Socio-economic Review* 4 (3): 379–416.

Kelly, Erin L., and Phyllis Moen. 2020. *Overload: How Good Jobs Went Bad and What We Can Do about It*. Princeton, NJ: Princeton University Press.

Kennard, Matt, and Ana Caistor-Arendar. 2016. "Occupy Buenos Aires: The Workers' Movement That Transformed a City, and Inspired the World." *Guardian*, March 10, 2016. http://www.theguardian.com/cities/2016/mar/10/occupy-buenos-aires-argentina-workers-cooperative-movement.

Klein, Naomi. 2009. "When Work Is a Crime. The Brukman Battle." In *The Silent Change: Recovered Businesses in Argentina*, by Esteban Magnani, 21–23. Buenos Aires: Teseo.

Kleinman, Sherryl. 1996. *Opposing Ambitions: Gender and Identity in an Alternative Organization*. Chicago: University of Chicago Press.

Knox, Angela, and Janet Walsh. 2005. "Organisational Flexibility and HRM in the Hotel Industry: Evidence from Australia." *Human Resource Management Journal* 15 (1): 57–75.

Kokkinidis, George. 2015. "Spaces of Possibilities: Workers' Self-Management in Greece." *Organization* 22 (6): 847–71.

Korczynski, Marek. 2005. "Skills in Service Work: An Overview." *Human Resource Management Journal* 15 (2): 3–14.

Kriauciunas, Aldas, and Prashant Kale. 2006. "The Impact of Socialist Imprinting and Search on Resource Change: A Study of Firms in Lithuania." *Strategic Management Journal* 27 (7): 659–79.

Krippner, Greta R. 2005. "The Financialization of the American Economy." *Socio-economic Review* 3 (2): 173–208.

Krippner, Greta R. 2017. "Democracy of Credit: Ownership and the Politics of Credit Access in Late Twentieth-Century America." *American Journal of Sociology* 123 (1): 1–47.

Kruse, Douglas L., Richard B. Freeman, and Joseph R. Blasi. 2011. *Shared Capitalism at Work: Employee Ownership, Profit and Gain Sharing, and Broad-Based Stock Options*. Chicago: University of Chicago Press.

Kunda, Gideon. 2006. *Engineering Culture: Control and Commitment in a High-Tech Corporation*. Philadelphia: Temple University Press.

Lafer, Gordon. 2004. "What Is 'Skill'? Training for Discipline in the Low-Wage Labour Market." In *The Skills That Matter*, edited by Chris Warhurst, Ewart Keep, and Irena Grugulis, 109–27. Houndsmills, UK: Palgrave Macmillan.

Lamont, Michèle. 2018. "Addressing Recognition Gaps: Destigmatization and the Reduction of Inequality." *American Sociological Review* 83 (3): 419–44.

Lapavitsas, Costas. 2014. *Profiting without Producing: How Finance Exploits Us All*. London: Verso.

Larrabure, Manuel, Marcelo Vieta, and Daniel Schugurensky. 2011. "The 'New Cooperativism' in Latin America: Worker-Recuperated Enterprises and Socialist Production Units." *Studies in the Education of Adults* 43 (2): 181–96.

Lavaca Collective. 2007a. "Hay que defenderlo a sangre." Lavaca.org, July 27, 2007. Accessed October 15, 2021. https://lavaca.org/notas/hay-que-defenderlo-a -sangre/.

Lavaca Collective. 2007b. *Sin Patrón: Stories from Argentina's Worker-Run Factories*. Chicago: Haymarket Books.

Leach, Darcy K. 2016. "When Freedom Is Not an Endless Meeting: A New Look at Efficiency in Consensus-Based Decision Making." *Sociological Quarterly* 57 (1): 36–70.

Lee, Caroline W. 2015. "Participatory Practices in Organizations." *Sociology Compass* 9 (4): 272–88.

Lee, Caroline W., Michael McQuarrie, and Edward T. Walker. 2015. *Democratizing Inequalities: Dilemmas of the New Public Participation*. New York: New York University Press.

Lee, Michael Y., and Amy C. Edmondson. 2017. "Self-Managing Organizations: Exploring the Limits of Less-Hierarchical Organizing." *Research in Organizational Behavior* 37:35–58.

Leidner, Robin. 1993. *Fast Food, Fast Talk: Service Work and the Routinization of Everyday Life*. Berkeley: University of California Press.

Levitsky, Steven. 2003. "From Labor Politics to Machine Politics: The Transformation of Party-Union Linkages in Argentine Peronism, 1983–99." *Latin American Research Review* 38 (3): 3–36.

Levitsky, Steven, and María Victoria Murillo. 2005. *Argentine Democracy: The Politics of Institutional Weakness*. University Park, PA: Penn State University Press.

Levitsky, Steven, and María Victoria Murillo. 2008. "Argentina: From Kirchner to Kirchner." *Journal of Democracy* 19 (2): 16–30.

Lewis, Avi, and Naomi Klein. 2004. *The Take*. Montréal: Alliance Atlantis.

Lichbach, Mark I. 1996. *The Cooperator's Dilemma*. Ann Arbor: University of Michigan Press.

Lin, Ken-Hou, and Megan Tobias Neely. 2020. *Divested: Inequality in the Age of Finance*. New York: Oxford University Press.

Llamazares, Iván. 2005. "Patterns in Contingencies: The Interlocking of Formal and Informal Political Institutions in Contemporary Argentina." *Social Forces* 83 (4): 1671–95.

Lopez, Steven Henry. 2007. "Efficiency and the Fix Revisited: Informal Relations and Mock Routinization in a Nonprofit Nursing Home." *Qualitative Sociology* 30 (3): 225–47.

Lorber, Judith. 1999. "Crossing Borders and Erasing Boundaries: Paradoxes of Identity Politics." *Sociological Focus* 32 (4): 355–70.

Magnani, Esteban. 2009. *The Silent Change: Recovered Businesses in Argentina*. Buenos Aires: Editorial Teseo.

Mansbridge, Jane J. 1980. *Beyond Adversary Democracy*. New York: Basic Books.

Manzetti, Luigi. 2009. *Neoliberalism, Accountability, and Reform Failures in Emerging Markets: Eastern Europe, Russia, Argentina, and Chile in Comparative Perspective*. University Park, PA: Penn State University Press.

240

Mapa Nacional de la Discriminación. 2013. "Segunda serie de estadísticas sobre la discriminación en Argentina." Buenos Aires: Instituto Nacional contra la Discriminación, la Xenofobia y el Racismo.

Marquis, Christopher, and Zhi Huang. 2010. "Acquisitions as Exaptation: The Legacy of Founding Institutions in the US Commercial Banking Industry." *Academy of Management Journal* 53 (6): 1441–73.

Marquis, Christopher, and András Tilcsik. 2013. "Imprinting: Toward a Multilevel Theory." *Academy of Management Annals* 7 (1): 195–245.

Martin, Patricia Yancey. 1990. "Rethinking Feminist Organizations." *Gender and Society* 4 (2): 182–206.

Marwell, Nicole P. 2004. "Privatizing the Welfare State: Nonprofit Community-Based Organizations as Political Actors." *American Sociological Review* 69 (2): 265–91.

Marx, Karl. 1973. *The Grundrisse*. Marx Engels Archive. https://www.marxists.org /archive/marx/works/download/pdf/grundrisse.pdf.

Marx, Karl. 1978. "The Eighteenth Brumaire of Louis Bonaparte." In *The Marx-Engels Reader*, 2nd ed., edited by Robert C. Tucker, 594–617. New York: W. W. Norton.

McAdam, Doug, Sidney Tarrow, and Charles Tilly. 2001. *Dynamics of Contention*. Cambridge: Cambridge University Press.

McSherry, J. Patrice. 2005. *Predatory States: Operation Condor and Covert War in Latin America*. Lanham, MD: Rowman and Littlefield.

Mears, Ashley. 2013. "Ethnography as Precarious Work." *Sociological Quarterly* 54 (1): 20–34.

Mellor, Mary, Janet Hannah, and John Stirling. 1988. *Worker Cooperatives in Theory and Practice*. Philadelphia: Open University Press.

Meyer, Adriana. 2017. "La resistencia del Bauen en tres frentes." *Página/12*, April 3. https://www.pagina12.com.ar/29499-la-resistencia-del-bauen-en-tres -frentes.

Meyers, Joan S. M. 2022. *Working Democracy: Managing Inequalities in Worker Cooperatives*. Ithaca, NY: Cornell ILR Press.

Meyers, Joan S. M., and Steven P. Vallas. 2016. "Diversity Regimes in Worker Cooperatives: Workplace Inequality under Conditions of Worker Control." *Sociological Quarterly* 57 (1): 98–128.

Michael, Robert T., Heidi Hartmann, and Brigid O'Farrell. 1989. *Pay Equity: Empirical Inquiries*. Washington, DC: National Academies Press.

Michel, Alexandra. 2014. "Participation and Self-Entrapment: A 12-Year Ethnography of Wall Street Participation Practices' Diffusion and Evolving Consequences." *Sociological Quarterly* 55 (3): 514–36.

Mische, Ann. 2009. "Projects and Possibilities: Researching Futures in Action." *Sociological Forum* 24 (3): 694–704.

Mishel, Lawrence, and Julia Wolfe. 2019. "CEO Compensation Has Grown 940% since 1978." Economic Policy Institute, August 14, 2019. https://www.epi.org /publication/ceo-compensation-2018/.

Moeran, Brian. 2009. "From Participant Observation to Observant Participation." In *Organizational Ethnography: Studying the Complexities of Everyday Life*, edited by Sierk Ybema, Dvora Yanow, Harry Wels, and Frans Kamsteeg, 139–55. London: Sage.

Moore, Sian. 2009. "'No Matter What I Did I Would Still End up in the Same Position': Age as a Factor Defining Older Women's Experience of Labour Market Participation." *Work, Employment and Society* 23 (4): 655–71.

Moreno, Graciela. 2020. "Cierra el Hotel Bauen después de 42 años: Se va la cooperativa de trabajadores." *BAE Negocios*, September 28, 2020. https:// www.baenegocios.com/negocios/La-cooperativa-de-trabajadores-del-hotel -Bauen-dejara-el-historico-edificio-de-Callao-20200928-0026.html.

Morgan, Kimberly J., and Ann Shola Orloff, eds. 2017. *The Many Hands of the State: Theorizing Political Authority and Social Control.* New York: Cambridge University Press.

La Nación. 2007. "Vuelve el recuerdo del Banade." May 13, 2007. https://www .lanacion.com.ar/economia/vuelve-el-recuerdo-del-banade-nid908115.

La Nación. 2014. "Bauen: Se vence el plazo para desalojar el hotel y hay tensión." September 10, 2014. http://www.lanacion.com.ar/1726026-bauen-se-vence -el-plazo-para-desalojar-el-hotel-y-hay-tension.

Nadler, Judy, and Miriam Schulman. 2015. "Favoritism, Cronyism, and Nepotism." Markkula Center for Applied Ethics at Santa Clara University, October 23, 2015. https://www.scu.edu/government-ethics/resources/what-is -government-ethics/favoritism-cronyism-and-nepotism/.

Neely, Megan Tobias. 2018. "Fit to Be King: How Patrimonialism on Wall Street Leads to Inequality." *Socio-economic Review* 16 (2): 365–85.

Neely, Megan Tobias. 2022. *Hedged Out: Inequality and Insecurity on Wall Street.* Oakland: University of California Press.

Nembhard, Jessica Gordon. 2014. *Collective Courage: A History of African American Cooperative Economic Thought and Practice.* State College: Penn State University Press.

Ness, Immanuel, and Dario Azzellini, eds. 2011. *Ours to Master and to Own: Workers' Control from the Commune to the Present.* Chicago: Haymarket Books.

North, Peter. 2007. *Money and Liberation: The Micropolitics of Alternative Currency Movements.* Minneapolis: University of Minnesota Press.

El Observador del Sur. 2020. "En plena crisis por la pandemia: Hoteles a la venta en Argentina." August 6, 2020. https://www.elobservadordelsur.com/en -plena-crisis-la-pandemia-hoteles-la-venta-argentina-n23223.

O'Donnell, Santiago. 2007. "El padre, el hijo y un espíritu non sancto." *Página/12,* August 21, 2007. http://www.pagina12.com.ar/diario/elpais/1-90028-2007-08 -21.html.

Ogasawara, Yuko. 1998. *Office Ladies and Salaried Men: Power, Gender, and Work in Japanese Companies.* Berkeley: University of California Press.

Omi, Michael, and Howard Winant. 2014. *Racial Formation in the United States.* 3rd ed. New York: Routledge.

Oseen, Collette. 2016. "'It's Not Only What We Say but What We Do': Pay Inequalities and Gendered Workplace Democracy in Argentinian Worker Coops." *Economic and Industrial Democracy* 37 (2): 219–44.

Otis, Eileen M. 2008. "Beyond the Industrial Paradigm: Market-Embedded Labor and the Gender Organization of Global Service Work in China." *American Sociological Review* 73 (1): 15–36.

Otis, Eileen M. 2011. *Markets and Bodies: Women, Service Work, and the Making of Inequality in China*. Stanford, CA: Stanford University Press.

Página/12. 2007. "El Bauen marcha contra orden de desalojo." August 6, 2007. http://www.pagina12.com.ar/diario/ultimas/20-89285-2007-08-06.html.

Palomino, Héctor. 2003. "The Workers' Movement in Occupied Enterprises: A Survey." *Canadian Journal of Latin American and Caribbean Studies/Revue Canadienne des Études Latino-Américaines et Caraïbes* 28 (55/56): 71–96.

Palomino, Héctor, Ivanna Bleynat, Silvia Garro, and Carla Giacomuzzi. 2010. "The Universe of Worker-Recovered Companies in Argentina (2002–2008): Continuity and Changes inside the Movement." *Affinities: A Journal of Radical Theory, Culture, and Action* 4 (1): 252–87.

Parker, Martin, George Cheney, Valérie Fournier, and Chris Land, eds. 2014. *The Routledge Companion to Alternative Organization*. New York: Routledge.

Pateman, Carole. 1970. *Participation and Democratic Theory*. Cambridge: Cambridge University Press.

Pateman, Carole. 1989. *The Disorder of Women: Democracy, Feminism, and Political Theory*. Stanford, CA: Stanford University Press.

Pateman, Carole. 2012. "Participatory Democracy Revisited." *Perspectives on Politics* 10 (1): 7–19.

Pearson, Ruth. 2003. "Argentina's Barter Network: New Currency for New Times?" *Bulletin of Latin American Research* 22 (2): 214–30.

Pérez, Marcos Emilio. 2018. "Life Histories and Political Commitment in a Poor People's Movement." *Qualitative Sociology* 41 (1): 89–109.

Pérez, Marcos Emilio, and Katherine Sobering. 2022. "The Persistent Influence of December 2001: Collective Action in Twenty-First Century Argentina." *Bulletin of Latin American Research*. Online first. March 7.

Pierucci, Fabian, and Federico Tonarelli. 2014. "Cooperativa de Trabajo Hotel B.A.U.E.N.: Una experiencia de autogestión y libertad." In *Crisis y autogestión en el siglo XXI: Cooperativas y empresas recuperadas en tiempos de neoliberalismo*, edited by Andrés Ruggeri, Henrique T. Novaes, and Maurício Sardá de Faria, 149–60. Buenos Aires: Ediciones Continente.

Pizzi, Alejandro, and Ignasi Brunet Icart. 2014. "Autogestión Obrera y Movilización Social: El Caso de las Empresas Recuperadas Argentinas en la Ciudad de Buenos Aires y Provincia de Buenos Aires." *Latin American Research Review* 49 (1): 39–61.

Polletta, Francesca. 2002. *Freedom Is an Endless Meeting: Democracy in American Social Movements*. Chicago: University of Chicago Press.

Prasad, Monica. 2018. "Problem-Solving Sociology." *Contemporary Sociology: A Journal of Reviews* 47 (4): 393–98.

Programa Facultad Abierta. 2003. *Informe del relevamiento entre empresas recuperadas por los trabajadores*. Buenos Aires: Secretaría de Extensión Universitaria,

Universidad de Buenos Aires. https://recuperadasdoc.com.ar/Informes%20 relevamientos/Informe%20Primer%20relevamiento%202003.pdf.

Rae, Douglas W. 1981. *Equalities*. Cambridge, MA: Harvard University Press.

Ranis, Peter. 2010. "Argentine Worker Cooperatives in Civil Society: A Challenge to Capital-Labor Relations." *WorkingUSA: The Journal of Labor and Society* 13 (1): 77–105.

Ranis, Peter. 2014. "Promoting Cooperatives by the Use of Eminent Domain: Argentina and the United States." *Socialism and Democracy* 28 (1): 51–69.

Ranis, Peter. 2016. *Cooperatives Confront Capitalism: Challenging the Neoliberal Economy*. Chicago: Zed Books.

Rao, Aliya Hamid, and Megan Tobias Neely. 2019. "What's Love Got to Do with It? Passion and Inequality in White-Collar Work." *Sociology Compass* 13 (12): e12744.

Rawls, John. 2005. *Political Liberalism*. Expanded ed. New York: Columbia University Press.

Ray, Victor. 2019. "A Theory of Racialized Organizations." *American Sociological Review* 84 (1): 26–53.

Rebón, Julián, Gustavo Antón, Jorge Cresto, and Rodrigo Salgado. 2006. "Empresas recuperadas en Argentina: ¿Una organización no capitalista de la producción?" *Organization and Democracy* 7 (1/2): 13–32.

Rebón, Julián, and Rodrigo Salgado. 2007. "Transformaciones emergentes del proceso de recuperación de empresas por sus trabajadores." *LabourAgain Publications*. http://www.iisg.nl/labouragain/documents/rebon_salgado.pdf.

Rebón, Nuria. 2019. "La Argentina tiene los sueldos ejecutivos en dólares más bajos de la region." *Apertura*, December 26, 2019. https://www.cronista.com /apertura-negocio/empresas/La-Argentina-tiene-los-sueldos-ejecutivos-en -dolares-mas-bajos-de-la-region-20191226-0004.html.

Reskin, Barbara F. 1993. "Sex Segregation in the Workplace." *Annual Review of Sociology* 19 (1): 241–70.

Reskin, Barbara F., Debra B. McBrier, and Julie A. Kmec. 1999. "The Determinants and Consequences of Workplace Sex and Race Composition." *Annual Review of Sociology* 25 (1): 335–61.

Reskin, Barbara F., and Irene Padavic. 1988. "Supervisors as Gatekeepers: Male Supervisors' Response to Women's Integration in Plant Jobs." *Social Problems* 35 (5): 536–50.

Reskin, Barbara F., and Patricia A. Roos. 1998. *Job Queues, Gender Queues: Explaining Women's Inroads into Male Occupations*. Philadelphia: Temple University Press.

Reyes, Victoria. 2018. "Three Models of Transparency in Ethnographic Research: Naming Places, Naming People, and Sharing Data." *Ethnography* 19 (2): 204–26.

Reyes, Victoria. 2020. "Ethnographic Toolkit: Strategic Positionality and Researchers' Visible and Invisible Tools in Field Research." *Ethnography* 21 (2): 220–40.

Rich, Adrienne. 1980. "Compulsory Heterosexuality and Lesbian Existence." *Signs* 5 (4): 631–60.

Rieiro, Anabel. 2009. "Gestión obrera y acciones colectivas en el mundo del trabajo: Empresas recuperadas por sus trabajadores en Uruguay." Master's thesis, Universidad de la República Uruguay, Montevideo.

Rivera, Lauren A. 2012. "Hiring as Cultural Matching: The Case of Elite Professional Service Firms." *American Sociological Review* 77 (6): 999–1022.

Romero, Lautaro. 2016. "Arte viviente en el Bauen." *Revista Cítrica*, November 14, 2016. http://revistacitrica.com/arte-viviente-en-el-bauen.html.

Romero, Luis Alberto. 2002. *A History of Argentina in the Twentieth Century*. University Park, PA: Penn State University Press.

Roos, Patricia A., and Barbara F. Reskin. 1992. "Occupational Desegregation in the 1970s: Integration and Economic Equity?" *Sociological Perspectives* 35 (1): 69–91.

Roscigno, Vincent J. 2011. "Power, Revisited." *Social Forces* 90 (2): 349–74.

Roscigno, Vincent J., and Randy Hodson. 2004. "The Organizational and Social Foundations of Worker Resistance." *American Sociological Review* 69 (1): 14–39.

Rosenfeld, Jake. 2017. "Don't Ask or Tell: Pay Secrecy Policies in U.S. Workplaces." *Social Science Research* 65:1–16.

Rosenfeld, Jake, and Patrick Denice. 2015. "The Power of Transparency: Evidence from a British Workplace Survey." *American Sociological Review* 80 (5): 1045–68.

Rosnow, Ralph L., and Gary A. Fine. 1976. *Rumor and Gossip: The Social Psychology of Hearsay*. Oxford: Elsevier.

Rothman, Joshua. 2020. "Same Difference." *New Yorker*, January 13, 2020.

Rothschild, Joyce. 2000. "Creating a Just and Democratic Workplace: More Engagement, Less Hierarchy." *Contemporary Sociology* 29 (1): 195–213.

Rothschild, Joyce, and Max Stephenson. 2009. "The Meaning of Democracy in Non-profit and Community Organizations: Charting the Currents of Change." *American Behavioral Scientist* 52 (6): 800–806.

Rothschild, Joyce, and Amy Tomchin. 2006. "Can Collectivist-Democracy Bring Gender Equality? The Efforts at Twin Oaks." In *Worker Participation: Current Research and Future Trends*, edited by Vicki Smith, 239–62. *Research in the Sociology of Work* 16. Bingley, UK: Emerald.

Rothschild, Joyce, and J. Allen Whitt. 1986. *The Cooperative Workplace: Potentials and Dilemmas of Organizational Democracy and Participation*. Cambridge: Cambridge University Press.

Rothschild-Whitt, Joyce. 1979. "The Collectivist Organization: An Alternative to Rational-Bureaucratic Models." *American Sociological Review* 44 (4): 509–27.

Roy, Donald. 1959. "'Banana Time': Job Satisfaction and Informal Interaction." *Human Organization* 18 (4): 158–68.

Rueschemeyer, Dietrich. 2005. "Addressing Inequality." In *Assessing the Quality of Democracy*, edited by Larry Diamond and Leonardo Morlino, 47–61. Baltimore, MD: Johns Hopkins University Press.

Ruggeri, Andrés. 2011. *Las empresas recuperadas en la Argentina, 2010: Informe del Tercer Relevamiento de Empresas Recuperadas por sus Trabajadores*. Buenos Aires: Ediciones de la Cooperativa Chilavert.

245

Ruggeri, Andrés. 2014a. *Informe del IV Relevamiento de Empresas Recuperadas en la Argentina: Las empresas recuperadas en el período 2010–2013*. Buenos Aires: University of Buenos Aires.

Ruggeri, Andrés. 2014b. *¿Qué son las empresas recuperadas? Autogestión de la clase trabajadora*. Buenos Aires: Ediciones Continente.

Ruggeri, Andrés. 2016. *Las empresas recuperadas por los trabajadores en los comienzos del gobierno de Mauricio Macri: Estado de situación a mayo de 2016*. Buenos Aires: Secretaría de Extensión Universitaria y Bienestar Estudiantil, Facultad de Filosofía y Letras, Universidad de Buenos Aires. http://www.recuperadasdoc.com.ar/informe-mayo-2016.pdf.

Ruggeri, Andrés. 2020. "Cooperativas de Trabajo y Empresas Recuperadas Durante la Pandemia: Impacto Sanitario y Productivo y Alcanes de las Medidas de Asistencia del Estado." Buenos Aires: Secretaría de Extensión Universitaria y Bienestar Estudiantil, Facultad de Filosofía y Letras, Universidad de Buenos Aires. http://www.recuperadasdoc.com.ar/INFORME%20DE%20LA%20ENCUESTA%20NACIONAL%20SOBRE%20EMPRESAS%20RECUPERADAS%20Y%20COOPERATIVAS%20DE%20TRABAJO%20EN%20LA%20PANDEMIA.pdf.

Ruggeri, Andrés, Desiderio Alfonso, and Emiliano Balaguer. 2017. BAUEN: *El hotel de los trabajadores*. Buenos Aires: Biblioteca Economía de los Trabajadores.

Ruggeri, Andrés, and Elisa Gigliarelli. 2021. "Argentina: Workers' Resistance to Macrist Neoliberalism." In *If Not Us, Who? Workers Worldwide against Authoritarianism, Fascism and Dictatorship*, edited by Dario Azzellini, 41–47. Hamburg: VSA.

Ruggeri, Andrés, Hectór Trinchero, and Carlos Martinez. 2005. *Las empresas recuperadas en la Argentina: Informe del Segundo Relevamiento del Programa*. Buenos Aires: Facultad Abierta, Facultad de Filosofía y Letras, Universidad de Buenos Aires, Programa de Transferencia Científico-Técnica con Empresas Recuperadas por sus Trabajadores (UBACyT de Urgencia Social F-701).

Ruggeri, Andrés, and Marcelo Vieta. 2015. "Argentina's Worker-Recuperated Enterprises, 2010–2013: A Synthesis of Recent Empirical Findings." *Journal of Entrepreneurial and Organizational Diversity* 4 (41): 75–103.

Scheffler, Samuel. 2015. "The Practice of Equality." In *Social Equality: On What It Means to Be Equals*, edited by Ivo Wallimann-Helmer, Fabian Schuppert, and Carina Fourie, 21–44. London: Oxford University Press.

Scheper-Hughes, Nancy. 2012. "Ire in Ireland." In *Ethnographic Fieldwork: An Anthropological Reader*, edited by Antonius C. G. M. Robben and Jeffrey A. Sluka, 219–33. Malden, MA: John Wiley.

Schlachter, Laura H., and Kristinn Már. 2020. "Spillover, Selection, or Substitution? Workplace and Civic Participation in Democratic Firms." SocArXiv. May 30. https://osf.io/preprints/socarxiv/684tf/.

Schneiberg, Marc, Marissa King, and Thomas Smith. 2008. "Social Movements and Organizational Form: Cooperative Alternatives to Corporations in the American Insurance, Dairy, and Grain Industries." *American Sociological Review* 73 (4): 635–67.

Schutz, Alfred. 1967. *The Phenomenology of the Social World*. Evanston, IL: Northwestern University Press.

Seim, Josh. 2021. "Participant Observation, Observant Participation, and Hybrid Ethnography." *Sociological Methods and Research*, February 10. https://doi.org/10.1177/0049124120986209.

Sen, Amartya. 2009. *The Idea of Justice*. Cambridge, MA: Belknap Press of Harvard University Press.

Sewell, Graham. 1998. "The Discipline of Teams: The Control of Team-Based Industrial Work through Electronic and Peer Surveillance." *Administrative Science Quarterly* 43 (2): 397–428.

Sherman, Rachel. 2005. "Producing the Superior Self: Strategic Comparison and Symbolic Boundaries among Luxury Hotel Workers." *Ethnography* 6 (2): 131–58.

Sherman, Rachel. 2007. *Class Acts: Service and Inequality in Luxury Hotels*. Berkeley: University of California Press.

Simmel, Georg. (1907) 2004. *The Philosophy of Money*. 3rd ed. Edited by David Frisby. Translated by Tom Bottomore and David Frisby. London: Routledge.

Simons, Tal, and Paul Ingram. 2000. "The Kibbutz for Organizational Behavior." *Research in Organizational Behavior* 22:283–343.

Smith, Vicki. 1994. "Institutionalizing Flexibility in a Service Firm: Multiple Contingencies and Hidden Hierarchies." *Work and Occupations* 21 (3): 284–307.

Smith, Vicki. 1996. "Employee Involvement, Involved Employees: Participative Work Arrangements in a White-Collar Service Occupation." *Social Problems* 43 (2): 166–79.

Smith, Vicki. 1997. "New Forms of Work Organization." *Annual Review of Sociology* 23:315–39.

Sobering, Katherine. 2016. "Producing and Reducing Gender Inequality in a Worker-Recovered Cooperative." *Sociological Quarterly* 57 (1): 129–51.

Sobering, Katherine. 2019a. "The Relational Production of Workplace Equality: The Case of Worker-Recuperated Businesses in Argentina." *Qualitative Sociology* 42 (4): 543–65.

Sobering, Katherine. 2019b. "Watercooler Democracy: Rumors and Transparency in a Cooperative Workplace." *Work and Occupations* 46 (4): 411–40.

Sobering, Katherine. 2021a. "The Emotional Dynamics of Workplace Democracy: Emotional Labor, Collective Effervescence, and Commitment at Work." In *Organizational Imaginaries: Tempering Capitalism and Tending to Communities through Cooperatives and Collectivist Democracy*, edited by Katherine K. Chen and Victor T. Chen, 31–54. Research in the Sociology of Organizations 72. Bingley, UK: Emerald.

Sobering, Katherine. 2021b. "Survival Finance and the Politics of Equal Pay." *British Journal of Sociology* 72 (3): 742–56.

Sobering, Katherine, and Pablo Lapegna. 2021. "Alternative Organizational Survival: A Comparison of Two Worker-Recuperated Businesses in Buenos Aires, Argentina." *Social Problems*. Online first. July 20.

Sobering, Katherine, Jessica Thomas, and Christine L. Williams. 2014. "Gender In/Equality in Worker-Owned Businesses." *Sociology Compass* 8 (11): 1242–55.

Stacey, Judith. 1988. "Can There Be a Feminist Ethnography?" *Women's Studies International Forum* 11 (1): 21–27.

Stack, Carol B. 1975. *All Our Kin.* New York: Harper.

Staggenborg, Suzanne. 1988. "The Consequences of Professionalization and Formalization in the Pro-Choice Movement." *American Sociological Review* 53 (4): 585–605.

Staggenborg, Suzanne. 1995. "Can Feminist Organizations Be Effective?" In *Feminist Organizations: Harvest of the New Women's Movement,* edited by Myra Marx Ferree and Patricia Yancey Martin, 339–55. Philadelphia: Temple University Press.

Stainback, Kevin, and Donald Tomaskovic-Devey. 2012. *Documenting Desegregation: Racial and Gender Segregation in Private Sector Employment since the Civil Rights Act.* New York: Russell Sage Foundation.

Steinberg, Ronnie J. 1984. "Identifying Wage Discrimination and Implementing Pay Equity Adjustments." In *Comparable Worth: Issue for the 80's,* edited by US Commission on Civil Rights, 99–116. Washington, DC: US Government Printing Office.

Steinberg, Ronnie J. 1990. "Social Construction of Skill: Gender, Power, and Comparable Worth." *Work and Occupations* 17 (4): 449–82.

Stinchcombe, Arthur. 1965. "Organizations and Social Structure." In *Handbook of Organizations,* edited by James G. March, 153–93. Chicago: Rand McNally.

Svampa, Maristella, Inés González Bombal, and Pablo Bergel. 2003. *Nuevos movimientos sociales y ONGs en la Argentina de la crisis.* Buenos Aires: Centro de Estudios de Estado y Sociedad.

Svampa, Maristella, and Sebastián Pereyra. 2003. *Entre la ruta y el barrio: La experiencia de las organizaciones piqueteras.* Buenos Aires: Editorial Biblos.

Sydow, Jörg, Georg Schreyögg, and Jochen Koch. 2009. "Organizational Path Dependence: Opening the Black Box." *Academy of Management Review* 34 (4): 689–709.

Taylor, Peter Leigh. 1994. "The Rhetorical Construction of Efficiency: Restructuring and Industrial Democracy in Mondragón, Spain." *Sociological Forum* 9 (3): 459–89.

Tilly, Charles. 1998. *Durable Inequality.* Berkeley: University of California Press.

Tomaskovic-Devey, Donald. 1993. *Gender and Racial Inequality at Work: The Sources and Consequences of Job Segregation.* Ithaca, NY: Cornell University Press.

Tomaskovic-Devey, Donald. 2014. "The Relational Generation of Workplace Inequalities." *Social Currents* 1 (1): 51–73.

Tomaskovic-Devey, Donald, and Dustin Avent-Holt. 2019. *Relational Inequalities: An Organizational Approach.* New York: Oxford University Press.

Tomaskovic-Devey, Donald, Dustin Avent-Holt, Catherine Zimmer, and Sandra Harding. 2009. "The Categorical Generation of Organizational Inequality:

A Comparative Test of Tilly's Durable Inequality." *Research in Social Stratification and Mobility* 27 (3): 128–42.

Tomaskovic-Devey, Donald, and Sheryl Skaggs. 2002. "Sex Segregation, Labor Process Organization, and Gender Earnings Inequality." *American Journal of Sociology* 108 (1): 102–28.

Tomaskovic-Devey, Donald, Kevin Stainback, Tiffany Taylor, Catherine Zimmer, Corre Robinson, and Tricia McTague. 2006. "Documenting Desegregation: Segregation in American Workplaces by Race, Ethnicity, and Sex, 1966–2003." *American Sociological Review* 71 (4): 565–88.

Tonarelli, Federico. 2020. "Las fábricas recuperadas recibirán ayuda del Estado." Radio Sur, May 12, 2020. https://www.radiosur.org.ar/noticia.php?id=11463.

Tope, Daniel, Lindsey Joyce Chamberlain, Martha Crowley, and Randy Hodson. 2005. "The Benefits of Being There: Evidence from the Literature on Work." *Journal of Contemporary Ethnography* 34 (4): 470–93.

Turco, Catherine J. 2016. *The Conversational Firm: Rethinking Bureaucracy in the Age of Social Media.* New York: Columbia University Press.

Uhler, Andy. 2020. "Hotel Industry Struggling during the Pandemic." *Marketplace*, September 7, 2020. https://www.marketplace.org/2020/09/07/hotel-industry-struggling-during-pandemic/.

Vaisey, Stephen. 2007. "Structure, Culture, and Community: The Search for Belonging in 50 Urban Communes." *American Sociological Review* 72 (6): 851–73.

Vallas, Steven P. 1990. "The Concept of Skill: A Critical Review." *Work and Occupations* 17 (4): 379–98.

Vallas, Steven P. 1999. "Rethinking Post-Fordism: The Meaning of Workplace Flexibility." *Sociological Theory* 17 (1): 68–101.

Vallas, Steven P. 2003. "Why Teamwork Fails: Obstacles to Workplace Change in Four Manufacturing Plants." *American Sociological Review* 68 (2): 223–50.

Vallas, Steven Peter. 2006. "Empowerment Redux: Structure, Agency, and the Remaking of Managerial Authority." *American Journal of Sociology* 111 (6): 1677–717.

Vallas, Steven P., and Angèle Christin. 2018. "Work and Identity in an Era of Precarious Employment: How Workers Respond to 'Personal Branding' Discourse." *Work and Occupations* 45 (1): 3–37.

Van Maanen, John, and Gideon Kunda. 1989. "'Real Feelings': Emotional Expression and Organizational Culture." In *Research in Organizational Behaviour: An Annual Series of Analytical Essays and Critical Reviews*, edited by Barry M. Staw and Larry L. Cummings, 43–103. Greenwich, CT: JAI Press.

Verba, Sidney. 2001. *Political Equality: What Is It? Why Do We Want It?* New York: Russell Sage Foundation.

Vieta, Marcelo. 2010. "The Social Innovations of Autogestión in Argentina's Worker-Recuperated Enterprises." *Labor Studies Journal* 35 (3): 295–321.

Vieta, Marcelo. 2019. *Workers' Self-Management in Argentina: Contesting Neoliberalism by Occupying Companies, Creating Cooperatives, and Recuperating Autogestión.* London: Brill.

Vieta, Marcelo, Sara Depedri, and Antonella Carrano. 2017. "The Italian Road to Recuperating Enterprises and the Legge Marcora Framework." Research Report No. 15. European Research Institute on Cooperative and Social Enterprises. https://www.euricse.eu/wp-content/uploads/2017/03/15_17-Rapporto-Vieta-Depedri-Carrano-1.pdf.

Viggiani, Frances A. 1997. "Democratic Hierarchies in the Workplace: Structural Dilemmas and Organizational Action." *Economic and Industrial Democracy* 18 (2): 231–60.

Wacquant, Loïc. 2015. "For a Sociology of Flesh and Blood." *Qualitative Sociology* 38 (1): 1–11.

Waldron, Jeremy. 2017. *One Another's Equals: The Basis of Human Equality.* Cambridge, MA: Belknap Press of Harvard University Press.

Wallimann-Helmer, Ivo, Fabian Schuppert, and Carina Fourie, eds. 2015. *Social Equality: On What It Means to Be Equals.* London: Oxford University Press.

Walzer, Michael. 1984. *Spheres of Justice: A Defense of Pluralism and Equality.* New York: Basic Books.

Warhurst, Chris, Chris Tilly, and Mary Gatta. 2017. "A New Social Construction of Skill." In *The Oxford Handbook of Skills and Training,* edited by John Buchanan, David Finegold, Ken Mayhew, and Chris Warhurst, 72–91. Oxford: Oxford University Press.

Weber, Max. 1946. *From Max Weber: Essays in Sociology.* Edited by C. Wright Mills and Hans Heinrich Gerth. New York: Oxford University Press.

Weeden, Kim A. 2002. "Why Do Some Occupations Pay More Than Others? Social Closure and Earnings Inequality in the United States." *American Journal of Sociology* 108 (1): 55–101.

Weeks, Kathi. 2011. *The Problem with Work: Feminism, Marxism, Antiwork Politics, and Postwork Imaginaries.* Durham, NC: Duke University Press.

Weick, Karl E. 1993. "The Collapse of Sensemaking in Organizations: The Mann Gulch Disaster." *Administrative Science Quarterly* 38 (4): 628–52.

Weick, Karl E. 2000. *Making Sense of the Organization.* Oxford: Wiley-Blackwell.

Westen, Peter. 1982. "The Empty Idea of Equality." *Harvard Law Review* 95 (3): 537–96.

Western, Bruce, and Jake Rosenfeld. 2011. "Unions, Norms, and the Rise in US Wage Inequality." *American Sociological Review* 76 (4): 513–37.

Wharton, Annabel Jane. 2001. *Building the Cold War: Hilton International Hotels and Modern Architecture.* Chicago: University of Chicago Press.

Wherry, Frederick F., Kristin S. Seefeldt, and Anthony S. Alvarez. 2019. "To Lend or Not to Lend to Friends and Kin: Awkwardness, Obfuscation, and Negative Reciprocity." *Social Forces* 98 (2): 753–93.

White, Stuart. 2007. *Equality.* Malden, MA: Polity.

Whyte, William Foote, and Kathleen King Whyte. 1991. *Making Mondragón: The Growth and Dynamics of the Worker Cooperative Complex.* Ithaca, NY: ILR Press.

Wiener-Bronner, Danielle. 2018. "Starbucks Achieves Pay Equity in the United States." *CNN Money,* March 21, 2018.

Wilkis, Ariel. 2015. "The Moral Performativity of Credit and Debt in the Slums of Buenos Aires." *Cultural Studies* 29 (5–6): 760–80.

Williams, Christine L. 1995. *Still a Man's World: Men Who Do Women's Work.* Berkeley: University of California Press.

Williams, Joan C. 2001. *Unbending Gender: Why Family and Work Conflict and What to Do about It.* New York: Oxford University Press.

Wilson, George, and Vincent J. Roscigno. 2014. "The Relational Foundations of Inequality at Work II: Structure-Agency Interplay." *American Behavioral Scientist* 58 (3): 375–78.

Wilson, William Julius. 1996. *When Work Disappears: The World of the New Urban Poor.* New York: Vintage Books.

Wooten, Melissa E., and Lucius Couloute. 2017. "The Production of Racial Inequality within and among Organizations." *Sociology Compass* 11 (1): e12446.

Wright, Erik Olin. 2006. "Compass Points: Towards a Socialist Alternative." *New Left Review* 41:93–124.

Wright, Erik Olin. 2010. *Envisioning Real Utopias.* London: Verso.

Wynn, Alison T. 2018. "Misery Has Company: The Shared Emotional Consequences of Everwork among Women and Men." *Sociological Forum* 33 (3): 712–34.

Zelizer, Viviana A. 1989. "The Social Meaning of Money: 'Special Monies.'" *American Journal of Sociology* 95 (2): 342–77.

Zelizer, Viviana A. 1994. *The Social Meaning of Money.* New York: Basic Books.

Zucchelli, Fernando Riva. 2014. "El Bauen, con desalojo en puerta." *Noticias Urbanas*, April 21, 2014. http://www.noticiasurbanas.com.ar/noticias/el-bauen -con-desalojo-en-puerta/.

Index

culture, 79, 128, 174–75; change and, 215n16; corporate, 74, 90, 94, 97; "dark side of," 212n17; egalitarian ethos, 11, 37, 54, 175, 205n32; sensemaking, 50–51, 211n1, 212n13; symbolic leveling, 10, 106–10, 119, 178. *See also* informal workplace dynamics

currency issues, 3–4, 123, 219n20; inflation, 124, 127, 183, 220n26

Deener, Andrew, 199

democracy, 2, 54, 179; in Argentina, 5–6, 20–21, 22–23, 208n7, 221n10; participatory, 50, 76, 83, 188, 196, 212n11; procedural *versus* substantive, 212n18; workplace, 12, 32, 48, 62–63, 72, 211n4, 224n9

democratic decision-making, 10, 14–15, 32, 47–72; free-rider problem, 128, 146, 177, 220n23; voting, 32, 37, 48, 51, 58–60, 74, 174, 215n13. *See also* appeals process; elections; informal workplace dynamics; participation; worker cooperatives

disciplinary sanctions, 39–43, 65, 68–71, 77, 116–17, 132; internal regulations, of BAUEN Cooperative, 40–43, 210n34

distributive justice, 8–11, 203nn14–15

Dodd, Nigel, 123, 218n10

economic crisis (2001), 17–18, 30–31, 92–93, 123, 188, 201n29, 202n4, 209n15; cacerolazos and corralito, 27, 208n13

egalitarianism, 8–11, 46, 97, 172, 177, 202nn11–12, 204n24; egalitarian ethos, 11, 37, 54, 175, 205n32. *See also* equality

elections, in Argentina, 151, 157–58

elections, in BAUEN Cooperative, 49, 213nn23–25; clientelism in, 61–65, 213n26; fairness in, 57–65, 176, 213nn23–29; favoritism in, 59–61, 213nn28–29

eminent domain. *See* expropriation

emotional labor, 75, 198, 214nn3–4; collective, 84, 90, 215n10

equality, 46; definitions and theories of, 2–3, 172, 177–78, 201n1, 202nn9–12, 203nn13–19, 204n22, 204nn24–26,

205n28, 223n4; formal, 33, 174; political, 48, 51, 58, 63, 174, 211n2; relations of, 8, 176; of status, 74. *See also* democratic decision-making; job rotation; pay equality

equality processes, 10, 178; inclusion, 10, 48–49, 178, 204n27; opportunity distribution, 10, 100, 178; symbolic leveling, 10, 106–10, 119, 178

equality projects, 8–11, 17, 177–80, 184–85, 205nn30–31, 223n6, 224n10

ethnography, 189–92; discrepant roles, 194–95; embodied costs, 196, 226n16; ethnographic toolkit, 196; field resistance, 195; immersion, 196–98; masking and unmasking, 193; observant participation, 189–92; organizational, 189–94. *See also* methodology

expropriation, 149–55, 157–62, 167–68, 183, 191, 221n5, 221n8, 221nn10–11, 221n17, 223n27; definition of, 150; process of, 152. *See also* legal issues

fairness: in elections, 57–65, 176, 213nn23–29. *See also* appeals process

Falklands War, 23

favoritism, 59–61, 213n28. *See also* elections; rumors

Federal Administration of Public Income (AFIP), 43. *See also* taxes

feminism, 204n25, 214n9, 225n2; feminist ethnography, 196, 226n15; feminist organizations, 206n41, 211n7. *See also* gender

Fernández Álvarez, María Inés, 100, 184–85

Fernández de Kirchner, Cristina, 158, 221n14, 226n14

financialization, 124, 136, 219n18

financing, 37, 44; challenges as worker-recuperated business, 31, 44, 163–64; the construction of the Hotel Bauen, 5, 22–23, 25–26, 208n12

firing practices, 54, 66–69, 101, 117, 132; theft and, 43

flexible informality, 75, 83

255

forbearance, 17, 149, 161, 220n1, 222n21
founding moments, 20, 32, 46, 97, 173–74, 207n4
Franklin, Benjamin, 120
free-rider problem, 128, 146, 177, 220n23
Front for Victory, 155, 157

Galeano, Eduardo, 180
Ganuza, Ernesto, 197
gender, 7, 53, 61–62, 86, 103, 108, 131–32, 173, 193, 212n10, 212n19, 213n20, 214n9, 215nn15–16, 224n14; gendered entry points, 104–5, 118, 217n17; in job placement, 99–100, 109–10, 216nn11–12, 217n27; organizations, as gendered, 12, 173, 206n40; wage gap, 9, 122, 137, 204n20, 218n5, 218nn8–9, 219n15, 219n21. See also feminism; job rotation
Goffman, Erving, 194, 226n13, 226n16
Google, 121, 220n31
governance. See democratic decision-making

Hanson, Rebecca, 193
health and safety codes, 43–44, 152–53
Hilton, Conrad, 1–2, 171, 172, 216n3, 223n2
hiring practices, 39–40, 41–42, 73, 77, 104–5, 110–11, 118, 145, 210n33
Hochschild, Arlie Russell, 75, 84, 214n3
Holland, Alisha, 161, 220n1, 222n21
Hotel Bauen, history of original business, 3–8, 21–28, 91–93; bankruptcy and crisis, 26–28; Bauen Suites, 24–25, 112–13, 195; financing construction, 5, 22–23, 25–26, 208n12; Iurcovich, Marcelo, 21, 22–23, 27; Mercoteles (Argentine firm), 27, 155–56; multinational capital, 24–25; precarious work, 25–26, 208n10; Solari (Chilean firm), 25–26
Hotel Bauen, recuperation of, 2, 28–46, 202n8; author's fieldwork experience, 13–15, 77–78, 187–89, 207n51; Callao Cooperative, 33; closure due to COVID-19 pandemic, 181–85, 200; occupation and movement building, 28–32. See also activist workplace; BAUEN Cooperative, formation of; legal issues; work sectors

hotels: hoteleros, 78–79, 83; managerial regimes, 75. See also service work, interactive
housekeeping, 45, 61–62, 79–80, 84, 92, 132, 142, 192, 217n17; concealment of labor, 37, 216n3; gendered entry points, 104–5, 118, 217n17; job rotation and, 101, 104–8, 112–13
housing cooperatives, 188

ideal worker, 76, 86–94, 146, 176, 215nn15–16; commitment, 89–91, 215n20; motivation, 86–89; political consciousness, 91–94. See also autogestión (self-management)
incentivizing work, 127–29, 142–46, 147. See also wages
inclusion, 10, 48–49, 178, 204n27. See also equality processes
inequality regime, 9–10, 204n26
inflation, 124, 127, 183, 220n26. See also currency issues
informal workplace dynamics, 49, 50, 174, 176; appeals process and, 66–72; elections and, 57–65; flexible informality, 75; participation and, 54–55. See also culture; job rotation
intentional communities, 49, 89–90, 223n32; kibbutz movement, 219n11
Inter-Cooperative Council, 188
isomorphism, 12, 207n2, 210n30
Iurcovich, Marcelo, 21, 22–23, 27

job rotation, 10, 16, 91, 96–119, 174–75, 191–92, 195; accessing opportunity through, 111–14, 217n26; administrative council, role of, 115; burnout and, 104–5; in conventional workplaces, 98–100, 216nn1–5, 216n9; as occupational re-sorting, 101–5; as punishment, 115–18. See also equality processes; skill, redefining; work sectors

Kalev, Alexandra, 99
Kanter, Rosabeth Moss, 89–90, 96, 112, 167, 223n31
Kirchner, Néstor, 28, 151, 155, 221n14

labor money, 144, 218n10; time banking, 123, 142–46, 219n13

labor process theory, 98, 214n4

landless workers' movement, 161, 209n24

lateral management, 75–76, 77, 83–86. *See also* management

legal issues, 17, 30, 31, 43–44, 149–61, 210n35; alternative organizational survival, 160–61, 222n18; eviction threats, 149, 155–57; law as politics approach, 151; legal gray zone, 149–52, 155, 169–70, 195. *See also* activist workplace

Macri, Mauricio, 58, 158, 159–60, 221n16; macrismo, 183, 224n3

Magnani, Esteban, 151

management, 75, 174; coordinators, 39, 41, 111, 142; lateral management, 75–76, 77, 83–86; managers, 38–39, 41, 111. *See also* autogestión (self-management)

Marx, Karl, 48, 123, 180, 224n14; Marxism, 162

Matanza, La (neighborhood), 78

meetings, of BAUEN Collective, 33–34; of administrative council, 51, 85, 106, 111, 114–15, 138–39, 188–90, 192; data collection and analysis of, 13, 190–92, 198, 199, 215n13; minutes of, 15, 37–38, 65, 67–70, 111, 129, 132, 153, 192, 198, 210n28, 210n34, 225n8; new member orientations, 33, 43, 73–74, 76, 81–82, 90; of sectors, 38–39, 51, 60–61, 191. *See also* Workers Assembly

membership, 64–65; asociados (voting members), 74; compañeros (worker-owners), 16, 74, 202n7, 214n2; hiring practices, 39–40, 41–42, 73, 77, 104–5, 110, 111, 118, 145, 210n33; turnover, 39, 104–5, 112, 114. *See also* firing practices; new members

methodology, 187–200, 225nn1–12, 226nn13–19; anonymity and transparency, 192–94; background, 13–15, 77–78, 187–89, 207n51; data collection and organization, 198–200; organizational ethnography, 189–94. *See also* ethnography

Ministry of Labor, of Argentina, 224n1

Ministry of Social Development, of Argentina, 224n1

Mondragón Corporation, 12, 206n38, 213n22

Morando, Mario: Morando Law, 153, 155, 156

National Commission on Disappeared Persons, 208n7

National Confederation of Worker Cooperatives (CNCT), 223nn29–30, 224n5

National Constitution, of Argentina, 151–52

National Development Bank, of Argentina, 23, 208n12

National Institute to Combat Discrimination, Xenophobia, and Racism, 217n25

National Law on Expropriation, of Argentina, 152

National Movement of Recuperated Businesses (MNER), 6–8, 28–30, 31, 150, 152, 202n6

neoinstitutionalism, 12, 206n43

neoliberalism, 5, 75, 94–95, 151, 188, 208n9, 214n6. *See also* capitalism

new cooperativism, 31

new members, 16, 73–95, 215n12; orientations, 33, 43, 73–74, 76, 81–82, 90, 215n13; probationary period, 40. *See also* autogestión (self-management); meetings; membership

Ni Una Menos (Not One More) campaign, 179

non-market interactions, 124, 222n26. *See also* survival finance

North American Students of Cooperation (NASCO), 188, 225n2

occupational re-sorting, 101–5, 118, 174. *See also* job rotation

occupation movements, 9, 31, 209n18, 209n23. *See also* worker-recuperated businesses

Open Faculty at the University of Buenos Aires, 31–32, 99, 206n46, 208n8

opportunity distribution, 10, 100, 178. *See also* equality processes

257

organizations: definition of, 204n23; as
enabling structures, 49; ethnography
of, 189–94; founding moments of,
20, 32, 46, 97, 173–74; as hybrids, 174;
organizational structure of, 37–40, 75,
210n30; organizational transformation,
12–13, 15, 36–37, 173–74; as racialized and
gendered, 12, 173, 206n40; survival of,
160–61, 222n18
outsourcing labor, 32–33, 134–35; burnout
and, 145; professional contracts, 109–10.
See also membership; overwork and
burnout
overtime work, 126, 132–35, 141–46, 165,
220n27
overwork and burnout, 17, 144–46,
215n18; everwork, 145. *See also* activist
workplace

participation, 10, 48–49, 50, 51–57, 196,
211n4, 212n10, 215n18; class discrimination in, 55–57, 212n19; conflict avoidance
and, 54–55; deliberative talk, 48, 211n1;
motivation, 86–89; observant participation, 189–92, 225n4; paradoxes of, 197;
pseudo-participation, 224n8; spillover
effect, 62–63; in the Workers Assembly,
54–57
participatory democracy, definition of,
212n11. *See also* democracy
Passeron, Jean-Claude, 197
pay equality, 10, 16–17, 91, 119, 120–47,
176–77. *See also* credit and debit;
survival finance; wages
Perón, Eva, 94
Perón, Isabel, 21
Perón, Juan Domingo, 22, 202n3
Peronism, 22, 202n7, 214n2. *See also*
politics
political consciousness: in ideal worker,
91–94. *See also* activist workplace
politics: certification, 221n3; elite cartels,
208n9; federal, 151–52, 157–61; law as
politics approach, 151; local government,
152–55
politics, national, 5–6, 151–52, 157–61,
208nn5–6, 208n9; military dictator-

ship, 20–23, 26–28, 202n3; Peronism,
22, 202n7, 214n2
Polletta, Francesca, 48, 211n1
populism, 151, 179
precarious work, 25–26, 177, 208n10;
rejection of, 35, 46
private government, 47–48, 54, 205n34
problem-solving sociology, 223n5
Productive Recovery Program
(Argentina), 224n1
psychological ownership, 90, 215n19

quinceañeras, 102, 137, 217n15

race, 16, 173, 188, 203n19, 214n9, 215n16;
Black civil rights organizing, 206n36; in
job placement, 98–99, 100, 216nn11–12,
217n19; organizations, as racialized, 12,
175, 206n40; pay inequality and, 122.
See also xenophobia
real utopias, 11, 180, 205n31, 223n5
recognition, 8, 31, 105, 178, 203n16. *See also*
equality
Recuperar program, 224n1
reimagining work, 31, 172–73; organizational transformation, 12–13, 15,
36–37, 173–74
reimprinting process, 20, 31, 33, 46, 174,
207nn1–4, 208n5
relational inequality theory, 9–10, 204n25
relational spaces, 205n27
Republican Proposal (PRO) party, 153, 157–58
Reyes, Victoria, 196
Richards, Patricia, 193
Rivera, Lauren, 106
Romero, Luis Alberto, 21
Rothman, Joshua, 8–9
Rothschild, Joyce, 49, 175, 211n5
rumors, 64, 176, 213n27, 225n7; watercooler effect, 59, 72. *See also* elections;
transparency

Scheper-Hughes, Nancy, 193
selective formalization, 41, 46, 97, 118,
174–75
self-exploitation (autoexploitación),
145–46, 215n18

Index

Sen, Amartya, 1, 9, 203n14
sensemaking, 50–51, 211n1, 212n13. *See also* culture
service work, interactive, 72–75, 79, 83–86, 217n20; compensation of, 128, 132, 177; cooperative hospitality, 72, 77–83; customer loyalty, 82; job characteristics, 99, 105–06, 177; self-management and, 74–76; solidarity and, 165–67; Statler Service Code, 216n3; surveillance and, 83. *See also* emotional labor
Sherman, Rachel, 45, 75, 216n5, 217n21
sin patrón (without a boss), 7–8, 223n28
skill, redefining, 16, 105–11, 118–19, 217n18, 217nn21–23; exceptions, 110–11; leveling human capital, 106–10
soccer, 21–23, 60, 91
social media, 14, 159, 182, 193; #TodxsConElBAUEN, 182
social movements, 160; embedded activists, 150, 158, 221n6, 222n24; in reimprinting process, 20; social change and, 162. *See also* activist workplace; worker-recuperated businesses, networks of
solidarity: with customers, 82; participation and, 95; rumors and, 59, 70, 72; service work and, 165–67. *See also* activist workplace
spillover effect, 62–63
Stainback, Kevin, 100
Stiuso, Antonio "Jaime," 195, 226n14
Supreme Court, of Argentina, 157
surveillance, 84–86, 128. *See also* lateral management
survival finance, 16–17, 121–22, 124, 136, 142, 146–47, 177, 184. *See also* pay equality
symbolic leveling, 10, 106–10, 119, 178. *See also* equality processes

Take, The (film), 13, 207n48
Tattoo Fest, 142–44, 220n33
taxes, 23–24, 43, 126, 151, 215n12
technology, 41–42, 43, 44, 84–85, 108, 212n10. *See also* surveillance
Telerman, Jorge, 155
Tilly, Charles, 204n25

time banking, 123, 142–46, 219n13. *See also* survival finance
Tomaskovic-Devey, Donald, 9–10, 100, 203n18, 204n26, 216nn11–12
training. *See* lateral management
transparency: bureaucratic secrets, 176; data, 192–94, 225n9; democratic, 44–46, 176, 210nn37–38, 211n39, 224n9; financial, 129–30, 220nn24–25
trustee, of BAUEN Cooperative, 33, 38, 44, 59, 71, 83, 87, 103, 107, 117, 137–38, 144
Twin Oaks Community, 219n11

unemployment, 3, 27–28; piqueteros, 6–7, 78, 215n11, 222n25. *See also* Hotel Bauen, recuperation of; economic crisis (2001)
unions, labor, 21, 98; Central Workers Union (CTA), 164; Union of Tourism, Hospitality, and Gastronomy Workers, 29, 209n18; worker-recuperated businesses and, 29, 159, 209n18
United States: Civil Rights Act (1964), 100; cooperatives and communes in, 49, 89, 206n36, 206n38, 213n30, 219n11, 221n5, 223n32; Equal Employment Opportunity Commission, 216n12; Equal Pay Act (1963), 218n8; pay secrecy in, 220n24
University of Texas at Austin, 188–89, 225n12
Utopia Café, 2–3, 37–38, 43, 55, 87, 114, 130–31, 134, 192
utopianism, 123, 150, 188, 219n11, 223n2, 223n30, 224n15; real utopias, 11, 180, 223n5; utopian demands, 179–80, 224n13

values, 1–2, 31, 50, 90, 173; rules tied to, 40–43; struggle to align with, 11–12, 32–33; value rationality, 49, 211n5. *See also* culture
Vieta, Marcelo, 75–76, 214n8, 222n22
voting, 32, 37, 48, 51, 58, 59–60, 74, 174, 215n13. *See also* democratic decision-making; elections

wage gap: gender and, 9, 122, 137, 204n20, 218n5, 218nn8–9, 219n15, 219n21; performance-reward bias, 122; unregulated pay variation, 130–32; vertical pay dispersion, 218n9

259

wages, 124–35, 219n20, 219n22; el básico (base pay rate), 124–25, 126–27, 129–30; as incentive, 127–29; overtime, 126, 132–35, 141–46, 165, 220n27; pluses (stipends), 125–29, 130; tips, 93, 130–32; travel stipend (viático), 126, 189; unregulated pay variation, 130–32; Workers Assembly and, 125, 126. See also pay equality; transparency

Walmart, 121, 218n3

Weeks, Kathi, 179–80, 224n13

Wilson, William Julius, 6

worker cooperatives: business models of, 11–13, 51, 205n35, 206nn36–37, 206nn41–43; hybrid services, 136; reimagining work, 171–73; theory and practice of, 49–51, 175–76, 211nn4–7, 212nn9–10, 212n14, 212n18, 224n12

worker-recuperated businesses, 6–8, 12–14, 20, 30–32, 46, 206nn45–46, 207n47, 209n18, 209nn20–25, 210n29, 222n23; Brukman (garment factory), 100, 149, 221n2, 222n25; Chilavert (graphics factory), 29, 209n17; FaSinPat (fábrica sin patrón), 166, 222n25, 223n28; FORJA San Martín (metallurgic factory), 207n48, 222n18; Industrias Metalúrgicas y Plásticas Argentina (IMPA) (metallurgic factory), 29, 221n11; job rotation in, 99–100, 216n10; "occupy, resist, produce," 28–29, 161; Zanon (tile factory), 38, 109, 166, 222n25. See also autogestión (self-management); Hotel Bauen, recuperation of

worker-recuperated businesses, networks of: Argentine Federation of Coopera-

tives of Self-Managed Workers (FACTA), 166–67, 223n29, 224n5; National Confederation of Worker Cooperatives (CNCT), 223nn29–30, 224n5; National Movement of Recuperated Businesses (MNER), 6–8, 28–30, 31, 150, 152, 202n6; Red Gráfica, 224n5

Workers Assembly, 38–39, 47–49, 52, 54, 57–58, 109, 129, 137, 140–41; activist workplace, role in, 158, 223n27; appeals and, 65–72, 116–17; collective authority, 32, 49, 57, 65, 74, 75, 174, 210n26; legal requirements, 33. See also appeals process; meetings; participation; wages

work sectors, of Hotel Bauen, 37–39; administration, 38, 45, 66, 84, 105, 107, 113–14, 126–27, 132, 136, 138, 141; custodial services, 59, 87, 103–4, 107, 117, 192; laundry, 88, 103, 217n17; press, 162–65, 188–89, 190, 222n25; reception, 78, 80–81, 82–83, 84, 85, 102–3, 107, 131–32; reservations and event planning, 101–2, 104, 132–34, 142–44, 217n15; sales, 110–11, 128–29; valet services, 77, 104, 116, 118, 131–32, 217n17. See also housekeeping

World Cup (1978), 4, 21–23

World Social Forum (2001), 94

Wright, Erik Olin, 178, 201n1, 223n3; real utopias, 11, 180, 205n31, 223n5

Wynn, Alison, 145

xenophobia, 117–18, 217nn25–26. See also race

Zelizer, Viviana, 124, 220n27